MW01341909

Gold Buckles Don't Lie

Gold Buckles Don't Lie

The Untold Tale of Fred Whitfield

Fred Whitfield

with Terri Powers

ISBN: 978-0-9894047-0-9

Printed in the United States of America

This book is dedicated to my fans.
Thank you for all of your support.
—Fred

CONTENTS

His grandfather, Edward Whitfield, used to hold him
all the time and even as a little baby, he was always looking up.
Big Papa would ask him, "Boy, what do you see up there?"
He said, "I'm gonna name him Moon
'cause he always looking up."

—Miss Marie

GIDDINGS

Each spring, the *Texas Calf Ropers Association* strategically planned their jackpot in Giddings around the San Antonio and Houston rodeos. It always drew some of the best ropers in the world simply because they were in the neighborhood and 1983 was no exception. They were all there. Roy Cooper came with four gold buckles, and another four to come; Barry Burk had seventeen trips to the NFR under his belt; Joe Beaver was still two years from the first of his eight world championships, but every cowboy in Texas knew where he was headed. It was an elite club indeed, and they had all taken pretty much the same path to get there. Most who succeeded at that level had families steeped in rodeo for generations who gave them all they needed to get where they were.

Alongside the cream, there was a crop of another hundred or so less-notable entrants, but until you saw them rope, it was hard to tell a hero from a hopeful. Except one. He arrived in a borrowed pick-up, pulling a borrowed trailer – he rode a borrowed horse and paid his entry fees with borrowed money. Few knew who he was when he got there. Everyone knew who he was when he left.

Roy Moffitt, the guy who had loaned him the truck, trailer, horse and money was with him that day in Giddings. He remembers thinking *oh my goodness* when he looked around and saw the competition. "Roy Cooper was an absolute legend at the time," says Moffitt. "And he was just one of several." None of it bothered Moffitt's young friend; in fact, that is just how he liked things – near impossible. It was on this day in Giddings, that Fred Whitfield beat the biggest names in the business to win the first round of the jackpot. He was sixteen years old.

That was a pretty big turning point and it was then I realized that I might have what it took. I was like 9.1 and I think 10 or 11 won second. I didn't end up winning the roping, but I ended up winning third in the average... and I beat some bad asses to do it. They knew then there was a star being born down here in Texas and people started talking. Just like nowadays, they talk about who's coming up, who's going to be the next phenomenon, and after Giddings, they were talking about me.

I probably won twenty-five hundred dollars, so me and Roy were on cloud nine. Back then, at my age, that was like winning the lottery. First, I had to pay Roy because it was his horse and his rig and his fuel and he paid my fees everywhere we went, so he got a percentage. Nothing from nothing leaves nothing and that's what I had without him – nothing. It wasn't like I come from absolutely nothing, but I wouldn't even call it middle class. It was lower class. But me and Roy had one of the best understandings in the world. Hell, there were times where if we didn't have enough money for both of us to rope, then he'd just enter me – he wouldn't even rope. Seriously, he'd enter me and say, "Stick it on 'em," and we'd leave with a boatload of money and be off to the next one.

Around the same time as Giddings, while I was still in high school, I took off rodeoing in Roy's rig with Spot, his Appaloosa horse. I went to Sonora, Del Rio, and some other places down there to about five of those AJRA [American Junior Rodeo Association] rodeos. I think I won first at four of them and second at the other one. It was in Del Rio one night that I heard this guy say, "I tell you what, there's a nigger come through here the other night on an app horse and I don't know who he is, but if he keeps roping like that, we're gonna know soon enough."

I didn't say much. I was the only black guy around there, and I'm thinking there ain't no way I can whip all these sonofabucks. I'll just keep putting these grass ropes on their ass and I'll show them who I am.

Chapter 1

Kluge Road

Growing up, I thought everybody lived like we did – but once I got out and looked back, I saw I was wrong. Most families don't try to kill each other as much as they did at my house. Through more than twenty years of interviews, I always painted a picture for the rodeo world that didn't even scratch the surface of how it had really been. I knew that when I finally told the truth it would have to be the whole truth, and the truth is that coming from where I come from, which was worse than nothing, it could have easily been the other way around. I could have been locked up or dead or just never had the opportunities I had. Thank God for Miss Marie, my mother.

We still call him Moon, but his name is Fredrick. I got the name out of a book at the hospital, and he don't really like that name so he makes it short. He don't have a middle name and his daddy don't have one. Fred was born at JD Hospital in Houston on August 5, 1967 and was seven pounds, six ounces. I was seventeen when his sister was born, eighteen when he was born, nineteen when Anthony was born, and so on and so on. He was my second child, so it was Tammy, Fred, Anthony, Loretta and Denise.

We lived on Kluge Road in Cypress, Texas, across the street from the Moffitts. The houses are still there where he used to play. Not our house, they tore down our house. Now I live right across the street with Miss Moffitt, Roy's mamma. I started working at the Moffitt's when I was nineteen, and when he was three, I started taking Moon with me. I did my work and Miss Moffitt didn't say anything about me having my kids with me while I worked, even two babies for a time. She played with them and was real good to them. After I went to work for her, Mrs. Moffitt started helping me a lot. She really did. They treated us like we was one of them.

It was her son, Roy Moffitt, that took Fred under his wing and that's how Fred started in his career. I never dreamed what would happen. I really didn't. By five, he was roping me. I'd be standing up washing dishes or cooking and all the sudden feel something go around my legs and it was Moon roping me. One day he roped me around the neck, and I said boy, are you crazy? Whatever he could find, he would rope with it. It was in his blood. He had a drive for it.

He won his first peewee rodeo at eight or nine years old, and after that, he went after it harder. Every day, we'd be down to the Moffitt's and I'd be inside cleaning and he'd be out there roping, sometimes just him and his brother. Anthony wanted to be a bull rider for a time, but he didn't make it. He would ask me why I paid for Moon and not for him. I said because I can't afford both of ya'll. Sometimes the guys at the rodeo would pay for Moon when I couldn't, so I sure couldn't afford both of them.

We were so poor that I gave Denise and Loretta away, Denise when she was six months old and Loretta when she was nine months old. I had five kids and couldn't take care of all of them. That's why I did it. My sister was married into a family with a woman who lost her baby in a fire. The lady wanted children so bad, so I let them talk me into giving Loretta to her. I have went to them and apologized, but I don't regret it because the people did good by my girls. Loretta's an RN, a head nurse where she work. She hire and fire, so she doing good for herself. And Denise stay in Baytown. Me and her don't get along. I've tried to reach out to her. I told her how much I loved her and how sorry I was for not keeping her. But she never forgave me.

Moon always loved nice clothes, especially blue jeans. I'll never forget his first day of school because he was so happy he had all new clothes. I didn't have enough money in the account, but I went to the department store and I bought my kids a bunch of school clothes anyway. I spent a hundred and ten dollars and the check bounced and Fred was so mad at me. He was little, but he was mad and said, "Mom, why would you do that?" I said, well, I thought I had enough to cover it. So it was either take the stuff back that they didn't wear yet or find the money somewhere. So Mrs. Moffitt gave me the money and they got to keep their stuff.

When Christmas came, they wanted gifts like the rest of the kids. So one year I bought them a used bicycle around June or July and I had a guy take it apart and paint each piece for me and then I wrapped them. Then, in November, I bought them coats and let them wear them until right before Christmas. Then I washed them and wrapped them and put them under the tree with the bicycle parts and by Christmas, they thought they had lots of gifts under the tree. I didn't want them to be the only kids in the neighborhood that didn't have a gift.

When they was little, we belonged to Rock of Salvation Holiness Church. My children participated in the choir and they participated in the youth department. Whenever they needed money for something at church, I would make pies and sell them and they would have their money. If each child was supposed to have like twenty-five dollars for a church activity, they had their money, because they got out and helped me sell pies. We used to go to church Tuesday night for Bible study, Wednesday night for choir rehearsal, Friday there was Bible study with the pastor and we went twice on Sunday. Oh, Moon hated church – he really did. You know what he said? He might get mad, but I don't care, he said, "When I get grown, I ain't ever going to church." He goes to church…but not my church.

Tammy got hit by a truck when she was four years old. I had left Willie Whitfield, Fred's daddy. We was always back and forth, and I had left him and went to my sister's. The kids was with me because I took them everywhere I went. My sister wasn't there, she was at the washateria, but she told me to go on in. I used to read those love magazines all the time and I was laying in the bed reading one at my sister's and the two boys was laying in the bed with me. Tammy was playing with her cousin Carla, my sister's daughter, who was older, and Tammy come in and asked if she could go across the street with Carla. I said no, because you might get hit. It was a real busy highway and Carla was only nine years old.

Well, I went back to reading my book and a few minutes later I hear *screeeeeeeech* and I run to the door. Carla met me at the door and say, "Aunt Marie, I turned her hand loose and she got hit."

Oh, I tell you, that hurted me so bad when I went out there. The boys were with me and saw it all. Tammy was unconscious. When the truck hit her, it throwed her on gravel and took all of this side of her off. When the ambulance came, I got in with her. By then my sister had come home from the washateria and I left the two boys with her. The ambulance was going so fast they almost turned over and Tammy hit the floor with me sitting there. I'm screaming and hollering louder than the ambulance and when we got to the hospital they took her on in and the doctor said that she had trauma and that she wasn't going to make it. That's what he told me in the waiting room. They had called a priest and he gave her the last rites.

My mother, she's dead and gone now, but she believed in God so much and she had this cloth that she had put blessed oil on. Some people laugh about it, but it don't matter, because I believe in the power of God, too. My mother took this blessed oil and she told me, she said, "Marie, let me go in there and let's put this on her and let's pray." She pinned it on the nightgown Tammy had on and my mamma prayed for her. Dr. Red Duke, that's who was her doctor, he's well known, he came in there and he said, "It don't look good." But when they changed her gown, the next lady had better news for us. They had said she was brain dead, that there was no movement in her brain, but she was coming around. So everyday my mamma went up there and prayed for her.

For thirty-one days, I lived there. I slept by Tammy on the floor, three or four months pregnant with Loretta and didn't know it. There was a chair in the hospital, but they didn't have beds like they do now, so I had no choice but the floor. I came home one day to get me some clothes and Miss Moffitt say Marie, you pregnant. I said Miss Moffitt, I'm not pregnant, but sure enough, I was pregnant with Loretta. When Tammy started trying to say stuff, the doctors was amazed and the first thing she said was Mama. I stayed there every day, bathing her and changing her so I could keep the blessed cloth on her and every day she improved. Tammy started coming around.

The day that they discharged her, they brought Fred and Anthony to the hospital to get her and it was the first time they had all been together since the accident. At first, they was both real careful with their sister because they knew she was hurt so bad. But about a week or two later, we went to a club and left Fred and Anthony at the house with Tammy. Man, I come back and they was roping that child so until she was crying. Before I even got in the house, I heard Tammy saying, "I'm gonna hurt ya'll if ya'll don't quit roping me." I walked in the house and boy, you could hear a pin drop. I said Moon, you wrong for that. You ain't got no business roping you sister.

She was well then…yeah, she was well. She had a head injury. She called her grandpa Big Papa before the accident and called him Mr. Muggins ever since she come home. I always thought it was mighty strange Tammy got hurt so bad by a car and then got killed in one. She was a person you needed to tell her you love her all the time, because she just didn't believe it. She loved her daddy and they got along good and Willie blamed me for what happened to her. He tried to kill me at the hospital. He tried to hit me in the head with a telephone, he sure did. He said it was my fault, but one of his cousins stood up and said, "No, it's your fault 'cause you won't leave her alone and she was getting away from you." See, Willie Whitfield would beat on me.

Willie's sister saw me one time and my eyes were swollen so bad I couldn't see.

She said, "Who did that to you?'

I said, your brother.

She said "What you going to do about it?"

I said nothing.

She said, "I'm going to tell you something right now, this is the third time he done did you like that. You better put a stop to it or he going to kill you."

I mean I wasn't doing anything, but I was pretty and had a nice shape and every time I tried to leave, he told me that if he couldn't have me than nobody else would. He said he'd kill me first. So, I decided that if he hit me again, I'm going to be ready. But I wasn't ready because I was scared of him. Then he did my eyes like that again and this next time I left with my three children tracking behind me, Fred, Anthony and Tammy. I couldn't even see out of one of my eyes. I said I don't know what I'm going to do. I don't have no money, I don't have no car, I don't know what I'm going to do.

I went over to his sister's, and she told me to go the police station and file charges on him and don't drop them this time. I said I would and I was walking to the police station and Willie passed by me, and hollered from across the street, "Yeah, I whipped you, you so-and-so, how do you like it?" I turned around and went back to the house.

I grabbed a twenty-gage shotgun that was there, but I didn't know how to shoot it, so I asked a neighbor man to come over and help me. He asked me what I was doing and I told him I was going to shoot Willie when he came back. He said, "He did your eyes like that again?" I said, yeah and I'm going to kill him. I promised not to tell nobody, so he showed me how to use that twenty-gage, but it kicked so bad when I fired it, I said I can't do this.

Then he told me the 410 would be better, so I got the 410 and shot it one time and it was a lot better. Then he left before Willie got home. I will never forget what happened then.

Willie got back to the house and came in there bragging about what he was doing in town. Anthony was three years old, and he grabbed Willie around the pants and said, "Daddy, Mamma gonna shoot you…Mamma gonna shoot you." He warned him, but Willie said, "Oh, that so-and-so ain't gonna do nothing."

When he said that, I grabbed the 410 from in back of the refrigerator, and I stuck it in his left side and pulled the trigger and his intestines came out the right side and was hanging out of his body. He reached for me and I didn't know what he was going to do, so I grabbed a butcher knife on the table and took out running. I heard the people across the way, Fred's cousins, holler "Oh somebody been shot."

I was wearing an old white meat jacket I always wore and it was covered in blood and I run out of the house and ran down to the Moffitt's. Mr. Moffitt was a detective and when I got there, I told him I just shot Willie. He said, "Is he dead?" I said, I don't know Mr. Moffitt, I just know I shot him. Mr. Moffitt called the police and told them I was at his house and we done called an ambulance. The ambulance got Willie and the police came down to the Moffitt's place and wanted to know why I shot Willie. I was sitting at the table with all of them and Mr. Moffitt said "He had a knife lying by him, did he try to do something to you?" I said no. Mr. Moffitt was trying to tell me to say yeah, but I said no. Then they say they was going to take me to jail. I was beat up real bad and Mr. Moffitt said, "Look at her face. You going to ask her why she shot him? He been doing this to her a while." Then he said, "Ya'll ain't taking her to jail."

Mr. Moffitt arranged it so the police would take me to pick up the kids and then take me to stay with a sister I got in Houston. He said that when things settled down, I could come back, but right now, I shouldn't go back to the house. But I wanted my kids. Mr. Moffitt told the police not to handcuff me and to take me to get the kids, but stay with me because some of Willie's sisters were crazy. When I walked in the house, Willie's family started calling me all kinds of names and saying what they was going to do to me and that I didn't need to shoot him. I said I just wanted to talk to my kids. But when I went in there, they was scared of me. My children was scared of me and they wouldn't come with me, and so I went on down to my sister's without Tammy or Fred or Anthony. But thank God, Willie didn't die.

Willie's sister, the one that told me to stop Willie from beating on me, me and her had a good relationship. She killed her husband. So after a few days, I called her and I told her where I was staying in Houston. My mamma said I shouldn't have did that, but I knew she wasn't going to tell them. She said the kids had been crying for me and they wanted me and that when everybody went to bed, she would bring them to me in Houston.

But Willie's daddy, Big Papa, said, "Tell her to come back home, she ain't got to leave. I got this twenty-gage and if anybody mess with her, they got to deal with me." He told Willie, "Sorry son, but you didn't have no business doing her like that because she's a good woman and she don't do nothing but take care of the kids, work and cook and keep this house clean. You didn't have no business to do her like that."

So, about three days later, I went on back home, and he told me, "Marie, if I'm not here, what you need to do is keep that gun by the door. If any of them come over here, shoot through the door." That's what his daddy told me, but I didn't have to shoot any of them.

Then Willie called. He couldn't talk because he had a trach, but he had the nurse call and tell me to come see him. And I did. And all of them was down there and they was calling me all kinds of names, but the nurse took me back there to see him.

Willie wrote a note on his little board, *You didn't have to shoot me.*

I was nervous and I wrote him back, even though he could hear me, I wrote him back, *You didn't have to beat me.*

After about two months, he got out of the hospital, and I took him back. He had plans to kill me, but I didn't know that then, so he got out of the hospital and I brought him home. The kids were all in the house one day and I was sitting there taking up some of Willie's pants because he lost so much weight at the hospital, and he come at me with a pair of scissors to stab me. Fred must have been about five and Anthony was about three or four, so they saw him coming to stab me and you know what they did to him? They grabbed him and tackled him down and hit him between the legs where he couldn't do nothing. Fred and Anthony took up for me and I said no child should have to go through that. I was tired of putting my kids through that and I left. But I came back again, yes I did. I came back again after he supposedly straightened up his life…again. It wasn't long before Willie did me like that again and I didn't do nothing but cry.

See, I'm proud of Fred because he could have been all messed up. But the boy done spent so much time with white folks that he prefers pumpkin over my sweet potato pie.

CHAPTER 2

WE JUST WANTED TO BE COWBOYS

No one remembers how Edward Whitfield came to be called Mr. Muggins or Muggy by everyone except his grandchildren, who called him Big Papa. The people of Cypress thought of him as a good neighbor and a hard worker – high praise for a country man. Muggins was a farmer who raised a few cows and pigs, kept some chickens and spent long days in his garden. He pulled his plow with a mule and people declared Muggins could train mules to do anything. He also trained some good hunting dogs. According to Roy, "Fred got his love of animals from his grandfather. Muggins was a good man and a hard, hard working man…Fred got that from him too."

Big Papa taught his grandsons to fish and to hunt the rabbits and squirrels and birds that were so abundant in the woods around their home. The family ate most everything they killed. Squirrels were a favorite and the boys learned to soak the squirrel meat in egg and milk to take out the wild taste. Hunting kept them busy and it put food on the table.

Muggins lived to be a hundred, but his wife, Miss Carina, died much younger. He was an outgoing person, while she was not as inclined to visit with the neighbors as her husband was. She did see a lot of the neighborhood children. With the nearest store at least five miles away, Miss Carina bought a variety of ice cream treats from the man who delivered the milk, marked them up, and resold them to the children of Cypress. Friends and family all describe her as "a nice lady."

Big Papa was already in his seventies when I was born. He favored me, but was not as tall. I don't think he was quite six foot and at that age, he wasn't real muscular and was pretty gray. He was lighter skinned than me and down the line, he had some Indian in him from way back when. He smoked, didn't drink a lot that I noticed – not like his son. We lived with him for years at his homestead there in Cypress where I grew up. I was raised out in the country in a little wood frame house that had been in our family for forty years, and I loved it because it was quiet. Life was never complicated. The only time my life was complicated when I was a kid was when there was turmoil with my parents.

My grandma was not a very big woman and she always looked kind of fragile to me. She had tons of kids to feed, so she was always around the house and usually cooking something. Miss Carina was strictly business and you seldom saw her laugh. Big Papa was good to her – any time he ever threw a fit, it was usually directed at my dad. Grandma died of cancer while I was still a little kid, and it wasn't a long, drawn-out deal. She got sick and forty-five to sixty days later, it was over. Miss Carina was the glue to our family, and always tried to keep peace. Once she was out of the picture, Big Papa took over. My granddad was stable – my dad was the one that created all the uncertainty around us.

I don't have many happy memories of my mom and dad's relationship. If he went out drinking and wasn't home by dark, there was going to be trouble later in the night. It might be two or three in the morning, but once he had some liquor in him, he'd want to come home and fight. I never understood that. I just learned to deal with it and going through all that as a kid made me a better man in the long run. As a young man with a hot temper, I've had my share of fights with women, but it didn't take me long to realize that if there's going to be friction between us, then we're not going to be together.

The one benefit from seeing all that I saw between my parents was that I learned how to treat women.

Our path did get rough when my sister was hit by that truck. My mom was gone at the hospital for a long time, but Big Papa saw that we got a bath every night and made it to school the next morning. Once Tammy got home, she was never the same. It done something to her mind and we knew that she was not a normal child after that. But she was my sister and I didn't care if she was different.

Me and Tammy and Anthony were kids who never had much, but I don't recall feeling like I was missing anything. We relished any opportunity to be around kids who had a lot of stuff, but then we'd go back to our world and were perfectly happy. Our childhood was very simple, and even when things went awry it was not a big deal. As long as there was food on the table and we had a few toys and we had a BB gun and could go out in the woods and go hunting, or go dig up some grub worms and go down to the fishing hole and catch some catfish, we had everything we needed. We all get older and our motives change, but I would give almost everything I've done to this point to go back to my childhood. I never dreamed that life would become as complicated as it has.

Big Papa would tell me all the time, "Boy, I seen it all, I mean, I've seen it all." He broke horses and that kind of stuff in his younger days before I was born. By the time I come around, he was done with all of that, but we would sit around, he would tell us the stories…and I would listen. Back then, when grown-ups were talking, kids didn't get to talk much. Miss Carina, had that old powdery snuff in the little can and if they were all sitting around talking and a kid said something, Grandma would look over and spit it in their eye. You got some snuff in your eye and that was the end of the conversation.

So us kids would just sit and listen and we'd hear them throw out names of guys that grew up around here and went to all the amateur rodeos. Ray Dyer, Ollie Ross – those guys were heroes in our minds, but they were just local guys that did well at local rodeos. I don't even remember the first time I watched my first National Finals Rodeo, which is sad, but these were our rodeo stars back then. We would see them at a rodeo, then go back to the house, and pretend to be them. My brother and I put a belt around one of us for a flank strap and one would be the bucking horse, the other one was the cowboy, and we were bronc riders. We played with it, but had no knowledge of what was really going on. We just wanted to be cowboys.

My mom worked for Joanne and Don Moffitt, which was a hundred yards from where we lived and I had been going there with her since I was about three or four. I found a lot of comfort at Joanne's house and she was good as gold to me and my family. I was there all the time, I ate dinner with them, I went wherever they went…I was just like an old shirt dragging along behind them. Even though I was quiet and reserved, somewhere along the way they saw there was a good kid in there and took a liking to me. Whether it was the way I did things or the way I carried myself in front of them, they felt I deserved a chance and they gave me that chance. Their son Roy was quite a bit older than me and had horses and calves and introduced me to rodeo. The best I can remember, I was five or six years old the first time I roped. It wasn't with real ropes because we didn't have any; we used cords off old vacuum cleaners or little nylon ropes or whatever else we could find. I was perfectly content with these because they taught me how to handle a rope, any rope.

My brother was the same way – we just wanted to rope. If a cat run by we'd rope him, if a chicken came around, we roped it. All of the animals knew if they came by us, they were going to get roped. It got to the point that my mom could be walking by and we'd be swinging a rope and get her by the foot. Tammy would get so stinking mad at us because we roped her around the neck. My brother got in trouble one time for roping a kid around the neck, and not knowing any better, the kid took off running. When he hit the end of that rope, it burnt his neck and looked like he almost hung him.

The cops got my brother and it was a big deal. We were pretty annoying when we learned to handle a rope.

My grandpa got me and my brother each a little black Shetland pony and we rode them so much in the summertime that the hair was missing off their backs. Once we had horses, we built an "arena" out back of our house out of plywood and pallets. For calves, we'd go around the neighborhood and catch dogs and get them hemmed up in our arena and practice roping them. We weren't cruel, but we'd rope them until they got out and then wouldn't see them until the next time we caught them. We roped off them ponies with old poly ropes that Roy had thrown away and we didn't have saddles or bridles so we tied a rope around their necks and rode bareback. We wore shorts and didn't have no shoes on and looked like a couple of wild little Africans on black ponies with the hair missing off their backs, roping dogs. Big Papa come back there one day and saw what we were doing and threatened to tear us up. But that wasn't the end – that was just the beginning. The dogs were our calves, the Shetland ponies were our roping horses and by God, we were cowboys.

Before Fred or Roy ever owned a horse or had an arena, there was Ollie Ross. Ollie was a cowboy who Roy claims was born a hundred years too late, but says, "He was our man." The boys would push calves endlessly for Ollie and his friends just for the chance to ride a horse and rope a few calves later. To this day, Roy says he can still hear Ollie saying, "You're burnin' daylight boys...burnin' daylight." He was a bashful man who preferred to rope in the slack instead of the rodeo as he needed alcohol and lots of it before he was comfortable around people. Ollie drank a half a gallon of whiskey a day and his health started to deteriorate at a very young age because of it.

Roy was about twenty-one and Fred around fourteen when Roy got a call late one night saying Ollie had ran his car off the bridge and into the creek just down from the Moffitt house. Roy got to the accident scene as they were pulling him out of the creek and cutting his pants off. Ollie, who still had his hat on, told the paramedics, "Just take me down to Roy's house and I'll be fine." But they didn't take him to Roy's and he wasn't fine. Ollie had extensive internal injuries from the wreck, and when they opened him up at the hospital, they saw the alcohol had also taken its toll. The doctors stapled him up and put him on a ventilator.

Ollie lingered for about a week and the boys went to see him every day, the last time being Halloween when they paid Ollie a short visit before leaving to a rodeo. Ollie died that night, an old man of thirty-three. At every National Finals Fred ever went to, he and Roy wished Ollie could have been there.

Ollie Ross lived half a mile down the road from us and had an arena. Before Roy had his arena, that's where we roped. If Roy had ten horses to ride, we'd saddle all ten of them and take them and the two Shetland ponies and we'd head off down there and rope at Ollie's. Kluge Road didn't have much traffic and we rode them horses up and down that road and hardly ever seen cars. We even drove calves down Kluge if we had to and would have little half mile cattle drives. We'd sing, "Going to the roping pen. Where ya'll going? We're going to the roping pen." God it was fun. And once we got to Ollie's, we helped the older guys rope and they let us ride calves and mess around and we would even get to rope after they were done.

By then, those Shetland ponies were trained roping horses. We'd rope a calf off those little horses then run down there with a string in our mouth and tie them, and our Shetlands would work the end of a rope like a full-grown horse. To those white boys with the best of everything, two wild black kids roping off black ponies, using strings and ropes others had thrown away and doing it just like they did was quite a sight.

Fred's brother, Anthony, nicknamed "Buggie" because of his fascination with bugs, also remembers childhood to have been adventurous and carefree. "We didn't have a worry in the world," he says. "We just woke up every morning and them Shetland ponies was right there waiting for us to get on they backs and start another day." Besides being their roping horses, the ponies were transportation any place the boys needed to go, including 7-11 for a Slurpee any time they could talk Big Papa out of a few dollars. Trigger was Moon's pony and Buggie named his pony Stud for obvious reasons, a name kept even after Big Papa changed his stud status.

Soon, word got around Cypress that the Whitfield boys could handle ornery little horses and people began bringing errant ponies in for a tune-up. After buying them for their children, many parents discovered that a pony-gone-bad is a big problem, but in a week or two Moon and Buggie would remake it into something the kid could actually ride. Business was brisk, with twelve or thirteen ponies being the most they had at one time, the average running about seven or eight. Big Papa was not happy about the herds of Shetlands in his backyard, but he admired the boys' gumption.

One summer Moon and Buggie worked for two long, hot weeks at a sand pit and were never paid the money they were promised. The boys went to the owner's house and took a few of his goats home in lieu of payment. They still weren't roping calves, but it was the closest they had come so far. Before the goats, it was chickens, dogs and the occasional sister or mother. Chickens proved to be rather frail stock and several gave their lives for roping. The boys hid the bodies way out in a pasture, sure, that their granddaddy would never even notice they were gone. A few days later, Big Papa surprised everyone with doughnuts, but Buggie smelled a rat and had his brother get him a doughnut before he took off and hid in the woods all day. See, Buggie knew they were in big trouble and the doughnuts were bait. When Moon reached back for his own doughnut, Big Papa caught him and "tanned him up good over them dead chickens." Buggie hid out as long as he could, but eventually had to come home, where he got his as well.

"Big Papa wasn't real tough on us," says Buggie about their grandfather. "He tried to make young men out of us the best he could." It was a big job as the brothers were daredevils apt to do anything, especially if they were told they shouldn't or couldn't do it. Even with the hardships, Anthony reminisces, "I would love to do it all over again. We had such a good time growing up and I wish I could turn back the hands of time to the old days."

Before they were even in their teens, everybody knew that Moon was the one with the gift. About his brother's incredible success that started so early, Anthony swears, "There ain't a jealous bone in my body and I'm glad for him." Maybe so, but Anthony will never forget the day when it was him that stood in the spotlight.

Miss Marie often took her sons to the "black rodeos" in Houston, where they met Rufus Green. An early advocate of the integration of rodeo, Rufus started as a fifteen-year-old ranch hand in Victoria, Texas who quickly demonstrated a keen ability to communicate with horses. He became one of the top horse trainers of his time, as well as a successful calf roper in the 1950's who was often the *only* black man at the more than two thousand rodeos he attended in his career. One of the first African Americans to receive a PRCA card, Rufus was also a founding member of the Southwestern Rodeo Cowboys Association, made up of black cowboys. Rufus passed away in 1982 at fifty-nine years of age, and in 2007, he was inducted into the National Cowboys of Color Hall of Fame. Among the accolades at his posthumous induction, Rufus was recognized for mentoring young people in all rodeo events, many who became top competitors. [*cowboysofcolor.com*]

After he got to know her boys, Rufus told Marie she should let them come spend the summer with him. Rufus had horses and cattle and mentored many young men and he assured her it would be a great experience for them. Marie hesitated as Mamma Stella, Rufus' wife, was rumored to be sort of mean and Marie didn't know if she wanted her kids there. But the boys pestered her until she let them go. Anthony reports that Mamma Stella was a little suspicious of them at first, but quickly warmed up and was very nice to him and Fred.

Rufus assigned each boy a horse for the time they were there and they practiced roping every day. There were also small ropings where the boys could compete for a dollar or two entry fee, but contestants also had to work the calves. It was at one of Rufus' ropings that Anthony heard them call his name for the breakaway roping, jumped on his horse, backed in the box, and roped the calf in an unheard of time of two or three seconds. "I was so excited," he says, "I beat Fred! I think I won about seven or eight dollars, and I was so happy."

Anthony alleges that "Fred was a lot of people's favorite for some reason" and never understood why his mother would pay for Fred to rope, but not him. "She'd say I couldn't beat Fred, so I never got to rope at the rodeos." As they got older, what interest Anthony did have in roping faded and he was content to help work the calves when Roy held jackpot ropings at his arena across the street. "I roped a little, but them old horses were so big and we was so little," he says. "I was used to roping on the Shetlands and when I got up on a big horse I didn't like it. It didn't even bother me if I didn't rope…I said I'm just going to play football."

Anthony recalls Fred's first real horse:

> It was a Welsh that our granddaddy bought him. He moved up from the Shetland ponies to a Welsh, which is a little bigger. I told Fred, you can't ride that horse like we ride these Shetlands…these Shetlands is broke in. Well he was hardheaded and he roped off that new horse all day. So when he finally put him up, he took the horse to the water and the horse was hot. I remember the old guys used to say don't give them no water, you'll kill them. I think the horse was smarter than Fred because the horse he wouldn't even drink no wa-

ter. Now Fred, he gonna take his hands and put it in the water and splash it on the horse's mouth. So we put him in the stall there at Roy's and we went home and got us some supper or what have you.

Later on that evening, my dad come home and he said, "Where that horse at my daddy bought you?" He wanted to see him so we go down to Roy's and we looked in that barn and his legs was straight up in the air. And boy, old Fred… he had such a look on his face. I said I told you you was gonna kill him; why you act surprised? I said you remember what Ollie done told you?

He was dead and my granddaddy was mad. Fred, he was so hurt and he cried. Yup, he cried a lot about that horse. I know my granddaddy didn't buy him another horse though. I think Roy helped Fred get his next horse, if I remember right, but it wasn't for a long time. We still had the little Shetland ponies.

When Big Papa found out about my new horse, he said, "Well I'll be damned, you rode him to death?" I bought him Friday, rode him all day Saturday and we went back over there that afternoon and he was lying dead in the stall. He just said to hell with this, I'm out of here and laid down and died.

Actually, it just looked like I rode him to death, but that isn't what happened. We never had a vet come or nothing, but the reason I actually think he died is we put him in them damn wood shavings and he ate them and it just killed him. But the joke was, "I can't believe it – he rode his frickin' horse to death," and it hurt me bad. And I owed three hundred dollars on a dead horse, so the chance of Big Papa getting his money back now was slim to none. Know what I mean?

Another animal that tore me up was our old black dog, Boone. One of Roy's girlfriends gave that dog to us and he was just like Old Yeller. He may not have been full-blooded, but he was part German Sheppard and if somebody jacked with you, he would attack their ass. Boone wouldn't let nobody mess with us. We could take him in the woods and if we run up on something, he'd find it before we did. He could even get your boots for you. I could be over at Roy's and tell Boone to go get my boots and he would run across the street and get them and bring them back. It's hard to get a dog to do that.

We'd had him probably six or seven years when one day we'd been down at Roy's roping and we were gathered up at the end of the arena, down there doing something. My brother come across the street to tell me to come home and Boone followed him. Before we even knew what happened, a car come down through there and run over him. He might have been all right, but he hit him and Boone rolled under the car, then the guy hit the brakes and stopped on him and killed him. It was horrible and I cried like a baby. I did. Other than my dad's drama, my animals getting hurt or killed are some of the saddest memories I have of my childhood.

The happiest time was when I was nine and went to my first rodeo and won. It was at Suburban, Texas, maybe sixteen miles from Hockley, where I live now. It's been a lot of years ago, but I remember I was winning the breakaway, winning the ribbon roping, winning the steer riding and maybe tie down or team roping...I remember I was winning four events. When I went back to the short round I had some problems, but I ended up winning second in the ribbon roping and it paid me twenty dollars. I left there on cloud nine. It was such a good feeling to win something the first time I ever left the house...unbelievable really. Roy was tickled to death, we were pumped up and high and mighty, not knowing what was around the corner.

That first one was a peewee rodeo and after that, there were youth rodeos and different little associations around here where I'd go and rope breakaway. I'd win a little money and it was like, man, this is easy. I loved it – I just loved the thrill of competing and beating other people. And I knew that if I was good enough to win a little bit of money now, it would only get better.

I'd be lying if I said that at nine years old I was dreaming of being a world champion. It was years later before me and Roy even started talking about the pros – and longer still that I realized that might be possible for me. I definitely wasn't groomed for it, like others were. Me and Roy knew Rusty Seawalt, who made the NFR a few times, and his dad, Ronnie, went several times and we felt that guys like that were born into the sport. The dad had rodeoed, the grandpa had rodeoed, the great-grandpa had rodeoed, but here I was, a young black kid that just happened into the sport. After my first win, I wasn't yet dreaming of a world title, but I was working at it a little harder. Winning just made me want to win more.

I would be across the street at Roy's and every day I would watch my cousins over at our place and every day it was the same thing. Whether it was nine-thirty in the morning or nine-thirty at night, they'd start a fire in a barrel and all their buddies would come by and they would smoke weed and drink and talk nonsense. One of them had played football and one of them had rodeoed a little, and they'd sit around getting drunk and talking about what they could have done and who they could have been. By the end of the night, somebody would say something like drunk people do and they were liable to pull a knife one night and a gun the next night and try to kill somebody. But the next morning they were back at the barrel drinking and talking about who they could have been.

At a very young age, I knew I had to escape all that. I never dreamed that roping would take me where it's taken me in my life, but I always knew that I had to find a way to escape. By the time I was ten or eleven years old, I would tell myself everyday that I wasn't ever going to be like them…sitting around talking about who I could have been.

Chapter 3

Moffitt Oil

In August of 1965, Joanne and Don Moffitt moved from a sub-division in Houston to Cypress, Texas where they could raise their two young sons in the country. Not quite a town yet, Cypress had a beer joint, a liquor store, a courthouse and a filling station all on Highway 290. After life in the big city, Joanne says, "You can't imagine what it was like here back then…there was nothing." Edward Whitfield owned the wooded land across the street and other than that, Joanne remembers only two other neighbors in the vicinity. "It was always happy here…not all the stress like nowadays."

Joanne had worked at the National Bank of Commerce on Main Street in downtown Houston until her first pregnancy, when she had to quit at four months as that was the bank's policy at the time. She stayed at home with her boys from then on, and eventually assumed the care of her father-in-law, who was in a hospital bed in her den. He had both legs cut off and was blind and other than pulling himself up to a sitting position from a rope hanging from the ceiling and dialing the telephone, he couldn't do anything for himself. Don Moffitt was away all day as a detective with the Houston Police Department, so Joanne hired a girl to help with his father. Shortly thereafter, Joanne came home and found both her father-in-law and the girl drunk. "So, Marie needed a job and I needed the help and that's just kind of how we all got started. Marie's little boy, who we called Moon and still do, was just a little kid that lived out here in the wilderness and he came with her."

Roy's dad was at work most of the time, but he still managed to stay on our asses. Maybe not on our asses, but he was always watching over us, making sure we did right and weren't screwing off anywhere. Roy and his brother Donnie would fight quite a bit, just like me and my brother did. Donnie is five years older than Roy, so twelve or thirteen years older than me, and he was never involved much in what we were doing. He was around, but Donnie had fancy trucks that he worked on and he liked lifting weights and chasing girls, not roping calves.

We couldn't always rope at Ollie's and we started going to different places to practice. If Ollie wasn't around, we usually went to Gold Mesa, which was two miles from the house. In order to go somewhere else to practice, we had to hook the stock trailer to the station wagon, load it full of calves, Joanne would haul the calves to wherever we were going, and then we'd have to turn around and get the horses. Roy had one trailer that would haul four horses. If you wanted eight horses over there...that's six trips to get horses and calves there and back. We had to make at least a couple of trips every time we went anywhere and it was a big ordeal.

I was always the chute help. Me and my brother were the little black boys that hung around the Moffitts and at first all they let us do was open the gate and untie calves. But people would ask who we were and Roy would tell them and I would get to know them. Then, when they were done roping, we'd get out there on our Shetlands and say man, you think we could rope a few? And they'd let us run a few calves. All that time roping chickens with extension cords and riding those Shetlands bareback paid off. We could handle a rope and we could ride. Today, I tell kids at my clinics that you can't learn to rope and learn to ride and learn to be competitive all at the same time. There are three different levels. We had total control over all of it and there was nothing awkward about what we did.

The Moffitts owned a vacation house on the Gulf in Matagorda, Texas, and in May of 1975, Don went there for the opening of shrimping season. Joanne and the kids stayed home because thirteen-year-old Roy was graduating junior high that Friday night and his brother was ten days from graduating from high school. The invitations to Donnie's party were already in the mail, and Don would be back in plenty of time for his son's graduation. But on Saturday morning after the junior high graduation, friends from next door came to tell Joanne that Don had suffered a heart attack and they were there to drive her to the hospital in Matagorda. The truth was that the heart attack had already killed him. He was forty-nine years old.

Joanne has no recollection of the next few weeks because her mother was feeding both her and Donnie copious amounts of Nyquil to keep them asleep. They were kept somewhat unconscious until the day Joanne's sister brought in a stack of mail from Moffitt Oil and asked what they should do with it. "I guess I woke up," Joanne recalls. "Two weeks after he died, I got up and it felt like I never went back to bed again."

At the time of Don's death, Moffitt Oil consisted of one truck and one driver and two gas stations, which he had inherited when his parents died. Joanne knew she could never go back to town to work and "leave the boys out here in this God-forsaken place knowing what they were going to be doing on those horses." Moffitt Oil was her only hope. A family friend said that if she was going to try to make a go of the oil business, she needed a new truck, a truck that turned out to cost more than what she had paid for her house. "God, that took nerve," she says, "but I had to make a living with it, so I got on the telephone." Cypress had been desolate since they moved there, but her children, who were now teenagers, came home one day excited about the new red light at Jones Road. Joanne could see that things in Cypress were changing. "I bought a truck and worked seven days a week, twenty hours a day and the business grew." Joanne's other big job was hauling Roy and his horses and his calves to practice every day and then to the rodeos on the weekends, which, "on top of the business, was killing me."

It almost literally killed her when a water moccasin bit Joanne while she helped Roy water his calves after they returned from a practice one day. On the way back to the house, she felt something hit the back of her foot… and then slither off. Joanne went to the barn for a hoe, found the snake and killed it, then went for help. It shook up her family so bad that they departed for the hospital without her, leaving her standing on the porch. They came back and got her, "And my mother, bless her heart, drove that car like it was a fire engine." Joanne told the doctor it was a water moccasin, a fact confirmed when Donnie arrived with the dead snake on a pie plate, which, he said, "Sure will clear out an elevator." She stayed overnight, went home the next morning and went back to work – the first order of business being to build a roping arena right outside her office window. She recalls that eight-year-old Moon watched with fascination from start to finish.

Joanne had her hands full with Moffitt Oil, taking us and the calves and horses to practice during the week, and then taking us to rodeos on the weekends. Just after I turned eight, she decided it made more sense to build an arena right there at the house. It was a full-size roping arena – a hundred and twenty foot wide and three hundred foot long with a barn back behind the arena along the easement. You pulled off of Kluge into their place and drove along the side of the arena on a paved road that went right up to the house. Man, we were in business.

At first, Roy's arena didn't have lights. When summer rolled around, it was hot as hell during the day, and we wouldn't rope much. You could run three or four calves and your horses were just spent from the heat. Hell, Joanne goes and spends four or five thousand dollars and put up lights on both sides of the arena. We aimed them right at the center so it was like it was daylight outside. It'd be a very comfortable eighty-five to ninety degrees at night and we got to where we'd rope quite a bit at night, sleep late the next day, run around until it got dark and start roping again. We couldn't wait for the sun to go down.

Up until now, I didn't have a saddle for my pony, but Big Papa bought me my first saddle when they built the arena. He paid somebody a hundred and fifty, two hundred bucks for it, which was like two thousand dollars to us. Finally, I have a horse and saddle and my best friend just put in a full-service roping arena right across the street. Look out. The arena was so new that the outside fence of the alley still had posts sticking up about a foot and a half. They had put a board on top of the posts on the inside, which was the arena fence, but hadn't done that yet to the outside fence of the alley. We were going to put a top board on it, but we were so busy roping and it was on the outside lane so there was never a chance of you catching a post roping a calf in the arena, so we hadn't gotten around to it yet.

I'd had my new saddle for about a month and was herding calves down the alley one day. I tried to rope a calf and roped one of them posts instead, tied on, going twenty-five or thirty miles an hour. It jerked the saddle horn completely off my new saddle and it looked like a saddle bronc riding saddle. I finally had a saddle for my Shetland and I'm looking at nothing but a big hole where the horn used to be. I was lucky it didn't rip me straight over backwards or the saddle horn hit me in the mouth as it come by and kill me, but I didn't see anything lucky about it at the time. There's no way to fix it other than put a new tree in it and that's another couple hundred bucks, so that wasn't happening. I had owned it for a month and I had to throw it away and go back to riding bareback. I was freaking devastated. The worst part was going home and telling Big Papa I had ruined the saddle he just bought me. He said, "What you talking about?" when I tried to tell him how it happened, and once he was clear, he said, "Well I'll be goddamned."

Even without a saddle, I got to where I was sticking it on them pretty good riding my pony. Then, every now and then, I got to rope off a real horse – but getting put on a big horse didn't happen every day. I had to turn out, untie and bring back a lot of calves for that to happen. It was usually a horse Roy wasn't real high on – he wasn't going to put me on the best one. It would generally be a practice horse that he'd let me run a few calves on, and it was a privilege to get to ride them. Just getting the chance to run a few on any big horse was a cherished opportunity.

After a few years, Roy started having jackpots at his arena all the time. When people come around that Roy thought was important, he'd still show us off roping on the ponies. But it did progress and I had more access to big horses and I got to where I was roping pretty decent. I won my first breakaway buckle in 1981 at one of his jackpots and gave it to some owl-headed girl somewhere along the way. The Moffitts had a pool table in their house so if it rained and the jackpot got canceled, we'd go in there and have pool games all night long. After a while, I got to where I was a pretty good pool shark because it rains a lot in Cypress. We had to be competing – we were constantly competing. We'd play pool for a hundred dollars a game at times. I never played golf much, but any time we went to the golf course and hit balls we had to bet on that too. Because of roping – everything we did was about competition. If we didn't have a bet on it and didn't have a chance to win something, then whatever was happening didn't matter to us.

With the arena in place, Joanne no longer had the task of getting the boys to practice, but there were still rodeos on the weekends. "I have sat in the rodeo arena in Brenham, Texas and watched the sun come up at youth rodeos," Joanne recalls. "I just couldn't do weekends and all week, too." Although, "nobody ever got hurt that I remember," Joanne thought Moon was too young and too little to participate. Roy didn't think so and Fred was letting calves out, driving the tractor and even roping a little. "They were always, always, in that roping pen," Joanne says. "You didn't have to make them practice – you had to make them stop practicing and go to bed." She recalls a mother asking her at a rodeo if she had to make her kid practice, to which she replied, "If I did, we wouldn't be here…I'd be home taking a nap."

Joanne still swears it was spending all week in the roping pen and all weekend at the rodeo that kept them all out of trouble. "Roy and Moon loved what they did and they were the best of friends." Roy confirms that, "Roping was a hundred percent of our lives; it's what we did all day, every day." Each Monday morning, Joanne planned her workweek around whatever rodeo was coming up the following weekend. Then on Friday or Saturday, sometimes even a Thursday, she loaded up Roy, Fred and all their stuff into a little Winnebago with the horse trailer behind it and went most any place in Texas. After they rodeoed all weekend, she drove the boys home on Sunday nights while they slept, often leaving them there until she woke them up for school on Monday mornings. Once home, Joanne was lucky to get a few hours sleep herself and then started the whole process over again.

Back when Roy wasn't even old enough to drive, Joanne took us to all our rodeos. She would load that RV full of food and drinks so we didn't want for a thing. Everything was self-sufficient, including an air conditioner and a little generator that we'd fire up going down the road and watch TV. It had a little bed over the cab and one of the couches turned into a bed, and we'd make us a ham sandwich or a bologna sandwich, get us a drink and some chips and kick back and watch TV until we got to the rodeo. Blow Pops were big back when I was a kid, and Joanne kept the RV stocked with Blow Pops. We also had those candy deals with the stick that you dipped in the tart stuff. You'd put the stick in your mouth and get a little saliva on it, then dip it down in that powder – it came in grape, strawberry and orange and was so sour. We had a lot of stuff like that and it was always fun to load up and go, whether we went ten miles or two hundred miles. They used to have youth rodeos at Giddings all the time, they had them at Gold Mesa, they had them at Hitchcock, which was south of us about seventy miles, at Suburban, just the other side of Tomball, and they had them at Conroe, Texas, which is forty miles from here.

I was always antsy before we left for a rodeo. For most of the youth rodeos, especially if they were far away, we had to leave on Thursday or Friday. If I knew we were leaving to a rodeo after school, I was antsy from that morning at eight-o-clock until school let out at two-thirty – just raring to go, couldn't wait to get there. When we finally got to the rodeos, the one thing I remember most was thinking about who was going to be there. Then, as I got a little bit older, I thought *I'm the competition this week...I don't have to worry about beating anybody but me.* That's what I always thought. Once you have a little bit of success, once you taste it, it breeds more success.

I was always different and people always made mention of it – something's wrong with him…what's his problem? I wasn't even interested in girls until after high school. If it didn't pertain to roping, it was of no interest to me. Roping is all I thought about, all I talked about, I craved it, it's all I ever wanted to do and girlfriends took time away from that. I had a couple along the way, but not like most guys. Once I got out of school, things started to change a little, but until about seventeen, eighteen years old, I just wasn't interested. I didn't have time for it.

At this point, Roy had some kind of two-horse inline that bounced around so bad you couldn't tell if it was unhooked or coming unhooked. It had a swivel and the tongue was actually on the axes so the trailer had some give and it wasn't so rough, but it was still rough. When I went by myself, I took the stock trailer because I was petrified of pulling that damn inline… but that was much later. Our motto was always "Drive a Volkswagen, ride a Lexus," and Roy always had nice horses. By the late seventies, Roy was giving twenty-five, thirty-thousand dollars for horses and that was unheard of back then. Some he bought from R.E. and Martha Josey, whose names are synonymous with rodeo. Roy just got to where he trusted them and if they thought they had a good horse, they'd call him and me and Roy would go out there and run a few calves on them. I don't know how many horses he bought from R.E. and Martha, but they were good horses that I rode sometimes at youth rodeos. Spot and Crisco were the two horses I probably rode the most. I think Crisco was Roy's best horse and he came from Ronnie Williams in Huntsville. Roy bought Spot from a guy there in Cypress.

It wasn't like I just got to run wild, but there was not boundaries on me from my family. I was a free spirit as a kid, but there were guidelines with the Moffitts. With the Moffitts, I knew that there was a certain way to act and a certain way to present yourself and I didn't differ from them. Now, once I got down the road or outside the driveway, I knew I could do whatever I wanted and pretty much get away with it. But as a kid, I was never a bad person and never took a chance on getting in trouble. I just never did. There was a certain code that I lived by as a kid and that code got me to where I am today. I think it was my approach and my attention to details. I showed up with an attitude that was all business – I wasn't there to play grab-ass with anybody. Any minute I spent jacking around took away from what I was there to accomplish…and that was to win. Period. I've always been disciplined and motivated and driven to have success. I've run off the course a few times, but there is a sense of urgency in me. The same attitude and work ethic I had when Joanne was driving us around to youth rodeos in that RV are the same principles I took with me to the PRCA later. That was my approach: we need to do this today, need to win, need to win, need to win. In my heart of hearts, I know that's how I developed into a world champion. Not only did I need the money, mostly I wanted to win because people said I couldn't do it. But I didn't listen.

About his young friend, Roy says:

> I don't know if being black limited Fred in any way, but I suppose any black man in the rodeo world is limited to a degree. I think those Bill Pickett rodeos are by invitation only and you don't see no white guys there. I used to give them black guys a hard time because I never got an invitation to a Bill Pickett rodeo. I would joke with

them when they'd show up at a rodeo; I'd say, "This ain't no black rodeo, this is a white rodeo. Hell, we can't go to ya'll's rodeos, how come you can come to ours and take our money?" Truth was, there were a lot of black rodeos we went to and we had a lot of fun.

It was early, really early, when we saw how good Fred was. He got real fast by the time he was just eight or nine years old, and I knew he was more than pretty good. He started roping breakaway but I didn't know if he would be big enough to flank and tie those calves – he was a scrawny sonofabuck. In high school, I got a truck with a camper and we hit the road without my mother. Fred was still a little kid, and we'd throw him in the camper because we didn't need his bullshit. Then, after the rodeo, we'd go to the bar and get drunk and Fred would be out in the camper watching the horses. Somebody at the bar always has to jack with the horses, right? And, in case any of us got drunk enough to want to ride them in the bar, Fred was there to stop that, too.

We'd video the rodeo and bring it to the bar and they'd show it on the big screen and we would watch it for hours. It was so much fun, but Fred would get mad because we'd stay at the bar all night and leave him outside. He'd tell us, "I ain't gonna be like ya'll, I ain't gonna be no akaholic." I did me some drinking, but still set a good example because he didn't want to be like me.

He got in the junior tie-down calf roping and then in the senior tie-down roping and he won at every level. When he got old enough to drive, I let him use my truck and my trailer and my horse to go to youth rodeos and he just dominated them. He dominated them. He won at youth rodeos, he won at high school rodeos, he won at amateur rodeos and he won at the pro rodeos. If he showed up, everybody else was roping for second. Whenever Fred roped, he won…simple as that.

At first, I roped and if we had enough money left over, Fred got to rope. But it didn't take long to put the shoe on the other foot and we paid Fred's entry fee first because he was most likely to win. Money didn't grow on trees and putting money on Fred was always a wise thing to do.

When we were kids, Roy Cooper was in his mid-twenties and winning world roping championships. He was the real deal and our calf roping idol at the time. In 1977, when I was ten years old, Roy Moffitt had an invitational roping in Pasadena, Texas, and invited Roy Cooper. I remember they added some money to attract some bigger names and Roy just called Cooper up and left him a message asking him to come to his jackpot.

Now Roy and one of his buddies would always call each other and say, "Hey, this is Roy Cooper can I talk to Roy Moffitt?" It was a big joke and made us laugh no matter how many times they did it. Well, one day we're there jacking around at the house and Roy's mom answered the phone and she yells upstairs, "Roy…Roy Cooper's on the phone." He come trotting his ass down the stairs and got on the phone and said, "Steve…you know this ain't Roy Cooper…" Turned out it was Roy Cooper and he ended up coming to Roy's jackpot.

Me and Buggie went too, and we got to see Sylvester Mayfield, Barry Burk, Dee Pickett and, of course, Roy Cooper. He had a big van, and a fancy horse trailer and a driver and when they got out of that van, they left it unlocked and the trailer open. So Roy introduces us to Roy Cooper and hang around with him a little bit and then they all left. When they did, we went off over there and got in his van and got to rummaging around in there, just playing like it was our own. Me and my brother played around in that van the whole time the roping was going on and we just had stuff everywhere, just like we lived there. When the roping was over, Roy Cooper comes back to his rig and finds us in there. We had stuff out of drawers and his things out on the ground, and he come in there and said, "What in the hell are you little old boys doing?" He scared us a little, but that was the highlight of the whole roping – hanging out in Roy's van having fun. We were goofy fricking kids and he was our roping hero.

CHAPTER 4

HOUSTON

In 1978, Marie shot Willie again; shot him six times and he lived…again. This was just after she shot at his girlfriend, explaining, "I was just tryin' to scare her, and she peed all over herself, then jumped in her car and backed off in the ditch." Her name was Peanut and she showed up at the Whitfield doorstep looking for Willie late one night. Marie had a pistol, which she kept, "up here in my bosom," and she fired off a few warning shots. While Marie watched and laughed, Peanut got her car out of the ditch and she went on home. Evidently a slow learner, Peanut continued to call and taunt Marie at her job at the Moffitts, telling her, "I'm goin' with your husband and there ain't nuthin' you can do about it." However, Marie could do something about it and she did, showing up at a club where she knew Peanut would be.

"I pulled her off that bar stool and I beat her good. I said this is for f'in' my husband and I hit her in the face and then I just beat her out of her clothes." The only damage to Marie was she lost a hundred and twenty-five dollars she'd had stashed, "up here in my bosom" as well. Peanut, on the other hand, ended up in the hospital for three days and sent Marie the bill.

"Willie come back on me for beatin' her," Marie recalls, telling her, "You didn't have to do her like that and now I'm gonna do you like that." Marie told Willie that if he stepped in the door, "I'm gonna kill you today." Big Papa said, "Kill him," and Marie commenced to trying. She pulled the pistol out, shut her eyes, and fired every shot she had, hitting him all six times from his cheek to his ass and down his legs. Fred was there for this one, too, and told his daddy, "Die. You need to die, 'cause you can't leave her alone."

Anthony confirms the obvious:

> Lawrd have mercy…they didn't get along. My daddy, he's like an animal. He would come home intoxicated and he would just start stuff. Mamma done cooked his food and put it on the table, but for some reason, he don't want that. He wanted to start a commotion for no reason. One time he was getting the best of my mamma, and we jumped on him. I think Fred grabbed his feet and I grabbed his head and we tore him up pretty good. I told Mamma then that it was time to go, but we didn't go.
>
> He come in about two or three that morning and raced the car 'til it seemed like the motor was gonna jump out of the frame. He was drunker than Cooter Brown and you could hear him in the room talking to my granddad, and Big Papa told him, "Boy, go on in there and go to bed." But he didn't listen. We were all in a bedroom with Mamma and my granddad had put a two by four up against the bedroom door so Daddy couldn't get to her. But he beat on that door and beat on that door and finally Mamma said, "Ya'll just get under the bed, I'm gonna kill him." I said, please Mamma no, please, don't kill him. She said, "Ya'll just get under that bed." I didn't know Mamma had bought a gun and he come through that door and he just kept'a coming. She let him have it and I mean the more she shot him, the more he came and finally he fell. I said Mamma, you done kill't him. But she didn't.

Willie was in the hospital for two months and it was about three months until he fully recovered. No main arteries were hit and they left one bullet in his butt and one in his cheek. The doctor said they would come out eventually and they did. Marie took Willie back when he got out of the hospital, but she reports, "He didn't beat me no more."

Marie had been selling cookies to her good friend – the judge. That, and the fact that Willie probably needed to be shot, kept her out of jail again. The judge asked Marie where the gun was and she said she didn't have it, which was true because Willie's sister had stolen it and already sold it. He warned her to make sure it didn't show up at the trial, and it didn't. Willie's cousin, Rose, who Marie considered a good friend, testified against her, telling the judge that "She carry a gun up in here wherever she go." Even so, at the end of the day, Marie went home.

Fred warned his mother that she needed to get away from Willie "before he kills you," and Anthony believed, "It was dangerous at our house and it was time for us to go." Still, they didn't go, but after the years of abuse, something inside Marie had changed. "I decided I was taking up for myself from now on and that's why I bought the pistol. I wasn't taking that crap anymore…he wasn't going to put his hands on me. No man is supposed to hit a woman and I knew that my children had been through enough and I wasn't gonna do it to them no more. Sometimes we do stuff and our kids suffer for it too."

Later the same year, Willie killed a man over a woman they were both seeing. He had blood all over him when he arrived home at his customary two in the morning and Marie asked what happened. Willie said, "I think I just killed a so-and-so." She asked whom and when he told her, Marie says, "I knew what it was about because I had heard all the rumors." Willie shot him in the back on a winter night at a busy nightclub and nobody there reported anything to anybody. The wounded man stumbled out back into a field and bled to death. That same night some nearby cows got out and when the farmer went looking for them the next morning, he found the dead man. The club was closed over the incident, Willie Whitfield went to prison, and his family got some much-needed rest from his torment.

There was a lot of talk about it and I heard it was over a girlfriend, but really didn't understand it at the time. I was ten or eleven and didn't know what to think. As a kid, I watched all the bullets and the drinking and the arguing and the handcuffs, and had I been older, I would have said I seen it coming. When he finally went away to prison, it was like thank God he's out of here. We thought he would be gone for ten years or so, but he was out in about five years. Things were peaceful – we didn't have to worry about nobody coming home picking on us, taunting us and stuff. Me and my dad have never been close; me and my grandpa got along a lot better than me and my dad ever did. I had a better life planned than what I had seen so far – I knew I would never end up like him.

That nightmare was finally over and then my mom moved me and Anthony to Houston with her and a whole new nightmare began. Tammy stayed in Cypress and I was glad because it was such a bad environment. I'd a rather been run over by a freight train than have to live down there. I didn't grow up in the perfect situation, but I was happy in Cypress and I was never happy in Houston. The first thing that got to me was the sirens. Mom rented a house in Acres Homes in a bad part of town, right in the hood. Our house was just off West Montgomery, a main street, and twenty-four hours a day, we heard sirens. We lived maybe a mile and a half from MC Williams, our new school. The first day my mom took me there and I enrolled in the seventh grade, I cried for two full hours. I was devastated for so many reasons. I was in an unfamiliar place with no sense of security and I didn't deal with it very well. It showed in my grades and everywhere else – I was depressed.

Mamma made us breakfast and got us off to school in the morning. I was always up early enough so I had enough time to kind of get my head on straight before I had to face another day of this bullshit. We walked to school and always had to allow time for a few scuffles on the way. We took a shortcut through some trees and other people's property, but there was no avoiding trouble. Until Houston, I'd been in school with pretty nice kids, but hell, we'd have to fight every day after school because somebody would want what we had. Most were inner-city kids and we didn't have much, but it was probably a little bit more than they had. By the time we got home in the afternoon and did any homework, the day was over. I played football, but that didn't last long. I would play in the games but I never went to practice and if you not going to practice you not going to be on the team long.

All of it was complete culture shock. I'd went from being out in the country with a lot of friends to getting thrown in with a lot of people I didn't know. I dressed different than other black kids, talked different than other black kids and had different interests than other black kids. I had a lot of trouble with it, but worst of all, there wasn't any roping in Acres Homes and that killed me. After roping every day of my life since I was a little boy, I'd have to come back out to Cypress to rope, so it was now weekends only. On Friday afternoon, my mom would drive me the twenty miles or so back to Cypress and I had about three places I could stay. There was Big Papa, my Aunt Velma or the Moffitts – I knew I'd be welcome at one of them. I'd rope all weekend and on Sunday night I'd catch a ride or my mom would come get me and head back to Houston for school on Monday. I was just trying to survive my circumstances…I was so disappointed, but I just kind of learned to deal with it.

Sometimes my mom and me would just show up at rodeos, she would pay my entry fees, and I'd borrow a horse. She had several friends who'd rodeoed and they knew her son was getting into it, so we'd use one of their horses, win a little bit of money and everything was good. Hell, when I was a kid, it only cost ten, fifteen bucks to enter some of these rodeos, which wasn't a lot of money. I'd win me a hundred, hundred and fifty, and be on cloud nine. That was enough to give my mom a little and still buy clothes, hats, boots, candy, ropes, food...just whatever I needed that week.

My brother fit in a lot better in Houston, but he wasn't that big on roping. He did it, but he didn't crave it like I did. Anthony kind of had a different attitude – it didn't take much to get him to fly off the handle. He was a bit of an outcast who would buck the system where I was just like a duck. It would just roll right off me, but Anthony would take it to heart.

Indeed, Anthony adjusted much better to life in Houston and has fond memories of his time there. He says that, "Mom was working two jobs and I would dress nice and had nice shoes and everything I needed, so I was happy there." Anthony was also the only one of her children that would accompany Marie to visit Willie while he was in prison. Anthony does admit that, "We had to fight every day 'cause they would try and take our money every day." Even so, Anthony functioned well in Houston, but says, "Fred never adjusted. He just did better out in Cypress. Before long, Fred went on back to Cypress and it was just me and Mom. I faded away from roping and me and Fred drifted apart."

I survived an entire semester because I didn't want to leave at the halfway point of the seventh grade. After that, I couldn't take any more of Houston. One day I went home and said, Mom, this ain't me. I said if I don't get out of here this ain't going to be good. I wanted to go back and live in Cypress. We kicked it around a little bit and she said I could do whatever was best for me. Thank God, she did, because there's no telling where I'd be today. I had the green light to go back to Cypress and I couldn't have been happier.

I lived at Big Papa's place at first, but he was older and things with him had kind of shifted, so I stayed with my aunt for a while. I didn't really care for that because she had too many people living with her and it was a day-to-day battle. We had like a compound with five wood frame houses. There was Big Papa's house; his youngest daughter lived in a house; my Aunt Velma and her daughter lived in the middle house; across the way my cousin Rosie had a house; and my dad's brother, George, and his family lived in the house in the back, which was kind of catty-cornered from our house.

Dinner was at my aunt's house at a certain time every evening, unless they barbequed, then everybody was outside together. It was more on the side of soul food with lots of fresh vegetables from my grandpa's garden. If I was there for dinner, I ate, but a lot of times I ate supper at Roy's. I spent most of my time at Roy's, but still needed a place to sleep and to shower in the morning for school. I had to go to school, no matter where I was living, and always wanted to dress decent and look nice. Wherever I ended up that night, I got up the next morning and went to school. I had to have responsibility, even at my age, because it would have been so easy for me to get lost in the shuffle. The pressure never got me; I just managed to keep a straight head and never really got into any trouble.

The minute school was out, I was back at Roy's and I'd stay there until after dark. I got very little schoolwork done, and could have done great in school if I would have applied myself. Rodeo has been like a disease to me ever since I picked up a rope and once it was in my blood, I did just enough schoolwork to get out. I didn't come home and study; I came home and roped. If I made a "C" on a test, shit, I'm in the house. If I had papers to do, I paid somebody to do mine. While I was in school, I was winning ropings, and I was liable to have a thousand, fifteen hundred on me. I'd just give some smart girl a hundred bucks to write my paper and then I would go home and read what they wrote. I'm not proud of it, but I did just enough to get by. I am completely different with my kids.

I grew up quick and discipline came from having to become a man at a very young age. I learned that if I was going to make it in life, it was going to be on my shoulders, and it made me very driven as a kid. Things were how they were and I dealt with it. I never felt hindered. I stayed with my aunt a little, if my grandpa was sick or something, then I'd go over there…I'd go back to this place or that place. The one bad habit I did pick up along the way is that whenever things got complicated, I'd drift off to another spot.

Still just thirteen years old, I went to work for a friend of mine, Frank Reeves, who had a septic system company. I was making a hundred and twenty five bucks a week working during the summer. We'd go over to one of the richest neighborhoods around here at the time, and tap sewers and that summer we probably put in two or three hundred of them. I'd work from about eight in the morning until about three in the afternoon, go home and rope, and that's all I did. I headed to Roy's right after work and we would tie calves, or doctor calves, or feed calves, and then we would rope at night. Monday, Tuesday, Wednesday we practiced, Thursday and Friday we were off to the rodeos. All along, I knew I was working towards something and that's what kept me going. I'd rope, rope, rope then go to a rodeo somewhere and win me four, five hundred and money wasn't a big problem that next week.

Eventually, I moved in over at Roy's just because I spent most of my time there and it didn't make sense for me to go back and forth. We just lived across the street, but to me, it was a better environment. Everything that I needed was right there – I had my own bedroom and I was more comfortable over there for many reasons. It was great.

Even though she no longer needed it to shoot Willie, Marie continued to pack a pistol in her brassiere. Roy Moffitt's wife, Trisha, recalls her rocking one of their babies who wouldn't settle down, until Marie realized, "I think that pistol's bothering him." She moved the infant off her chest and he settled right down. You would think people would learn, but when Fred was about sixteen years old, he got a little smart-alecky with his mother and she pulled her gun on him too. Fred has yet to find the humor in it, but Marie still loves to tell the story.

Fred made me so mad one time. He was with Roy Moffitt and had won some money and I asked can you let me have some? He had won about eighty-five dollars and I wanted about twenty. He said no, I ain't giving you nothing. When he said that, I slapped him, and when I slapped him, he raised his hand up. I pulled my gun out of my bosom and fired a shot over his head. I said boy, the day you hit me is the day you hit that floor. He took out running and yelling, "Mamma crazy." I never had another problem with him no more 'cause he knew I meant business.

Marie was still headquartered in Houston, but came out every weekend to do Fred's laundry and check on him. She recounts the weekend he mentioned his living arrangements were about to change…

Moon lived at his grandpa's place and then one day he says, "Mamma, I'm gonna move over there with Miss Moffitt. Roy said it was okay."

I said what did Miss Moffitt say?

He said, "Well…Roy said it was all right."

I said I'm going over there and talk with Miss Moffitt.

He said, "No Mamma, Roy taking care of it, don't say nothing to Miss Moffitt."

I didn't say nothing and next time I come out here, he done moved in with them. He was happy there and Miss Moffitt always knew what was going on with them kids. By now he was in high school and busy roping all the time, he really was. I know the first time Roy tried to get Moon to be with a girl Roy laughed at him because he didn't want to stop for girls, all Moon wanted to do was rope. Once they got big enough to go by themselves, I trusted Roy to do that. I went to the rodeo with them one time, but it was the

> worst mistake I ever made. Roy like to have killed me. I like to have had a heart attack. He was taking that Winnebago across the road and he made it go eighty-five, trying to scare me. I said Roy, I'll never ride anywhere else with you. Roy has always been a real down to earth person and he would give him the clothes off his back if he could help him.

Roy says that as awful as it was for him after Fred left for Houston, he knew it was worse for Fred. He recalls that Fred would come back on weekends and stay with Muggins and the weekends began to last longer and longer until Fred was finally back in school in Cypress.

> Fred lived with Muggins and got himself up for school and was very disciplined, even as a little bitty boy. There was way too many living over there and some kind of trouble all the time, so eventually, he just moved in with us. He's my friend, but he's been like my kid – hell, he's been like a father to me a few times. I hate to admit it. I took care of him and watched him very, very close.
>
> My mother would leave her desk to go cook dinner and then go right back to work. She worked all the time, but there was dinner on the table, there was breakfast, there was lunch, there was snacks. Fred would rather go without than have any part of the free lunches at school, so I made sure he always had lunch money. Good food on the table and lunch money.
>
> I also made sure he had money to rope and I kept him on good horses. I think that's one of the contributing factors to his early success, he stayed on good horses. Fred's horsemanship is just like his roping – he is a master who makes any horse look good. He could crawl on anything and win, so he could damn sure get things done on a good one. Me and Fred had big plans to go pro. I had the fi-

nancial resources to do it and I wanted to try it while I was young. I was okay at it, but when you compare yourself to Fred Whitfield? Give me a break. Fred was head and shoulders above the best at every level. In youth rodeos, in the amateur rodeos, he beat them in every facet of the rodeo world. Then he turned pro and he did the same thing.

I don't know what would have happened if he didn't have me. It doesn't matter. It happened the way it happened and it all worked out just fine. My only regret is that we didn't get pictures of any of it. That's what I learned from all this – take pictures. I wish I'd had some of myself and I sure wish I had some of Fred. From the pros on, Fred's got a lot of pictures, but at youth rodeos, we didn't care about pictures. We'd go to a rodeo and people would be selling pictures and we'd walk right by them. My son started racing motorcycles and there was always someone there at the racetrack taking pictures – I bought every picture they took…I didn't care what he was doing or how he was doing…I wanted a picture of it.

At about fifteen or sixteen, I got to winning a little bit at the amateur and the youth rodeos and became more aware of what I was doing. I knew I roped better than most and other people noticed it too. I was still a kid, but people around me who were knowledgeable about the sport, started whispering "This is that Whitfield kid…he does this and he does that…" every time I backed in a box. It started to creep into my mind. Then pretty soon the word on the street was that I wasn't going to be big enough. They started saying things like, "He can get it around their necks fast, but he can't get down there and flank them and tie them." I was a skinny kid and never even started growing until after high school. When I got out of school, even my first year at the National Finals, I was a shrimp. Finally, I just had to show them I could flank and tie a damn calf.

Roy was having a jackpot there at his place and a guy that Roy knew rolled in and unloaded a high dollar horse out of his trailer. He was the biggest redneck that God ever put on this earth and I knew he'd been talking trash about me. Him and his bunch went to Cypress Creek High School and I went to Cy-Fair, so we were already kind of rivals. Before long, we agreed to a match for a thousand or fifteen hundred dollars, of which I had none. Roy put up my share. It was raining, I'm talking raining straight down, and we were ignorant for doing what we did because I was riding a twenty-five thousand dollar horse myself…one of Roy's best. I'm talking the arena is knee deep in mud and they canceled the actual roping, but the match had to go on. Before long, I bathed this dude with them poly ropes, do you hear me? I beat him every which way you could beat somebody and then some. Then I started to whip his ass with a rope for talking trash. After that, the talk was back to, "That Whitfield kid, he's really going somewhere…"

The first time I took a truck and trailer and went to a rodeo by myself was a very big deal that I will never forget. I had it all planned out and went to the Moffitts and asked them if it was all right to take a rig and a horse for a few days. I was going to Round Top, Texas, probably sixty or seventy miles from Cypress, and I was going to be there Wednesday, Thursday, Friday, Saturday and then come home on Sunday. They trusted me to make good decisions and not get in trouble and it meant a lot as a sixteen year old to load up the rig and take off by myself. It was exciting and scary going off by myself, especially since I didn't have a driver's license. I just had a learners permit.

I had the four-horse trailer and a '77 double-cab Chevy 454, brown to match the trailer, and took Spot and maybe another one. It was spring break, probably around mid-March, and I headed to Round Top and stayed with a buddy of mine, Craig Bower. We were going to practice that week and go to the rodeo that weekend. While I was there, we get to goofing around one night and decide to go to town to see what trouble we could get into. We had us a few beers and were feeling a little froggy on our way back home from town. I'm driving with three or four kids in the truck and speeding down a gravel road when somebody said "watch this curve," but it was too late. If I would have tried to go around the curve, we probably would have rolled it, so I just run this sonofagun off in the ditch. We're going sideways and slid into a culvert and it hit the front wheel and bent the rim. Oh my goodness.

Now we got to walk back up there to his parent's house and tell them what happened and have them pull it out of the ditch. His daddy was so mad. He asked us what happened and we told him we just had a little accident. He asked us if we were drinking, and we said, "No sir," of course. Now I've got to find a wheel that matches the one that was on there, but I was there a few days and got it all situated. I never scratched the truck nowhere else but that rim and I had replaced it with a new one. The coast was clear.

I come back home and a couple of days went by and Roy says, "What did that wheel cost?"

What wheel?

He said, 'Don't bullshit me, I already know what happened."

Bad news travels fast and he knew everything. He said, "When I trust you off with my vehicle, the first thing I don't want you doing is drinking and the second thing I don't want you doing is speeding." Luckily nobody got hurt. I wasn't going that fast, but it was fast enough to run off the road with four or five high school kids with me who'd been drinking too. So, I come clean and got through that deal. There has been so many set-backs. It's hard to put into words, but my path to where I am today hasn't always been easy. It's not the way you would draw up a plan to be an eight-time world champion, but it's the way things went – just the way it happened. Then the next thing you know, all the stuff happened with Joanne.

While Fred and Roy dreamed big dreams and hatched grand plans for the big time, Joanne continued building her business. To this day, she sometimes still answers a ringing phone with "Moffitt Oil."

> I was just doing what I was supposed to do, what I had to do, and business just went up, up, up. I guess I got more secure when Chevron came along and started giving me all those plaques that I still have in my office. I started in '75 and in 1994 or '96 I got a plaque for being one of the top ten women owned businesses in Texas. I had to move to a bigger bank. In all those years, I did not leave this office in the daytime. Even if I had a doctor's appointment, I went at 5:00 because I panicked at the thought of turning anything loose to anybody else…until 1981.
>
> It was Christmas morning and I have always had Christmas morning breakfast at my house, still do, for the entire family. It's the only time I make Eggs Benedict and they all come…family, kids, grandkids, great-grandkids. In my dining room, I had a ceiling fan and I climbed up on a stool to turn the light on, and fell off. My head missed the concrete step by that much. Of course, I screamed. I screamed and screamed I was in so much pain. I just knew my tailbone was broken because it hurt the worst. As it turned out, one arm was broken once and the other one was broken in two places. My tailbone was okay, it just hurt. I've got a picture of me sitting there Christmas night with both arms in a cast held out in front of me with a bar in-between to stabilize them. Overnight, I went from being in control of everything to being in control of nothing.

At this point, just as their sons had done, Miss Marie moved in with Miss Moffitt, because, "She couldn't even wipe her butt. She sure hated that I had to do that for her, but she couldn't do it. I did her hair, too, and oh, I made such a mess out of it. I got the rollers all tangled up and I said Miss Moffitt,

I cain't do white folks hair." But Joanne had bigger problems than her hair, and the only one who could help now was Roy.

> I jumped in her spot because the day after Christmas, business had to happen and there was no one else to sit behind that desk. That put an end to all my rodeo plans and it was heartbreaking at the time. I had no idea what my mother was doing all those years. She used to beg me, "Sit here and listen to what I have to say." I always said these hands were made for roping, not working, and I didn't have time for that nonsense. To a degree, I wish I would have because when she broke her arms, I walked directly from the rodeo arena into the office. I did it my way a lot of the time and after she got well, we worked side-by-side for many years. She trusted me.
>
> Being from a rodeo background, I wanted to grow the business and be competitive...competition was fun. It bothered me to put away my rodeo plans, but business turned me on too. Closing deals gave me that euphoria, that high, that rodeo did. Then my girlfriend got pregnant and we got married – and all the sudden, I'm a grown-up. We moved into a doublewide there at Mom's, didn't have no extravagant lifestyle at the time, and for the next thirty years, I sat behind a desk. If I wasn't going to win gold buckles, I was going to win in that office.
>
> I still had all my rodeo dreams come true through Fred. My mother didn't put a rein on what I could and couldn't do with the finances of the company, so I finagled ways to fund Fred's deal. I gave him the opportunity he deserved and Fred carried on for both of us. People have asked me many times if I knew Fred was going to do what Fred did. I said how in the hell are you going to predict that? I knew he was a gifted roper who needed a chance; I didn't know he was one of the greatest cowboys that ever lived. I'd have taken better notes if I had.

We were going to rodeo together. Me and Roy was going to go on the road together and be professional cowboys, side by side. But in 1981, all the sudden life hit him right square in the face and he had to go to work. Roping was second then, but he still maintained his love of it for me and made sure I had money and a truck and everything I needed to get down the road. He said, "You're gonna be a star some day," and I said, "I won't let you down."

Chapter 5

Bad Dads

With Roy's new responsibilities at the office, Fred now took himself to the youth rodeos. "Fred was already on top of his game," Roy says. "But there was some jealousy as I recall, and he had to do everything just right." He adds that, "When I was with Fred at the rodeos, I didn't see him any different than anybody else and I didn't let him get treated any different. They weren't going to give him no hard time." However, Roy wasn't at the rodeos as much anymore.

Roy let me take Spot and I went to hauling him around and winning money hand over fist. This horse was phenomenal. Spot didn't have the speed as he got older, but when we got our hands on him, this sucker worked and was as solid and honest as the day is long. Roy knew how to buy good horses and he could afford them, so we had some horsepower. Spot was one, Crisco was another, and then he had a dun mare that was awesome, too.

The parents at the youth rodeos didn't like this black guy showing up with this ugly-ass spotted horse and whipping their kids like I did, so they changed a lot of the rules trying to keep me out. Pretty soon the word on the street was that I wasn't going to school and wasn't passing and shouldn't be allowed to rodeo. I promise you I am the reason behind the no pass, no play rule when all of the sudden you had to start showing your report card at high school rodeos. They were sure that would keep me out, but I was going to school and passing all my classes, so that didn't work. Then they tried to put in a rule that you couldn't share the same horse at the high school finals. Damon McVay, who is still a good friend of mine, went to Cy Creek and I went to Cy Fair, and we both rode Crisco at the last couple of rodeos one season. I think we won first and second in the calf roping, first and second in the ribbon roping. They thought, oh no, they're going to win everything at the finals and we can't let that happen, so they tried to put in a rule where we couldn't ride the same horse. You got to be kidding me – what other rule are they going to come up with?

I was getting tired of the battle. When I finally got to where I could really rope, I tormented them just a little because I knew there wasn't anybody around those youth rodeos that could beat me. By then, I'd worked my tail off to the point where it was like a man roping against kids, and I was almost a guaranteed check. From the time I was sixteen until here recently, I knew what I could do with a rope and knew that it would take a bad situation for me not to win. But that roping in Giddings is the first time I got to really test myself.

We knew before we went that a lot of those guys would be there and it was a huge moral boost as a young kid to compete against the same ropers I'd been watching on TV at the National Finals. I knew in the back of my mind that I was good enough, but I hadn't yet been thrown in there with all the sharks. Back then, that's what we called them, and I still do to this day. There's kids coming up all the time and everybody talks about how good they are, but they're just a big fish in a little pond. Bring them on out in the ocean with the sharks and let's see how they fare. Because in the ocean there's great whites, there's tiger sharks, there's bull sharks, hammerheads…a lot of creatures that come at you from all angles. There's danger in the ocean and not a lot of security when you're not as tough, mentally or physically, as the predators. So the ocean used to be our analogy about rodeo. Guys could hang around here and not go far from home and have some success, but the PRCA is the real measuring stick. If you can jump in the ocean and swim with the sharks, then you knew you were pretty good.

It was a year or two after the Giddings roping, in like '84 or '85, when me and Ross Hinds went to Durant, Oklahoma to a junior roping and blew the engine in our truck leaving the roping. We were stuck for a few days and didn't have anybody to stay with, so I had a friend call Roy Cooper and tell him we needed a place until we got a new engine for that truck. We ended up staying at Roy's place. Back then, they had those Winston Tours, so Roy was off in Washington or somewhere at one of those, but his wife was there and Lisa put us up at a little bunk house back there and put our horses up, too. I'm on cloud nine. We're missing school, we're hanging out at Roy's place – we were doing it.

Probably about Wednesday, Roy flew in and was going to take us to Denton where somebody else would pick us up and take us on home. We load a few horses and get in his van and we're driving along when Roy pulls into this store on the side of the road. You know what this crazy sucker does? He says, "Man, I need you to get behind the wheel because I'm fixin' to go in there and rob this store." I looked at him like, man, as much as you win rodeoing and you're about to rob this store? I was a nervous wreck, you hear me?

Then this sonofagun pulls out a gun, cocks it back, gets out of the van and goes in the store. A few minutes later, he comes running out of there and yells at me to take off, so I took off. I'm like seventeen years old, and I drive a little ways and then I asked him, "How much you get?" He started laughing and told me that place was a gun store that repaired guns. That gun he took in the shop had been jamming and he left it in there to get it fixed. I said, I can't believe that. Hell, I don't know no better. He tells that story to this day – the time I drove the getaway car for Roy Cooper.

On October 31, 1983, Willie got out of prison and Marie allowed him to parole at her home. By the end of November, after all the fireworks, Marie ended it for good. "It only took one month for me to throw his clothes outside and not ever let him back in my house. That was it – no more me and Willie. I called his brother, I said you got to come get him because he can't stay here. I found out he was worser than he ever been." Willie blamed Marie because she and his own sister talked him into taking the .38 he killed the guy with and turning it and himself into the police. His lawyer said that was the worst mistake he made. Willie said, "I listened to ya'll and it got me ten years."

Fred told her she was crazy to let him come back, but Marie says she felt sorry for him because nobody else would let him stay with them and he had to have somewhere to parole. Because of Willie's delicate legal situation, Marie is clear that "He didn't put his hands on me because I had the upper hand on him. I told him flat out, I mean I told him flat out, if you put your hands on me, I swear to God I will kill you this time. So he didn't hit me no more."

I never knew what my mom was thinking when he come home that time. She said "We're gonna try and make it work," and I thought my goodness gracious. "Gonna try to make it work." If I light a cigarette lighter and burn you, aren't you going to move back? The next time I light it, aren't you going to be standing a bit farther from me instead of standing right next to me. She was advised by his sisters, by my grandpa, by her family, even by me and my brother and sister that it was a bad idea. Why would you continue to put yourself in that situation? I don't know what she was thinking or feeling at the time – I'm just a kid on the outside looking in, but still knew when to remove myself from a harmful or dangerous situation.

Things had been so peaceful while he had been away. Life was finally something we could call normal, and we had not been under any pressure from him coming in late at night and wanting to fight. The seas were pretty smooth while he was away, then all the sudden he reappears and the water started getting a little rougher. The first day back he was pretty quiet and subdued because he hadn't been around us in years, but it wasn't long before he was feeling right at home. Back then, you didn't have to go to no halfway house. Now they let you out and you have to go to a halfway house for a certain amount of time before they release you into the population. I think he was just standing there when he got out and they picked him up. I was totally against it, totally against it, but it turned out I didn't have anything to worry about. She threw him out for good not long after he got there and he didn't have any impact on my life anymore.

It was just a bad mix because my mom didn't back down, I'm telling you, she did not back down. All the years of abuse led to her having to stand up for herself because she didn't at first. She was scared to death of that dude before she figured out she had to do something to him or he was going to kill her. I hear stories about women in that situation all the time and it brings stuff up that I witnessed, but I was able to escape and survive and I try not to let it affect me. It hasn't overall, but it's there. It's locked away, but it can be opened up. It's just like any wound that is healing – if you pick at it, it's going to bleed again.

Anthony concurs that life was peaceful with his daddy in the penitentiary, and while Fred had no contact with his father during his incarceration, Anthony visited Willie consistently. "Mom would go up there and see him, and out of all the kids, I would be the only one who would go with her. He told me that when he got out he was gonna buy me something because I come to see him." Upon Willie's release, Anthony's loyalty was rewarded with a Moped and a Jeri curl. In Houston, the Moped was practically as good as a car, on top of his great new hair, and life in the big city was good.

That summer, when he went to visit Fred and Big Papa in Cypress, Anthony took the Moped with him. The boys had stayed up late roping that night before, and Fred had to be at summer school early that morning and tried numerous ways to wake Buggie up to take him on the Moped. Buggie told him to take it himself, but that wasn't what Moon wanted and he continued to pester his brother. The last straw was when Moon hit him in the chest and Buggie got up and chased him, grabbing an empty beer bottle on his way. Once outside, Buggie threw the beer bottle and hit Fred in the back of the head and he promptly collapsed, bleeding from the head. Big Papa called their mother and when Marie arrived several hours later, Anthony reports that, "Moon was still laid out in the yard, but he was breathing – I made sure he wasn't dead and by now, he had even stopped bleeding. Old Fred was laying there playing possum for his mamma." Anthony recalls that his mother was beside herself over what he had done to Fred, because, "This was her golden boy, this was her roper. After that, every time we would get into it, I would reach back there and touch that scar he still has and he would quiet down."

We were totally different, me and my brother, and by a certain age, I knew I was the favorite and he knew it too. He had a big chip on his shoulder and people didn't warm up to him as quickly as they did to me. We grew apart when he moved to Houston, but he was out there where he liked it and where he could play football. He tells the story, "Well they paid his fees, but didn't pay mine," but he had the same opportunity I did. He just didn't work at it like I did. He didn't put forth the effort and I never felt guilty because I had no reason to.

In late 1985, I got a job over in Conroe riding and training horses for Bill Butaud and teaching his son Casey to rope. He approached me about living over there the night I met him, and told me, "You don't even realize your talent…I can make you a star." He said he had some nice horses and would pay me to rope and ride them, and that if I ever wanted to get somewhere, he was the man that could get me there. That's what the guy told me the first night I met him. They had an aluminum trailer from here to there, they had a red and white Chevy truck that was all souped up with stripes down the side of it, and I'd heard people talk about the Butaud's having plenty of money. He paid me three hundred bucks a week and gave me a brand new 1986 truck to drive, which was a gold mine at the time. I couldn't go wrong – I was going to get out of school and get to rope everyday and that's exactly what I wanted to do. I talked to my mom, she wasn't much for it; I don't think I even said anything to Roy, he wasn't roping, and I was just gone. I didn't have anything to lose, so I left Roy's and moved in the house with Bill and his family.

It was my senior year and I had gone to Cy-Fair from seventh grade until then, but I transferred to Conroe High when I moved. I was on work release from school and would take Casey to his school in the morning, then go to high school until about eleven and go home and train horses until dark. Bill had Ben Rice and a girl working there and they had from five to fifteen head of horses saddled, and most of them ridden, by the time I got home from school. I would go in and change clothes, put on my boots and hat, whether it was shaped half-way decent or flat as all get out…and then I would rope. I'm telling you what, I would fricking rope.

By the summer of 1986, I had graduated high school, and was riding at least thirty horses a day. Bill would sell the horses I trained and some of them summer months I run two hundred calves a day, sometimes more than that. It was a hell of a deal. I drove a brand new truck, had plenty of money and got to rope and ride every day.

I knew when I went there that I would have everything I needed for roping. Then I found out what I had to endure to have it, starting with the dogs. I don't know what Bill was up to, but he always kept a herd of those Rottweilers and Chows around the house. At night he locked the gate at the end of the road and he turned them loose and I guarantee there wasn't nobody coming on the place. Those dogs would chew your leg off if they didn't know you. Bill was a gourmet chef, so we ate the best food you could possibly eat every night, but he drank all the time. He got up and brewed his coffee, then he got out the *Dewar's* and start pouring every morning. Bill was always in a hard-core bad mood and I still remember comments he made to me over the years. Anytime you done something wrong, you would get a cussing and it was like being in boot camp around there, almost like being in the army. He was a perfectionist and I think that he meant well, it just didn't come across that way.

I was his cash cow. That first summer I was there, we probably sold sixty horses, and that was his goal. I probably would have been there a lot longer, but after everything he said when I started, Bill actually didn't want me to rodeo. Bill Butaud was an s.o.b. but his son Casey became like a brother to me and still is today.

Casey Butaud was fourteen-years-old when eighteen-year-old Moon came to live at his house. Casey had decided he wanted to learn to rope and Ben Rice, who worked for Bill, started taking Casey to the Cypress Rodeo. Casey recalls that, "Moon was the champ over there – he won the breakaway, the tie-down… he won everything at the Cypress Rodeo." Calvin Greeley, who also worked for Bill, introduced the two boys and they quickly became friends. Bill had been pondering hiring somebody else to ride for him, and Casey got him over to meet his new friend and his father hired Fred on the spot.

> So Moon showed up at the house in a few weeks and my dad put him in the same room with me. He had probably five shirts, five pairs of pants, one pair of cowboy boots and a rope can and that was all he owned. He had quit high school, but my dad talked Moon into finishing school because he only had one class a day for one more semester. So Moon went back to high school every day after he took me to school. We'd get up and go eat in the mornings, go to school, and come home and rope all afternoon. We had two

queen-sized beds there in our room, so at night we'd lie in bed and talk about roping and going pro and winning gold buckles.

Moon's background was real simple: he didn't have a whole lot, his mom cleaned houses for Roy's mom's family, and his dad made some bad decisions. I think Moon had some heartfelt issues with his dad like I do with my dad, but he never talked a whole lot about it. When I was having trouble with my dad, he said something real brief like, "My dad's a sorry dad," but not much more than that. His dad wasn't around until Moon started doing well professionally as a cowboy and anytime his dad called, he wanted something. He'd ask to see him, but it was just a pretense to get money out of Moon. He'll never get to have a real dad, but I think all of this is what made Moon as great as he is.

My dad's a bad dad. Like Moon, I been through similar stuff. My dad's never been in jail or got shot, but he's really hateful. Our lives have been real different, but similar too. My parents divorced and it got so bad that I learned at an early age to forget a lot of the bad stuff that Bill said to me and did to me. As an adult, my wife and my grandparents have asked me about Bill, but to be honest, I can't remember. Not that I wouldn't tell them, but I can't recall a lot of it. I guess that's the way I learned to deal with it. Bill didn't really whip me much at this point, he was past the whipping stage, but he was real negative, real derogatory towards me and Moon.

But Moon is just one of those never give up, never say die, kind of guys. When he first got to our house, he was an athletic person and he had the ability to rope, but all of that was so unrefined that it was ridiculous. I think two things happened to Moon while he was with us that moved him so much further along. What Bill does is he beats you up so bad and runs you down in different ways that it makes you mentally strong. So Moon had both of those two things helping him, he roped all day every day and he had Bill giving him so much hell and treating him just like a second-class citizen. Moon already had his perseverance, but my dad's torment drove Moon, at least part of the way, to be as great as he was as a professional cowboy. Bill changed his game, the mental part of it, by breaking him down so much, and Moon succeeded because he learned how to overcome what my dad did to him. I know Moon could have done it without my dad, but I think the mental part of working and living with Bill prepared him for how they treated him in the PRCA and the things that were said in a more direct, derogatory, in-your-face manner. Bill prepared him for that level by treating Moon like trash.

When he moved in there with us back in the eighties, there wasn't hardly any black guys that roped, much less rodeoed. There's a lot more now, but then it was rare, rare, rare. Moon dealt with a little bit of racism rodeoing in the south in that kind of country environment, so mentally he had all of that to deal with. We would practice all week and sometimes my dad would let us leave on Saturday and Sundays to go to ropings and jackpots and little amateur rodeos. At eighteen, nineteen-years-old, Moon was winning as much as all the top guys from around here. What was cool that I always remember is Moon setting the calves in there so he could try to rope them literally before he got out of the box. I mean it was amazing and I started telling him that he could beat anybody and that belief in him just grew and grew and grew. He was going to these small ropings and starting to tie them in under seven seconds, which nobody could do, especially at his age. Moon was just one of those rare guys that could do that and he won every roping, he won every jackpot, he won everything he went to – it was crazy. Everything we went to, Moon won first. But they always messed with him – and he was with me and my dad the day he had enough of it.

Moon was in the senior division and I was in the junior division, and I remember we were at a high school rodeo where twelve flat was winning first. Moon roped and tied his calf in a short eight, like 8.2, 8.5, and they flagged him out because of something about his sleeves. Even my dad said a few things to the judges about it, but it was one of those times when we could tell it was racial. I mean I've just never seen something like that happen in all my life…in all my life, and I've been to a bunch of rodeos over the years. They were trying to hold him down so bad that even my dad had to say something about it. This stuck to Moon and we talked about that for weeks and months and even years; all the way to the pros we talked about it. It was one of those things that stuck in Moon's head forever. It got inside of him like a lot of things have, and I think it made him persevere and try harder. White cowboys could be real hard on Moon and at the same time, he's kind of one of them because he's always been in that white environment. First Roy and his family, then my family, and just from being in rodeo in general for his entire life, he has a lot of the same characteristics of any normal white southern rodeo cowboy.

It was bad whenever I went to high school rodeos. All the other kids I competed against had their own horses, the best money could buy, and I had to make do with whatever I could. After I left Roy's, I had to borrow horses and I'd show up in a raggedy two-horse trailer I had bought with money I'd saved while the rest of them showed up with the best of everything in their fancy-ass rigs. I didn't have nothing of my own and I'd show up with this guy one week and that guy the next week and this horse one day and that horse the next day. But I stuck it on them every time because they didn't work at it like I did. You never seen a guy give a roping lesson like they got at those high school rodeos.

The last straw came at a high school rodeo one Sunday afternoon in Belleview, Texas. I went over there with Casey and when we left home I forgot a shirt, so I had to wear one of his. Well hell, his shirt sleeves come to like right here on me, so I got to roll one up so it doesn't restrict what I'm doing, but I left the other one down. And I run out there, and I think 12.1 or 12.2 was winning the rodeo and I was like 8.4 and I threw my hands up. I get back on my horse and see that this guy is waving his flag. I'm like, what the hell? And he rides up there and tells me I was disqualified because I had my sleeve rolled up.

My mouth just dropped open. I had a meltdown and just threw a fit. I'm talking about a cussing, wall-eyed fit. This rolled up sleeve had not been a problem before I whipped another rich white kid. I was mad enough to fight, but first, I tried to reason with them, and couldn't reason with them. Then I got off and tied my horse up and tried to talk to them again and this time they threatened to kick me out. I said, you sonofabitches ain't going where I'm going anyway. I wasn't going to mess with it anymore. They said, "We're gonna ban you," and I said stick it right up ya'll's ass because the next time ya'll see me, it will be on TV. This is a true story and I wish I had it documented somewhere.

I wasn't going to jack with it anymore. It was just too big a hassle and that was the last one I went to, but I dominated them while I was there.

CHAPTER 6

THE POND

Casey says that Bill would keep between seventy-five to a hundred horses all the time at his place and buy a hundred to a hundred and twenty-five fresh calves every month and "all we did was run them out for Moon."

> Some days he would ride some twenty or thirty horses and would run two hundred calves a day. It wasn't like he'd come out there and rope five or ten – he would rope and rope and rope. I would bet that back in their youth, all the greats, Roy Cooper, Joe Beaver, all of them would get to fifty to seventy calves in a day and say, that's enough. I let most of those calves out for Moon and I never once heard him say "I'm tired…my hands hurt…I don't want to rope no more." I never heard him say he didn't want to go to a rodeo either.
>
> Bill showed a lot of roping horses to buyers, and the whole routine was sort of like at the rodeo. Moon would put on a cowboy hat, starched shirt, clean jeans and boots like he was at the rodeo and then Bill would give Moon his instructions. "Okay, Joe Smith is coming to look at this horse for ten thousand dollars; we're going to show him these three horses, I want you to run three calves, four swings and a wrap…" With my dad, you could never let the horse have a problem, never make a bobble, never let the horse look weak and Moon set every one of them up with no mistakes. He got into those scenarios and by the time Moon was nineteen, he had went

through it so many times that he was like a robot.

The likes of Roy Cooper, Tom Ferguson and Joe Beaver – the who's who of calf roping and rodeo, started showing up to buy horses. These guys are saying to my dad, "Man, that black boy can rope…that black boy can rope." They used a little different terminology than that, but they all said the same thing. I was letting the calves out and it was more impressive to watch Moon rope than the world champions that showed up to try the horses.

In my opinion, that's what helped make Moon so great – the opportunity to rope literally hundreds of calves a day. This wasn't one day a week; they would rope like this five or six days a week. The other people who worked for Bill would bring the horses to Moon ready to go, he'd go rope off them, when he was done with that horse, they'd have the next horse ready for him and he'd rope off that one…and this would go on all day. He wouldn't tie all those calves down, but he would tie a big part of them. He'd ride old horses, he'd ride young horses, he'd ride problematic horses, and he'd ride sour horses, so he got that horsemanship. Moon was smart enough and tough enough to take advantage of working for Bill instead of letting him beat him down.

I've always had thick skin and Bill's torment bothered me, but it didn't usually linger. I could take a twenty-minute ass chewing, but then it got to where it was every day. Then it got to where I was in trouble for everything I done and just couldn't do enough right for him. He was going through a divorce with Casey's mom and having to give up a lot of money and he was a horrible drinker, so it was bad. But I was making money and was saving most of it and working towards where I wanted to go. It wasn't costing me a dime to live and I was pretty conservative with my money while I was there. I'd go to a jackpot and win fifteen-hundred dollars and I'd get to put thirteen-hundred in the bank. At the end, I had somewhere around thirty thousand dollars saved up.

Lots of famous people from the rodeo world came over there to buy and sell horses, and after I left Bill's, I knew I was going where they were. Roy Cooper came over there; his brother, Clay Tom, bought a couple of good horses; DR Daniel come and tried some, he was a big name back in the day; Joe Beaver bought Pat from Bill, the horse he won the world on in 1985. That was Bill's most famous horse deal, when Joe bought Pat from him.

I still took a lot of crap because of the color of my skin, but by now I'd had years of it. It was just a fact that there was always somebody going to jack with me, always somebody who was going to say something. It happened at the Smith Brothers Jr. Championship Roping one year with a guy who later won one world title. He had been bumping his gums and it got back to me that he was saying, "I'll match that nigger." I said I ain't afraid to rope him – we can rope for a bullet or we can rope for money, make it light on yourself – sky's the limit for me. That pissed them off even more. But I just never backed down, and not that I was a big tough bad guy, I just felt like if I stood my ground there would be less of what was going on. I figured if I shied away from it, that it would intensify, so I just never backed down. I was in a position to dictate what happened by then, so say what you want, but take this ass whipping with it. That's roping; it wasn't always fighting. I did it when I had to but I didn't leave home with the intention that I was going to have to whip somebody today – it wasn't that bad. I whipped them in the arena, and that was usually good enough, and that's what happened with that guy.

That Smith Brothers roping was in July every year and it's where all the top guys in the world from 16 to 19-years-old come together for a big jackpot. I went to it twice and won second twice. One year I borrowed a horse from Ronnie Williams that was probably one of the best in the world at the time. Roy Cooper rode him at the Finals twice and I'd got to riding him a little bit and I'm telling you what, he was the real deal. So I won second both times – the first year I broke a rope and that's why I didn't win it, the second year I got beat by some accident I can't recall. I'd also been to Barry Burk's Junior Roping and beat some up-and-coming nineteen-year-olds who could damn sure rope, and I left those competitions without a doubt in my mind that I was real. They knew it too.

Casey recalls the changes in Fred:

> Those Smith Brothers ropings were big defining moments for Moon. Kids come from Canada, the east coast, the west coast, and all over these southern states to compete at this deal. It was big entry fees, big calves, big arena, long scores and a professional type environment. Both years he technically out-roped about two hundred kids all across the United States and Canada, but both years he had fluke things happen. I can remember his confidence growing after that first year. I could put my finger on it; and when we left that second year, he had changed. He was that much better a competitor, that much better calf roper, and that much more confident in himself outside the little local Texas amateur stuff he'd been doing. He just got elevated at that point.
>
> I loved Moon and everywhere I went, I wanted Moon to go. My grandparents and my parents were all wealthy white people and I wouldn't go to any of their fancy holidays or family events unless Moon could be there, too. I made it clear that if I went, he was coming. My grandparents let me bring him at Christmas, but my dad didn't like that at all. About half the time I would ride with Moon and we would go in a different vehicle than my family and show up together. I don't know if Moon knows this, but at Christmas, I told my grandparents they had to buy him presents too. The first year he

> was there, they didn't even want to talk to him. I made them accept him in our lives, but it took a little bit of behind the scenes massaging to make them realize how much I thought of Moon. My dad still always tried to treat him like he was just the help. Being a Texan, I ain't saying I ain't been a racial guy, but that's never come up with me and Moon. We've had our fights, our ups and downs, our life situations, but his color just never mattered.

Casey says something about his grandparents being racist, but I never saw that. If they said it to him, they never said it to me. He's telling the truth; I just didn't see that. I only went to their place a few times, and it was something else. They were rich, and they're still rich, so I'm sure they were kind of that way. The only black people that were around them worked in their house, and now all the sudden you got one that's living with their grandson. I'm sure it didn't go over very well. Even so, I never saw Bill as being a racist person – he didn't come across like that to me. If I had thought that, I wouldn't have been living over there. He wasn't prejudiced – he hated everybody the same.

It was the summer of 1987 when me and Bill Butaud had our last blow up. It was after the NARC [North American Rodeo Association] Finals that summer. The NARC is where all the amateur associations come together and they have one big finals in El Paso. I went with a guy named Tommy Balloosic and he come by Bill's to get me and Bill really didn't want me to go and that was the reason we got into it. Working for Bill, I had to stay there and ride a bunch of horses and he didn't want me rodeoing much. He wanted me to stay there and be his slave, because he cared about selling horses, he didn't care about rodeoing. The thing about that is when you got good horses and you take them out to rodeos, they're a lot easier to sell. That was my pitch to try to get to go a few places – you can't sell them at home, nobody sees them. But he didn't want me to go nowhere…I mean it was alright to go to Field store which was just down the road, but anything else made him mad. He wouldn't even let me take a horse, so I actually borrowed a horse of Joe Beaver's. I just loaded up and we went to El Paso.

We're at the NARC Finals and I roped and didn't do no good the first round, maybe won a little bit of money in the second round, and while we're out there, we blew up Tommy's truck. Now we're stranded in El Paso, seven hundred and fifty miles from Conroe. We'd been out there since Tuesday but couldn't get a ride out of there before it was over on Sunday and Bill was not happy about that. Now, I work for the guy and I understand that, but I had to call him and say, man, I don't know when I'm going to be back home. Well he's mad.

He said, "I can't believe you ain't coming back here. We got horses to ride, we got this to do, we got that to do...somebody wants to come try some horses, and I need you to show them..." He roped a lot on his horses, but when customers came, I rode them because I could make them look like a million dollars even if they were dinks. On top of Bill being mad at me, I got to get this horse back to Joe because I said I'd have him home. Finally, we got Tommy's truck fixed, a new motor that cost seventy-five-hundred dollars, and got home. By the time I make it back, I'd been gone about nine days.

There was a guy from Pasadena who had come to Bill's to try this horse, and I drive in and they were down there in the round pen and Bill's got horses lined up. I went to the house and changed clothes and go down there. It was in the spring, probably about three thirty, four o'clock, and when I get to the round pen, he don't say a word to me. I walked right by him and he didn't say hello, go to hell, nothing. Now the guy that's there to try the horse, he says, "Damn son, where you been? I been sitting on this board fence for a week waiting to try this horse." I didn't back up. I said you probably should have got up and walked around if you been sitting there waiting for me that long. It was pretty quiet the rest of the day.

Now Bill, he's a big time chef and that night he cooked a big old fancy meal, but I didn't go downstairs to eat. I stayed up there in Casey's bedroom and took a shower. I just sat on the bed and thought about it for a minute, and thought well, the inevitable has happened. I ain't putting up with no more of this and I started packing.

Casey come in and said, "Man, what are you doing?"

I said dude, I'm probably going to check out.

He said, "Moon, I don't want you to leave, please don't leave," but I said I've had enough. We'd bonded pretty good me and him and got to be pretty tight. His dad was a jerk and he treated Casey like he treated me, so he and I got to be like brothers. He said, "Moon, please don't leave, please don't leave," but I said man, it's time for me to go. I threw all my stuff in a bag and went to the barn.

Bill came out there and said, "What the hell are you doing?"

I said I'm done.

He said, "Man, you can't pull up and leave like this, what the hell's wrong with you?"

I said I can't do it no more. You don't want me to rodeo, you don't want me to go nowhere, you want me to stay here and make all these sorry horses look good so you can sell them. I make three hundred bucks a week and you're getting all the glory.

The more I roped, the better I was getting, and I'd had it in the back of my mind for a while that it was time to make the leap. Tonight was as good a time as any. Sometime in here, I'd bought me an old raggedy three-quarter ton truck, and had a little raggedy one-horse trailer and I had a five-year old mare that I'd been training on that belonged to Roy Moffitt. I loaded it all up and left there that night. I didn't know where in the world I was going to go.

Casey says it had been building for a while and that "Bill wasn't shocked Moon was leaving; I think he was sort of expecting him to leave." He says that his father knew Fred would do well without him and that he couldn't stand the thought. "Even though Bill could have helped Moon, he never would and always kept his thumb on him. It's the most unexplainable thing to me – he don't like to see you do good." Casey adds that although it was for all the wrong reasons, his dad did have a significant impact on Fred's career because of the invaluable experience in roping and enduring mental torment, both of which he would need where he was going.

> Moon knew what was coming. That night there was a lot of name-calling and a lot of threats: "You ain't going to amount to nuthin'...you're just a piece of trash I got off the streets..." Anything he could jab, prod or poke to hurt somebody, that's what he did. I was hurt and didn't want Moon to leave, but neither one of us was going to stand up to Bill. Looking back it was best that Moon left because if he wouldn't have gone that night he could have stayed caught up there longer because it was easy in a way.
>
> Bill had a lot of money, a lot of horses, a lot of calves, all the stuff Moon needed and didn't have. God only knows how many more years Bill could have suppressed him. He kept us all on a tight rope with *his* horses, *his* ropes, *his* money, and Moon had no choice but to leave and figure it out for himself. Even if the stuff was Bill's, he couldn't take the talent away from Moon, he couldn't take away the experience of winning everything, he couldn't take the knowledge he had gained from being there and roping so much. Moon had it all now and it was time to go and implement it, so I think it was good that he left.
>
> Roy gave Moon a lot and helped him along, but Roy sort of turned his back on him a little bit there and that's why Moon got off track. It was a hate-love deal with them for a few years, but Roy wound up helping him financially and that's how he got to the pros.

That was always Moon's deal, to get enough money to get out of this cutthroat amateur circuit and go to the pros. That was his only goal and we often talked about that. He was always saying, "I got to get money, get horses, I got to go…" But we always knew he was going to the pros; we always talked about winning the world or making the Finals…all the good stuff.

I will never forget Bill cussing him and calling him names and putting his finger in his face that night. It was a big deal in my young life because I came from a divorced family, and so did Moon, and we clung to each other a lot. Moon's not a real emotional guy, and he gets real distant when things are bothering him. My dad hurt him bad and Moon told me, "Man I got to go, I just can't live like this. I'm sorry you have to, but I'm going to go on with my life." Neither one of us are big talkers, so it was all pretty short and sweet. I loved him like he was my brother…and then he left and went on with his life. From here, he ended up being with you-know-who for about a year and that turned out to be pretty radical.

It was about a year or so after he left our house that he got on drugs. Rodeo is a small world and they act like it's a big movie star world and coke was the in thing to do for even the best cowboys in rodeo back then. I wasn't rodeoing, I was sixteen years old, just a kid in high school, but people started telling me Moon's doing this and Moon's doing that. I hadn't talked to him in a month probably and one night he calls me and says, "Casey, I need you to come get me and take me to Cypress." I said all right, where you at? When he told me whose house he was at, I should have known right then what he was up to.

I had a nice Mustang sports car my mom bought me, so I go over there about nine o'clock on a school night. Moon gets in the car and he's got a rope can with him that he puts in the backseat of my car and we take off. I'm a bad speeder and I'm going fast and he's telling me to watch it, but he always did that. I'd say okay, okay, and keep speeding. Finally, he said, "You got to slow down." I asked him what the big deal was since I had a radar detector and he pulls that rope can out of the back and opens it. Inside of it was a big old bag of cocaine. I never really did any drugs, and I sure as hell never saw that much. I asked him how much he had and I don't remember exactly what he said, but he said it was a lot and that if we got pulled over we were going to jail for a long time. I went the speed limit the rest of the night.

When he got out of the car, I said man you shouldn't be doing that. Even as a sixteen-year old kid, I'm thinking he's going to prison. Of course, he lived through it, but that's how I found out for sure that Moon was involved in drugs. I never really questioned him about it again and I didn't think it was my place to judge him. I always cared so much about him, but I didn't say don't do this, don't do that, I just said be careful. Whatever you're into, just be careful…something like that. But this was not really Moon – he's more focused than that; he's more on track compared to the older guys he was doing it with. I think it's something he regrets. He got out of his element and was influenced by his peers, which was rare with him.

After I left Butaud's, I called my mom and told her I might come and stay with her a little bit. I dropped that mare off at Roy's and moved in with my mom for a little bit. It didn't last long. One day she said she was going somewhere and then circled back trying to catch me with girls in the house, which she did. She said, "I don't know what in the hell you think you're doing – I ain't runnin' no whore house." I didn't stay there long. Then me and my brother got an apartment down in Houston and that didn't last long either. Me and him could not get alone, so I left there, too.

From there, I drifted around and stayed with a guy who was a pretty successful roper at the time and me and him got on drugs and I stayed on drugs for about a year. It was cocaine and hell, we'd rope all day and all night on that stuff. I'd drive the guy around while he did his thing and was pretty much his go-fer. He'd make deals and I'd pick it up and drive it around and make deliveries for him. He was just using me so he wouldn't get caught. I stayed there doing this for damn near all of '88 and I'd done run through all my money and was just living day to day.

During the Finals one year, some guy he was doing business with called and told me to tell him that if he didn't have his money by the fifth round, he was going to show up out there and break his arms so he'd never rope another calf. I let him know the guy called and they needed their money. I said I don't know what your deal is, but you probably ought to pay them.

So we had a couple of little dope deals going on when he come to me one night and said "Man, I need to tell you something."

I said what is it?

He said, "If we ever get busted, you take the rap and I'll get you out of trouble."

It was just like the light come on. I thought this dude thinks I'm stupid. I never said it to him, but in the back of my mind, I wondered just how stupid he thought I was.

I don't belong in a cage and the thing that always scared me about drugs was jail. When I was doing it, that's what I was thinking about...what if I get caught, what if I get caught, what if I get caught? I was always paranoid about getting busted and that kept me from getting any deeper into drugs than I went. I'm not going to say peer pressure made me do it because obviously, I wanted to do it and nobody held me down and stuck a straw up my nose. But I was always around older people and they did it, so I did it. I knew it was a dead end street. As counterfeit as my dad was, he told me one time that I could do whatever I wanted to, but if I ever got caught with drugs

I was on my own. That was in the back of my mind during this whole time. I left there and I decided that drugs weren't the way and decided that I didn't want to jack with it no more.

My mentality was always to be the best, and to be the best in the biggest field. When I was winning all this stuff around here, it meant a lot and it was financially prosperous, but the whole time I had my sights on being in the ocean. I was in the pond around here and it was fun and all that was grand but I wanted to beat the best. I was always looking up; I wasn't ever looking back. Right before my rookie year, I just walked away from it and have been drug free since then. I said it ain't me, I don't want to be associated with it, and when I was done, I was done. There wasn't no relapses, there wasn't no shrinks, there wasn't none of that. I've talked to a shrink before but it wasn't about drugs…it was about women.

Hell, Roy will tell you he done it too. When I got back to Cypress, he was pretty much the same way the rest of us were.

Roy discusses Fred's true "addiction":

> Yeah, Fred had a little run there with the coke, but it didn't last long. I had a run with it as well, so I probably didn't set a great example in the drug arena because I liked cocaine, too. I mean that was what you did in the '80s; you snorted cocaine. I don't know if it's still in the rodeo world, but at that time, there was a lot of cocaine going around. You could drive more, you could do everything more. It was cool, stay up for a few days…line it up and let's keep rolling.
>
> This was early, early in Fred's career, even before his rookie year, and they got to using coke, him and his friend. I wasn't around a whole lot at that time – I was at the office, but I had heard about it and knew it was going on. One time him and some girl come by my house and there was some cocaine involved. He got sick as hell,

drinking and doing coke, and I said maybe that will break him of the habit. Somewhere along the way he got broke of the habit. It was recreational drug use, whatever you want to call it, because he wasn't addicted to cocaine. Fred never had a drug addiction, Fred never had an alcohol addiction – Fred had one addiction and that was roping.

Chapter 7

Bless Her Heart

By late 1988, I left drugs behind, but not before my little habit cost me the thirty thousand I had saved up at Butauds. I'd also blown up my truck so it wasn't running, and I knew I had to do something different – I needed to change my environment completely. I came home and stayed with my mom for just a little bit, then drifted on to La Porte, Texas and landed at the Knox's, Wayne Knox and his wife Shawn, which was the best place for me. I met them through Stephen Perry when he come up to Bill's and bought a couple of horses and we got to be friends. Wayne and Shawn and Stephen Perry are still good friends of mine to this day. Wayne has done well for himself with a pipe company they owned in La Porte and they now have a thousand acre ranch just twenty miles from me. They have been up here about ten years, but when I moved in with them at La Porte, they were building a house there and we lived together in a little apartment in the barn – a barn the size of a house. Besides the part we lived in, there were stalls inside and outside, wash racks, a drive up deal where you put your tractor, and you could still park three big trailers inside it. It was huge. The apartment was part of the tack room and it had a living room, a little kitchen area, one bedroom and one bathroom. They would get up in the morning and shower and then I would shower and we worked hand in hand in a very small place. I had been around Wayne, but didn't really know him when I moved in with him and Shawn. I showed up and they invited me to rope and ride their horses. I stayed the first night and the next thing you know it was three or four nights and the next thing you know, that was my address.

For the most part, I've always fit in and been accepted wherever I am. Some of it had to do with my talent, but I'm a trustworthy person who was appreciative of what people did for me. Before long, I got settled in and they knew I wasn't going to run up eight thousand dollars on their American Express, so they turned me loose with checkbooks, credit cards, horses, trucks, trailers, whatever they had, and we had so much fun…we had some good times. Bubba Paschal, another good friend and sponsor to this day, lived just down the road, and that's how I met him. Bubba has an older brother, Shane, and we would rope together every day. Wayne kept calves and had a nice set-up; an all pipe arena and big pens; he had four or five good roping horses and Shawn run barrels, so she had two or three horses. There was plenty to do there and I would get up every morning and swim her barrel horses in the little swimming deal she had for them. When I first got there, most of the time she would want to swim them herself, but then she figured out I knew what I was doing and trusted me with her horses.

The story I told people about my background was that I grew up in Cypress, my dream is to rope and be successful in rodeo. Other than that, I didn't disclose a lot about my family life to new people. I wasn't going to tell anybody my dad killed somebody and went to prison. The people who knew me well, knew about that, but as I got older I never talked about it in articles or interviews. I don't think it's something you need to go talk about every day; it's nothing I'm proud of, but I dealt with it.

The first thing Wayne and Shawn Knox make clear is that, "He's not Fred Whitfield to us; he's still Moon, but nobody else calls him that anymore, so we try not to." Wayne says that he roped calves for a short time in his "first life," the one where he was a kid married to somebody else. It was after Wayne met and married Shawn, "the love of my life," that he decided he wanted to rope again, and heard that Bill Butaud's was the place to get a good horse. It was there that the Knox's met Fred, but didn't know him that well – until he moved in.

Shawn says that, "It's hard to give an accurate record of Fred to anyone who doesn't know him. He was always such a whiz kid…such a whiz kid." She says that one day he just moved in and for a year they bunked together in two tiny rooms – she and Wayne in the bed in one room and Moon on the couch in the other room. Shawn says she did feel like his mother while he was away from his own mother, but that she never had to clean up behind Fred because he took care of himself. "I did wash his underwear, but other than that, he was independent." Wayne takes it from there.

> Bill Butaud was known for being a big drinker, for having lots of money and for having good horses. Fred worked for him and that's where we met him. Even when he was working for the other side and trying to sell you a horse, Fred was honest and Fred was true. Fred did things on a horse that made you think if he could do it then I can do it too. When I first tried to rope off that horse I bought, I must have hit the ground a thousand times. Fred was eighteen or nineteen years old at the time, and could ride a horse and make it look like magic. He was so talented that he could make a not-very-good horse look great, so it was incredible what Fred could do on a good horse.
>
> Bill Butaud would drink like you couldn't believe, and I never knew exactly what happened between him and Moon, but somehow after Moon left Butaud's, he came to our place. It was kind of like a bridge for Fred and it was another world for him. I kept twenty or twenty-five roping calves and when I left for work in the morning, he would be roping and tying calves and when I came home in the afternoon, he would be roping and tying calves. Every day, all

day long. On the weekends, me, Shawn, Bubba, Shane and Fred all rodeoed together and had a great time – I mean we had some good times. We all loved going to rodeos, we loved roping and we loved to be around people who loved it too. A lot of guys saw how talented Fred was and they didn't like it; some of the rednecks couldn't stand the color of his skin. He had ninety-eight percent more horsemanship than anybody else around and could take a colt and beat any of them. They didn't like it. He never talked about becoming a world champion, he never bragged, he never said he could do it; he never talked about any of it. He just wanted to do the best he could with what he had. He wanted to make a living roping calves...he was talented at it and he loved it.

We didn't know much about his early life, but Fred knew how to make it work with nothing. He didn't need anybody or anything. I think if you dropped him out of an airplane in China, he'd end up in the same place in life as he is right now – he would figure it out. You see the killer instinct in Fred. He has heart. I love him so much, and he's so honest that people either love it or hate it. He doesn't know any other way – it's just not him. He never took a shortcut in any of it and it makes Fred mad when somebody tries to cut the corner. Even at that young age, Moon's integrity, his hard work, his dedication, was all there and it's because of his heart and his try that Moon got where he did. He earned it and he deserves it.

He's been exposed to everything there is. I've been with him a few times and he probably kept me in line when I should have been keeping him in line. He does that for a lot of people...a lot of people. I don't think Cody Ohl would be alive without Fred Whitfield and that's the truth. He's a unique person.

I stayed at Wayne's in 1988 and a little bit of '89 and was twenty-years-old now. I was having a great time, but I wasn't really going anywhere. I learned a lot at Bill's and I learned a lot at Knox's, but I knew deep down inside I had to go back to Cypress where it all started. I wasn't raised in the best environment, but there was no doubt in my mind that's where I should be. I went back and stayed a little with my mom, then I'd stay at Bubba McDonald's for a while – he's another good friend that I spent a little bit of time with. Bubba was about five or six miles from Roy's, and he had an arena out in his front yard and we roped a little bit. But Moffitt's was the most secure place I had ever known and I could have some normalcy there. A lot of people have done a lot for me over the years, but Moffitt's was a sanctuary where I could be sane and truly be home. I also knew there was a place for me to go to work and if I showed the work ethic and the drive that I had always shown, a way would be provided for me right there.

I went back to Cypress and sat down with Roy and told him my dreams and my goals and everything I had been doing. I had a heart-to- heart with him and said this is where I want to go. I said man, I know the last few years haven't been exactly what we wanted, but I really want to rodeo. I said I'm ready to get it together because right now I'm just not headed in the direction I want to be going.

Roy gave me a job and my title was "Lube Distribution Manager" at Moffitt Oil. I was more a warehouse flunky who drove a truck and delivered oil, but the deal was I worked a little and roped a lot. I'd had a few other jobs as a kid. I sacked groceries in my sophomore year of high school, and I could not have been more miserable at all of them, do you hear me? Jobs were like having wisdom teeth pulled out without Novocain. But the fall before my rookie year, I had a job and was working and saving money. I had tossed away some valuable years and had some catching up to do, but I wasn't too far off track.

When I showed back up at Roy's, the arena was gone and a parking lot for all his eighteen-wheelers was in its place, so we built a new arena on the easement behind his house. You had to go through a strip of woods, about forty feet, and then right on the other side of the woods was the arena. The power company gave us the okay to build an arena under the guy wires back there on the pipeline. Roy had a house over there with a swimming pool and all that stuff and he put a barn behind there, too. I was in a good place because I would work all week and then on the weekends I'd load up a few horses and go to the rodeo. If I won a thousand or so, than I'm that much more to the good. I got my permit in '88 and won $19,000 on it so I was eligible for PRCA rodeos in '89. It was all falling into place, but I wasn't quite ready yet, so I stayed put for now.

Even though I was back in Cypress, I stayed away from my grandpa's place. I'm not saying I didn't want to be around my Big Papa or my sister, but there were so many people coming in and out of there. My aunt would always bring outsiders in and there were always different people there – I wasn't better than them, I just didn't want to be in that circle. I would go and visit Big Papa and Tammy, but my dad was usually around too, so I never hung out over there much. Tammy was close to my dad and once I got a little older, I never had any use for him. I tolerated him because if I didn't, he was going to probably kick me or stomp me or beat me…at the very least, he would talk to you like you were a fricking dog. I would acknowledge him and navigate my way around him when I saw him. I didn't want much to do with him. He knew I was scared of him and so that just made things worse. Once I got away, I stayed away and that's sad because Big Papa did a lot for me. But I had outgrown everything that went on over there…totally outgrown it all.

Tammy and I were close and talked all the time. The only time she and I had a problem was over the choice of guys she hung with and in my mind, that's why she's not here anymore. That brain injury when she was a kid permanently affected her emotionally and she was never the same after she got hit by that truck. Tammy got pregnant at an early age and had a couple of kids and just made a lot of bad choices. I know it was because she wasn't always at the top of her game mentally. I had kind of gotten away from the house when the accident happened and she got killed.

On a quiet Sunday afternoon in February 1989, Marie and Roy were at his house watching *Pee Wee's Big Top* with his three children while his wife was in the hospital for a hysterectomy. Earlier, Marie had seen flashing lights going down Kluge Road and told Roy, "Somebody done had a wreck. I bet it was Willie..." Before long, one of the cousins from the Whitfield place came running across the wooden deck just outside. She was yelling and screaming and didn't stop to knock before she swung the door open and said "Marie, Marie…Tammy dead, Tammy dead…" Roy helped Marie sit down.

"Bless her heart," Roy says. "Tammy had some problems because of that accident when she was a kid. It wasn't nothing bad, but she changed…and now this."

Marie recounts what happened earlier that day:

> It never dawned on me when I saw them lights go by that it was my daughter. Tammy was twenty-two years old and didn't know how to drive. Roy came down earlier and said you need to go talk to Tammy because she's drinking and she says she's going somewhere with some guy and the kids are crying. I went and got Tammy's children and talked to them. They needed some Valentines for school, so I took them to the store and when I come back, they said, "Talk to Mamma because she's been drinking and she's fixing to go somewhere." I tried to talk to her, which she wasn't talking to me because somebody reported her for not taking care of her kids and CPS had took them and give them to me. I had them for ninety days and CPS said they could go back and when they went back, Tammy was doing all right. But then she started drinking and I didn't know it.

> Later that afternoon, she left her house driving this man's truck and hit a tree about a mile and a half from the house. When the people got there to tell us, my stomach fell. It was Rosa who run in and told us. She's seventy-seven years old now and still lives over there. She said, "Marie, there's been a bad wreck and Tammy is dead."

Roy called his mother to stay with Marie and he went down the street to the crash. Just as he got there, the helicopter took off with the passenger, while Tammy was still in the vehicle. She had been pronounced dead at the scene. By now his mother had arrived with Marie and Roy kept her away because, "She was crazy by that time…by then Marie was gone…she had lost it." Roy says he stood between Marie and the truck Tammy was still in, trying to keep her away from it, and, "There were cops everywhere, there were lights everywhere, the helicopter was taking off…it was wild. It looked like a movie. It was terrible…terrible."

Tammy had driven into a big tree on a curve and the motor came into the cab and crushed her. She was killed instantly. Marie recalls trying to get to Tammy, but says the police told Roy and Mrs. Moffitt, "Don't let her see her because her body's in bad shape." Marie says she always thought it was strange that Tammy was hurt so bad by a truck when she was four, and now she'd been killed in one. She says that Fred and Tammy were very close and that, "When we buried her, Fred couldn't take it. When we walked in the funeral home…Fred couldn't take it. I asked his wife if he ever talks about it, and she said he don't talk about it. He holds things in."

It was in '89, the year before my rookie year, and Roy called me and said I needed to come right home. I was at Bubba McDonald's and I said what the hell's going on. Roy said, "Your sister's had a wreck and she didn't make it." I wasn't but twenty minutes away and when I rolled up over there, there were people everywhere and cops everywhere. They done had her covered up down the road and I didn't go to the scene. I guess it was an hour or so after she had passed that I found out about it and so they had the scene secured. They didn't even take my mom down there because she was wigged out.

I pulled in the driveway and there stood Roy. I said, dude, what's going on? He gave me bits and pieces of the story and I could not believe what he was telling me. There was conflicting stories; some people said that when they left Big Papa's Tammy was driving, some people said she was a passenger, but the fact was she was driving. My sister did not have a driver's license and should have never been driving with her mental condition, let alone when she'd been drinking. I guess they were going to the store and got to arguing and ended up hitting a tree and the steering wheel hit her in the chest and just crushed her. Tammy had been dating this counterfeit s.o.b. and we never really found out the truth. I think they were fighting and run off the road a mile or two from the house, hit a tree head on and it killed her. We could never get the final details, and that sorry sonofabitch is still alive to this day. They cut the tree down not too long ago.

Every time I think about it, I wonder if I had been around if I could have kept it from happening. I was always the one who would speak up and get involved if I was around somebody and saw them doing something wrong. If I would have been there that day and she would have been drinking, she might have got in that truck, but it wouldn't have been behind the wheel. That's the part that still bothers me.

William "Bill" Pickett (1870–1932) was the first black rodeo athlete ever inducted into the ProRodeo Hall of Fame. Billed as "The Dusky Demon" on show flyers, Bill Pickett was one of the Wild West Show's more colorful characters, and is also heralded as the original creator of bulldogging. His method differed somewhat from today's steer wrestling in that Bill Pickett took down steers by biting their lips, as dogs did. It's said he learned his technique as a cow puncher who watched "catch" dogs use the same technique on cattle in the thick Texas underbrush where swinging a rope was useless.

In the Oct. 11, 1931 edition of the *Tulsa World News* an eyewitness account describes Bill Pickett's performance at a "show" as rodeos were then called: "The steer lunged into the arena ... Pickett's horse plunged full speed after it...the rider leaped from the saddle. He turned a complete somersault along the length of the steer's back, flying out and down over the curved horns... to fasten his teeth in the side of the steer's mouth. With sheer strength he dragged the running behemoth's head to the tan-bark, thrust its horn in the ground, and forward momentum threw the steer hocks over horns in a somersault of its own."

After his days in the Wild West Show, Bill Pickett worked on a large ranch in Oklahoma and it was here that he was killed by a bronc in the spring of 1932 at the age of sixty-two. His grave is marked with a sandstone tombstone that reads, "Bill Pickett-C.S.C.P.A," which stands for Cherokee Strip Cow Punchers Association. Today, Bill Pickett Invitational Rodeos (BPIR), a circuit for African American competitors intended to educate the public about the role of African American cowboys in the history of the West, continue in cities large and small across America. [*billpickettrodeo.com*]

I've had this scar on my face for a while – I got it in a bar fight in California in '89 after a Bill Pickett roping out there. I'd been seeing a girl from around Austin, a black girl, and this half-black, half-Indian guy had been trying to steal her away from me. A few weeks before California, we'd been in Austin and had a little encounter with him after the rodeo. Me and my girlfriend and Dana Williams and his girlfriend were sitting in a Denny's at around two-thirty in the morning when him and his friends come in and sat in the booth next to us.

"Boy, that sure is an awful pretty young lady you got with you," he said, "She should be with me."

I said really. I got up and I stood out of the booth and said, hell, she can get up if she wants to.

They called me a smartass and this, that and the other, and we didn't say much or do nothing. There was four or five of them and two of us, so we just finished eating and left.

Then I run into him in a bar out there at that rodeo in California and he told me, "When this bar closes, I'm whipping your ass." I said well, I guess I got an ass-whipping coming because I ain't going nowhere. When the bar closed, he pulled a knife on me in the parking lot and cut real deep into my face; he was trying to cut my throat and damn near got it done. When he did that, I got a tire tool out of the back of somebody's truck in the parking lot, and I'm talking wailed on this sonofabitch for so long that he couldn't see or walk by the time the cops and the ambulances got there.

This all happened about two-thirty or three in the morning and they took me to the hospital and stitched me up. It took thirty stitches on the outside and six on the inside where he'd cut so deep it broke the white pigment of my skin. Just as soon as they were done, I went to fricking jail in Livermore, California, which was the first and only time I been in jail. I had enough money on me to bail out, but they wouldn't let you bail yourself out, so I stayed in jail for about twelve hours.

I'd done called Roy two or three times, but he was out of town and since I wasn't having no success getting him, I had to call my mom. We had to hire a bail bondsman, and I'm talking to my mom from jail telling her to go to the bank and withdraw some money and get it wired so I can get my ass out of here. My mom's like, "I talked to the guy and he's gotta do this and he's gotta do that…I got to get the money out of the bank…" just on and on. I said, I'll tell you what, if ya'll don't get me out of here by noon, I'm done with all of ya'll. I'm telling you, done…just write me off.

So about noon that day, they started throwing out them orange suits, getting ready to transport the people that weren't getting released anytime soon to the prison. I'm thinking, oh, man…I done been on the phone all night, I ain't slept a wink, and, yeah, I'm in a lot of pain. Those stitches got that cut all pulled together and it was leaking a little bit, but I wasn't worried about that, I was worried about getting my ass out of jail. About twelve-thirty that afternoon they come in and said, "Whitfield." I said, oh yes. So I finally got out of that jail cell and I tell you what, I ain't got a clue where I'm at. I was lost in Livermore, California.

Cell phones was not available back then, so I had to find a phone and I'm trying to get in touch with the guy I went out there with. Finally, I called the fair grounds and got a hold of him and told him he needed to come get me because I had been released. I catch a ride back over there to the hotel and I gather up all my stuff, left my horse and everything else out there, and got on a plane and flew home. After getting sliced up in a bar fight that night, I didn't want to be there no more and it felt like rodeo was over for me. I came home, but had to go to court out there several times to get out of that deal. It was a lot more trouble than I bargained for and it damn near got me killed.

I had a good friend of mine, Jackie Fitzgerald, and we run into the guy the next winter, and Jackie begged me to let him kill the guy. He said, "I guarantee you, I'll take that dude out…" And I said nah, don't do that because it's going to come back to me.

But that's what happened…it was over a girl.

CHAPTER 8

RANDOM ACTS OF VENGEANCE

In 1947, African American cowboys of the era formed the Negro Cowboys Rodeo Association, which evolved into the National Black Cowboy Association and today boosts a membership of twenty thousand. One of its earliest members, Calvin Greely was also one of the first black men to integrate what was then called the *Rodeo Cowboys Association* (RCA). An all around cowboy during the 1950's and 1960's, Calvin was a "role model and stepping stone for other young black cowboys," who was sometimes made to ride after the main performance of the rodeo. While he competed on the professional circuit, Calvin Greely never qualified for the National Finals.

At the 1982 National Finals Rodeo, Los Angeles cowboy Charles Sampson won the bull riding world title and became the first black man in history to wear a PRCA gold buckle. Sampson gave a lot of the credit to Myrtis Dightman, a bull rider from Houston, who, in 1966, became the first African American to qualify for the NFR. From 1966 – 1972, Dightman only missed the NFR once and ended up third in the world in 1967, but never got a gold buckle.

"I've had a lot of old white cowboys come up to me and tell me he got the worst shaft in the world, that he should have been a world champion," Sampson says of his mentor. "I heard all these stories about how tough it was for Myrtis to win, how the judges cheated him and how he couldn't get into some rodeos. But he never talked about those things. All he ever said was ride hard, try hard, and enter as many rodeos as you can."

It was rumored that a few unscrupulous stock contractors assigned Myrtis the meanest bulls they had, and then, like Calvin, made him wait until spectators had left the stands before letting him make his ride. At a rodeo in Little Rock, Myrtis was denied entry because the gatekeeper could not believe a black man could be a rodeo contestant. His bull was turned out, but the misunderstanding was corrected and he was later allowed to ride. Dightman also said he spent more than one night sleeping in the back seat of his car rather than risk being turned away from a hotel.

Myrtis once asked his friend Freckles Brown what it would take for him to win the world title. Freckles replied, "Keep riding a bull like you've been riding and turn white." However, his achievements were finally recognized when, at age sixty-two, Myrtis Dightman became the first living African American cowboy inducted into the National Cowboy Hall of Fame in Oklahoma City. [*Andy Smith, Conroe Courier; cowboysofcolor.org*]

As far as having black heroes that rodeoed, there was a select few, and I got older and got to meet them and come to understand all the obstacles that they had to go through just to have a chance to go and compete. At one time, Myrtis Dightman and me were both endorsed by the same hat company and I got to be good friends with him. He would tell me all these wild stories about how back in the sixties they'd make him ride his bull after the rodeo. This is not something I dreamed up. These stories are true and Myrtis told me this with his own lips. These guys paved the way, but it was still far from a clear-cut path to where I was going. Knowing what they went through made it a little easier, but it was still tough, it was still complicated. That's just the truth, whether you want to hear it or not.

To this point, pretty much everything I used, Roy Moffitt paid for. He bought this and we shared that and it had been that way for a long time. Now, I needed some money to buy my own truck, my own horse. I'd never won any high school titles, but I'd been going to amateur rodeos and winning pretty good. I realized it was time to get me a bank account and start saving some money to get ready to jump out into the ocean with the sharks. That's where I wanted to be.

The biggest amateur rodeos at that time were Pasadena, Rosenberg, Angleton; then Clem McSpadden had that Bushy Head roping every year where they added like ten thousand and roped out in a pasture. I went to all of those rodeos and from September 1, 1989 until October 15, 1989, I won thirty-five-thousand dollars roping. I won Rosenberg, I won Pasadena, I won Angleton, and I won like ten thousand at Clem McSpadden's. And I went up against the best of them to do it. Roy Cooper, Dee Pickett, Barry Burk, the whole herd of them, roping calves, I guarantee you, that weighed three hundred and sixty pounds. Some of their tails drug the ground, they were so big. And I did it all on a horse I borrowed.

I come home and, hell, all of the sudden I got me some dough built up. So Roy said, "Listen, we're going down to the bank and we're going get you an account set up. Buy yourself a new truck and let's start looking for a horse to buy." This was late in the year in '89, almost 1990; I went down to Lawrence Marshall Chevrolet and bought a brand new 1990 maroon 454 extended cab truck. Things were rolling and I was in high cotton, you hear me? 1990 was going to be my rookie year – I was going to the pros.

Kansas City was my very first pro rodeo after I'd filled my permit. I didn't win the whole thing, but I won quite a bit there, maybe second or third. Denver rolled around in January and I won good there, next was Fort Worth and I didn't do very good at Ft. Worth, but then I won quite a bit at San Antone. Houston rolled around and I won money there. Before you know it, I'm fricking number one in the world by March of my rookie year, and I'm telling you what, we couldn't be happier. Roy's excited, I'm excited…and I still don't have a horse. Number one in the world and I don't have a horse.

In the spring of 1990, I heard about a pretty good horse right here in Cypress that I should take a look at. The guy lived about eight miles from me and it was raining, but I wanted to ride the horse, so I threw a saddle in the back my truck and went over there. His name was Ernie and this sucker was beautiful – a buckskin, black mane and tail. I thought *man, oh man*. So, I saddle him up and lope him around a little bit. Roy drives in a little later and we're looking at this horse. He says, "Hell, run a couple on him." I back in the box and he stands just like a statue. I run one and it was like holy moly. So, I run another one and another one and he just gets better. After I'd run about four calves, Roy says, "Don't run no more on him. We need to take him to the house and rope on him and see if he's that good." The guy said we could take him for a while and if we decided to buy, he wanted ten thousand for him. I said okay.

We get him home and Roy asks me again what I thought of the horse, and I told him he was unbelievable. I roped two or three times on him there at the house, I'm telling you it was a match made in heaven. It's about mid-April of 1990 now, so I decide I'm going to load this horse up and take him to a few rodeos. I went back east with Rusty Young and Dan Webb and won three rodeos in a row on this horse, and I'm telling you, we're roping some big soggy calves. This sonofagun was like being tied to a freight train. I was like 9.1 at one of them rodeos, when twelve might be winning second at a pro rodeo and that was unheard of. So I call Roy and I say man, we need to get the money together.

In the meantime, the guy calls Roy and says another guy just offered him fifteen thousand for the horse. Roy called and told me that, and I said, you got to be kidding me. I said, you tell him I'll be home in two or three days and we'll just bring him back. He's straight up screwing us and I ain't going that route. When I left his house that day, he wanted ten thousand, and now he wants five thousand more because I won three rodeos in a row on him?

Roy told me to hold on and not worry about the money, he'd call the guy. He called him and said, "Hey, we got a problem. When Fred picked that horse up from you, you only wanted ten thousand. Now that he's won these three rodeos on him, bam, bam, bam, three in a row, why'd the price jump five thousand?" The guy said he had a legit offer for fifteen thousand, and Roy said we'd give twelve five today and to go pick up the cash from Mrs. Moffitt. I had me a horse.

Roy's memories of how Ernie came to be differ slightly from Fred's...

Did he tell you the story of the first horse he ever got? I don't know if he told the whole story or not, but he gave me a hard time saying that horse ain't no good. I told him there was this dun horse named Ernie for sale down the road. We knew the horse because we seen him every weekend and I said that's a pretty good horse, Fred. He said, "That horse ain't no damn good." He was giving me a hard time, right? I said let's just go try him, let's just try him. The guy that had been riding him was just a mediocre calf roper and they didn't win no money on him, but that horse still looked good to me. I saw potential in that horse, so I said: Fred, just keep an open mind and let's try him.

So we went down there and Fred got on him. I knew what was going to happen, I knew what that horse was going to do, so I took a video camera with me. Sure enough, that first run he worked half-assed like he always did, didn't do nothing good but didn't do anything too terribly bad. Second calf, he did a little better, third calf he come on strong. I think we might have run about five calves on him and he just really fired on the last two calves, worked really good. So that was enough and we put him up because we knew he was sound, didn't have no leg problems, you could grind him forever. Fred didn't want to admit I was right, he was thinking that I'd been away from rodeo too long to know what I was talking about, but I had the damned video.

To make a long story short, we bought Ernie and Fred went on to win rookie of the year on him and he won the world on him. I'm not going to say Ernie was the greatest horse he ever had, but I am going to say I was right.

I went to winning left and right on that horse, but Ernie hadn't been hauled a whole lot, and he was getting a little nervous. June rolls around, I about got this horse blowed up because I have been rodeoing my ass off. I'm number one in the world with people all around me, with stuff going haywire, and this fricking horse is about to have a nervous breakdown. I put ten thousand miles on him in forty-five days and he was in culture shock. We had come from Texas, where it was like eighty-five degrees and now we were in Redding, California where it's forty and raining and this great new horse I got gets sick, I'm talking sick. I let him rest for three days, but then he quit eating. He was bad sick. I had gone to California planning to make about five rodeos and then hit Helldorado Days in Vegas on the way back, but Ernie ain't ate or drank in three days and he's the only horse I got.

I'd been training a little dun mare as a back-up horse, but I went with three other guys in a four-horse trailer, so I could only take Ernie. Finally I told them, look man, I got to get this horse home. We were in my truck and somebody else's trailer, and I don't remember who, but one guy just threw a big fit. He said, "Man, you can't just leave us high and dry." I told them they could take my truck and I'd catch somebody going back to Texas, but I knew if I didn't get this horse home, he was going to die. I finally got Ernie home and took him to the vet I'd been using who I thought was pretty good and they give him a bunch of pills, but this horse still hadn't ate or drank coming on five days. This is when I met Doc Currie who is my vet to this day. I took Ernie over to Doc's and he said that horse was hours away from dying – hours. Doc Currie saved him, but I had to stay off him for a month, so now I'm without a horse again.

I'm back to borrowing horses, but everything was still peachy, and I'm rolling around in the top five in the world standings. By now, summer rolls around and I decide to rodeo a little bit with Sylvester Mayfield. He was a renegade, runaway, sonofabuck. Never mind the details, going off with Sylvester was a nightmare.

After Myrtis and Charlie, before Fred, there was Sylvester. The NFR's third African American, the first in a timed event, Sylvester Mayfield qualified twice and was one of the top calf ropers in the world during the mid-eighties. He went to the Finals in 1985, the first year it moved from Oklahoma City to Las Vegas, and again in 1987. Even so, black cowboys hitting it big in the PRCA was still unheard of. By the early 1990's, approximately one hundred of the ten thousand members of the PRCA were African Americans [*Eileen Daily, answers.com]*, as the combination of racism and economics continued to make it near impossible for most to compete at that level. Well, one was doing all right for himself ...at least that's what they were saying in the papers.

> *Houston Post, March 1, 1990:* Number three in the world, Fred "Moon" Whitfield is achieving instant success on the Professional Rodeo Cowboy Association circuit without a traditional rodeo background – no ranch, no rodeo heritage. As a rookie, he had already placed at ten of the winter rodeos, and earned $15,447, more than half of it at San Antonio. [Number one was Joe Beaver with $21,272, number two was Mike Johnson with $19,341.]
>
> *The Daily Sentinel, Grand Junction, CO., June 23, 1990*: Fred Whitfield...and his horse were spectacular Friday night. A 22-year-old rookie from Cypress, Texas, Whitfield has taken the pro circuit by storm.
>
> *Rodeo Sports News, Spring 1990:* Placing third and winning

> $8026 at San Antonio in February followed by significant wins in March at the Rodeo Royal in Calgary and the ABC Rodeo in Lubbock Whitfield established himself as a contender in the calf roping and shoots holes in the worn out stereotypes of black athletes. Unlike most cowboys, Whitfield has neither a ranch background nor a tradition of rodeo in his family. About Roy Moffitt, Whitfield says, "Roy's been a father figure to me. He taught me right from wrong." Roy says, "I'm awfully proud of Fred. We both hope he'll make it to the National Finals Rodeo."

I didn't set out to hide anything from anybody, but nobody ever 100% researched everything in my life. They took it for what I was saying. I told the truth, I just didn't tell the whole story. I wasn't lying, I just felt like my business was my business. I kept it to myself and those who knew me best knew about my life. I've never had anything to hide.

When I was with Sylvester I don't win a lot and everyday I'm dropping in the standings…ninth, eighth, eleventh... About that time, Roy Cooper hit me up and said, "Man, you want to rodeo with me?" I said yeah – I'll finish the fall with you. So it was late July and I get hooked up with Roy, and we go up to the northwest and win a little bit. He let me ride Topper, everybody's heard that name before, so I'm riding his horse and having quite a bit of success. I was lucky my rookie year. I rodeoed with Dan Webb, Russell Young, Sylvester, Roy Cooper, right down the line and most rookies don't get to do that. I think it contributed a lot to the success I was having and if I'd been down a ways in the standings, who knows if they'd have even given me the time of day. I've figured out over the years that everybody wants to be around a winner.

Roy Cooper and I went for a little while and I had some success, but after awhile it just felt like I was his driver. Roy had access to airplanes and people would fly him around and do everything for him, so we weren't rodeoing together as much as I was just driving his horse around. He was letting me ride his good horse, which was great, but I left Salt Lake in late July headed to Cheyenne and I said, Roy I really appreciate it, but I think I'll buy me a dog. At least I'll have somebody to talk to while I'm doing all this driving. I said man, you get old Topper and find him a ride because I'm going to do something different than this. And it wasn't a bad break up or nothing; we just went our own ways. By now, I'm back on Ernie and we got ready to go to Cheyenne.

Roy Moffitt says that he has been a Fred Whitfield fan for a long time, and was personally involved in all aspects of his professional career, especially in the early years. "I followed him closely, but I was working and all my energy went towards building that business," says Moffitt. "I had kids and a family, but I also had Fred and the success of Moffitt Oil helped Fred get where we wanted to get him to go." Roy had the PRCA number memorized because he frequently called it to pay entry fees and fines, and he and Fred conferred daily on the telephone. Then one day Fred called to say he was done with all of it and coming home.

> I think he was in Nampa, Idaho and he said, "Man, I'm comin' home. I am digging a debt with you that I will never get out of." I said let me tell you something, I'm sitting here working eighteen hours a day and I need you to give me a reason to do it. You just keep getting your hands up in the air. You worry about winning first…let me worry about this money deal for a while…forget about the damned money. I wanted to get that financial pressure off him and I knew he felt that pressure and I knew how bad the stress was trying to be a competitive calf roper, running up and down the road and financially he just couldn't see the light at the end of the tunnel. He couldn't get there from here in his eyes and I told him to go on

and let me worry about the money and so he went on. He had too much talent to let money woes mess everything up, which it does for so many people. It was no secret where he was headed by then. Maybe two or three weeks later, he won Cheyenne and qualified for the NFR by late summer his first year out.

Cheyenne is in July, and he called me up after he roped his first one and said "You gonna come out here?" I said you rope your second one and let me know how you do. There is two and a short at Cheyenne and I was going out there if he made the final cut. As soon as he made the short round, I flew out there and watched him win the whole damn thing. His rookie year and he wins Cheyenne – the daddy of them all. Oh man, was I glad I went.

Me and Roy done some of the craziest things back then. Nowadays you couldn't get away with the stuff we done back then – you'll get killed in a heartbeat. I match roped a guy in 1990 for five thousand dollars at the Phil Line Roping. To be real honest, we had the money, but we didn't have the money…we had a guy with us that we could get the money from if we lost. It started when this guy walked past me and said, "I'm about half drunk and I don't think you can catch ten today." I said sir, I'm not going to back down from you and since you been drinking, and since I can't catch ten today, let's just put up five thousand. So the guy walks out in front of the box before I run the first calf and he says, "We got another five thousand we want to bet against the nigger." I said I don't have no more money to bet, but I'm not going to listen to you talk to me like that, so you need to just get out of the way and watch me stick these grass ropes on your ass. And that's what I done – I stuck it on his ass; do you hear what I'm telling you?

Then, when the roping was over, they didn't want to pay us and things got a little testy right quick. Roy was running around looking for somebody's gun because we was going to vigilante these sonofabitches. It was serious. We got our money, but as soon as we did we got the hell out of there. We didn't even unsaddle the horses; we just loaded them and left because them rednecks were not happy about me taking their five thousand. Roy went down the road throwing their hundred dollar bills out of the truck window, just throwing them out. I said Roy, you're a freaking idiot; you're going to get us killed man. I've had some of the best times of my life with that guy – he's probably the best thing that ever happened to me.

Roy tells his version of the Phil Line match roping.

> That pissed me off – those guys walking around talking like that to him. Five thousand dollars was really five thousand dollars in them days and on top of that they were trying to throw more money at us than they thought we could handle. I wasn't scared to bet them and Fred damn sure wasn't scared to rope against them. Fred would rope for his life because he is so freaking competitive.
>
> We ended up getting paid, but I just knew we was going to have to fight our way out of there. We were young and it was the major leagues. And he's lying about the hundreds – it was twenties. I was just getting that drink on and talking smack – "We got a lot of problems, but money ain't one of 'em" All of it was for show.

Fred and Ernie opened the 1990 Cheyenne rodeo with a mediocre 14.2 in the first round and came back with a 12.0 in the second round to make the final cut. Fred went into the championship round in fourth place, behind Mike Ray, the arena record holder, Herbert Theriot and Dee Pickett. When it was all over, Pickett had trouble with tying, Theriot broke the barrier and Ray was the last man with a chance to beat him, but just didn't get it done. With another 12.0 in the final round, Fred Whitfield was the first place winner of the 1990 Cheyenne Frontier Days Rodeo and received a check for $13,174.

Just after I won at Cheyenne, I knew I had made my first National Finals. I was wore clean out, so I came home and rested for a few weeks and then took off out northwest. The latter part of that year I didn't have near as much success as I had the first part. If I had, I would have gone to my first NFR in a better position and things might have been different. Me and Ernie got to where we weren't getting along and I took him to Richard Stower's out there in Oklahoma to ride for a few months. I'd done won Cheyenne riding him and been to some rodeos over in Kansas and Oklahoma in late August and this horse had been working his guts out. Then all the sudden, he give up. He was tired, just like I was. I have a horse that can stop and jerk a house down, and by late October, I knew I couldn't take him to the Finals.

Brad Riney brought his horse to the San Angelo Roping Fiesta and I rode him and won money. He felt real good at that roping and Brad thought I ought to consider riding him at the Finals. I'd roped one on this horse and he'd run three jumps before he ever stopped, but not knowing I was going to be in a shoebox out there at the Finals, I said sure. I had a horse to ride, so I got on a plane to Las Vegas – there ain't nothing to worry about.

Before I ever left for Vegas, I knew I had the rookie of the year won. It was already in the bag, and I was the second rookie to ever make the Finals. Joe Beaver went to the Finals and won the world in '85, his rookie year, but that was it at that point. Me and Blake Krolczyk flew to Vegas and showed up there the day before the Finals started, tickled to death. It was happy times. His mom has set us up with a rental car and we roll up to the Hertz counter, but ain't neither one of us twenty-five and they won't rent us a car. We didn't have no cell phone, so we went around the corner and got on the pay phone with his mom. She told us what to do and what to say, and we go back over there and get us a Towne Car. We leave the airport and we got that thing on two wheels, I'm talking about smoking it down. Hello, Las Vegas.

Once we leave the airport, I start to see a few of the guys and they're like "Man, where you been?" I just got here, what do you mean where have I been. That's when they told me I'd missed the welcome reception, where you get your back number and all your information for the NFR. This deal had already started a few days ago and I thought you just showed up and roped. I didn't get off to a very good start at the rodeo either. At the first performance, I missed. I don't even think I caught the first two or three I run. After being the 1990 PRCA Rookie of the Year by more than twenty thousand, after staying well into the top fifteen all year long, after going to the Finals in fourth place in the world, I ended up in seventh place when it was all over.

I didn't let my guard down as much as I got a little content with just qualifying and didn't prepare to be there the same way I'd prepared to get there. I just made some bad decisions. I should have called somebody who had been there a few times and asked for a little bit of advice, but all I cared about was I was headed to Vegas. I might have been happy to get there, but I was mad at myself when I left Las Vegas. Troy Pruitt won the world that year and he's a great guy and a good friend of mine. But I let this one get away, just like in '92 and '93, when I got me a girlfriend and wasn't really focused on what I should have been focused on.

My winnings for the first year were $74,095, including $15,330 I won at the NFR, and I was into the Moffitt's for right around thirty grand. Roy said "I'll tell you what, give me nine thousand and keep the rest to start '91 on." And that's what we done. Most people would have said give me my money. Most people would have said give me your fifteen thousand and you better come up with another fifteen or you're going to be in a bind. Roy was like having a bank with no interest. I had a checkbook with both our names on it and it didn't matter if I wrote a check for two thousand or twenty thousand, it was covered. If you got that kind of security and you're good at something, all you got to do is go do it. And I did.

CHAPTER 9

THE OCEAN

Well hell, the story has got to be told. I met her in Cheyenne during my rookie year and we were together a long time – almost five years. It was love at first sight. Roy Cooper invited me to somebody's wedding and I met her there. I don't even remember who was getting married, but it was at the reception that I run into her. I was wearing a cow print jacket…black guy in a white hat and cow print jacket. Don't laugh – that was the style back then. She come by and started jacking with me about that cow print jacket. I thought hum, she's pretty good looking, probably five seven or so, blond hair, green eyes. I might need to meet her. We got introduced and went out bar hopping after the reception. I got her phone number and called her a few times and we just got hooked up. By '91, we were living together.

I had dated, but as far as I can remember, she was the first girl that I ever cared for. I can't put my finger on why, but I just fell head over heels for that owl-headed woman. At the start, we didn't fight all the time, but after we'd been together about three years, around late '93, things started to turn. She was devious, she was manipulative, and everywhere we went everybody was always drawn to her and she had to be the life of every party. It wasn't jealousy; it just got to the point where it was annoying. There were happy times, but they were few and far between.

I guess the biggest complication with our relationship was that her parents didn't like me. It was the first time they'd ever had anything to do with a black person, especially one that was dating their daughter. Then she moved to Texas to live with me and her mom and dad had a fit with it. For a going-away party, they threw everything she owned out in the front yard and said "I can't believe you're going down there to live with that…" blankety-blankety-blank. Naturally, that put a strain on things too. When the in-laws hate you, you're doomed from the start. I showed up at their house with her one year for Christmas and I don't think her dad said one word to me. Christmas holidays, and I mean not *one* word. I guess I had to be in love to put up with that.

I was getting all kinds of outside advice on my relationship from a lot of people who were concerned about what it was doing to my life and my career. Everybody except my mom. My mom just loved her; this girl who had her so snowed. Roy didn't care for her at all, but that was all about rodeo. "You need to leave her alone, you need to focus on your rodeo, you're doing this and you're doing that…" I tried to not make waves and just kind of ride the fence, but it all created friction. Now that I look back at it, now that I'm a lot older, I probably should have listened. After things went down the way they did, I realized if I would have got her out of the way, I'd a been a ten time world champion instead of eight. I guess it was all just part of the process a guy goes through in life.

He had been out of it for several years, but in 1990, Casey Butaud decided to revive his roping career and his dad promised to help him. By the spring of his senior year, Casey was roping again and doing well enough on the amateur circuit to make it to their finals that year. Before he even graduated, he and Bill had fallen out again; Casey moved in with his mother in the 'burbs; left his horse at a friend's; borrowed a truck – "things were just all crazy." By mid-summer, "a guy we all know named Stephen Perry" said he could ride with him and Casey was once again on track.

This is Moon's rookie year and by now he had that girlfriend. Me and him get to talking and Moon says that if I will come and help him drive, he will pay my fees at the permit rodeos and I could ride his horse and we could travel around that summer and rodeo. I said all right. So I get in with him, and me and him and that girl take off together. We go to the first permit rodeo and I win the rodeo, so I filled my permit like right now. Back then, once you filled a permit, you could rodeo the rest of the year and didn't have to buy a card. I wanted the full six months to rodeo on the rookie deal, so I didn't buy a card and some places we went to, I could rope, some places I couldn't.

Her and Moon hadn't been together long at all at this point, but they ended up together for years. I don't think he had any serious girlfriends until her. When Moon found her, he found something he liked and that he wanted. She was beautiful, blond-headed, wealthy and educated. She had everything going for her – on paper. He was younger and a little less mature, and I think a lot of that relationship was mental for him. He had it in his heart, but I think he had about half in his heart and the other half was just because she was what he wanted.

After about six weeks of rodeoing together, me and Moon start arguing real bad. He argues and gets pissed off and gets an attitude about everything. I've got a temper, but our personalities are totally different. Sometimes I just wanted to ask him, dude, what are you so pissed about *today*? What is it today, Moon? I mean, are you broke? Did you break your arm? Did your horse die? But none of that has happened – he's just pissed off. He's one of the top ten guys in the world, has a great horse, a trailer, a camper, a truck and a beautiful, rich girlfriend and he's pissed off most of the time. Finally, we had a falling out where it all really went down and I'll never forget it because it's such a western story.

Her parents were real wealthy and money was never an object for her. We were in Colorado Springs for a rodeo and one day all three of us go in some western store and she says "Casey, I want to buy you a new straw hat and some new boots." I said great. My family had money, but they wouldn't give me any of it, so I was happy to get a hat and some boots.

Moon comes up and says "What in the hell are you doin'?"

I said I'm getting a hat and some boots.

He said, "Who's paying for that?"

I said, she said to get it.

He says "Hell no, she ain't paying for your hat and boots."

I said, well, I ain't got no money.

He said "Then you ain't getting no hat and boots."

She is standing right there and starts telling Moon that she *is* going to buy me a hat and some boots, and he comes back with, "I'm getting just a hat – and Casey don't need nothing." Then him and I start to go at it a little bit and finally I just said to hell with it, I don't need a hat and boots. He said, "You spoiled little brat, you got everything given to you your whole life." I said a few things back, not a lot, and he's pissy to me until we get back to the Pikes Peak or Bust Rodeo.

Sylvester Mayfield used to work for us and was friends with my dad, so I knew him really well. Well, he's there and Joe Beaver's there and Moon starts really giving me hell in front of Joe and Sylvester. Joe takes me aside and says, "Hey, ya'll are always going to fight, that's how you two are…so I'm going to take you with me." I said I don't want to go with you, Joe. If I wasn't going to be with Moon, I wasn't going to go.

I've done quite a lot of rodeoing in my life and most of it was because of Moon. When it was clear we weren't going to get along and it wasn't going to work, I went back home to do something different. I think I was there more to be around Moon …I think it's always been that way. That night it got so bad that I got on a plane and flew home and I didn't rope again for a very long time. I went in the military sixty days later.

Roy confirms his pessimistic view of Fred's love life at the time, but admits, "At that point, there wasn't a whole lot I could do other than be there for him, just be the moral support for Fred." Yeah, provide moral support and make sure the love birds stayed out of the Las Vegas city limits for anything other than roping.

She was a fiasco. She rodeoed with him and every time we went somewhere, even to the National Finals, they were fighting. I was worried to death that it would mess his mental game up, but he proved me wrong because nothing can mess him up. But I finally got to the point one time at the Finals when I threatened him – I said we're going to have to keep your ass about a hundred miles outside of Vegas. He was going through his relationship issues, and I thought we're going to have to stay outside of town where there wasn't a casino and there wasn't all the riff-raff. I don't know the name of the place we stayed that year, but I said get out of these lights, get out there and chill, you know… we can go back to town when it's time to get ready to rope.

I've told Fred, and I've told reporters before, that back in them days it was fine for a black baseball player or a black basketball player to have a white girlfriend…nobody frowned on that. But I was afraid that in the rodeo world that would be looked at differently by that crowd. My comment to Fred was that it might limit his number of endorsements. Other than that, it was irrelevant to me who he slept with. But I don't know how it could have been any different because he wasn't in an environment to find a black woman, never in his whole life. Fred is whiter than I am, but he had a lot of controversy and it was a tough deal for him. I mean, we're talking over twenty years ago in the rodeo world and Fred would take it straight up. He lived it every day, I didn't.

Casey says that what Fred did professionally was just part of the story, and that he had challenges his fellow competitors didn't have to worry about.

It's easy to see all the accolades, his accomplishments, the money he's earned, but to see the true Fred is to see what he overcame to do what he did. No mom and dad who could help him, no money, no horses, no rodeoing background…and if that wasn't enough obstacles, they tried to run him off the first five years he was in the pros. They gave him so much hell that most anybody else would just go home and stay amateur or quit rodeo altogether and get a job. Anybody else would have said I ain't going to listen to this…I mean it was bad.

I don't know if he's talked about this, but I been at an amateur rodeo with him where they said, "Oh lookie here, we got two of a kind…we got a black calf and a black cowboy." At the PRCA, there was a group of them that would call him "nigger" before he roped to try to get him all messed up. I don't know how much of this he's told people, but they would literally call him "nigger." It was that bad and when he came into the arena, that same bunch would boo him. They would go to bars and try to run him out of there. They would threaten to beat his ass if he showed up someplace they didn't want him. And in the right environment they would sort of bulldog him around and put their hands on him. They attacked him racially, they attacked him mentally, and some of them attacked him physically.

He was pretty good with it and tried to keep to himself, but Moon's really tough. He's a tough man, big and strong, and he'll take up for himself. He ain't going to beat up the whole town, but he'll fight and he wound up whipping a lot of them. There was a pack of them and over time he started singling a lot of them out. He knew better than to hit one guy when there was three or five, but over the years, he wound up getting back at them. And after the first five plus years or so, it started fading out.

They knew he was a champ, they knew he was great. They came to know in their minds that if they called him that name or not, that it didn't matter. No matter how they treated Moon; he always let them know that he was going to win and they couldn't deny it when he made it as big as he did. His presence and performance spoke for itself, and so that kind of treatment faded out to some degree.

I personally don't think I have a bad attitude. It can be brought out, depending on my surroundings at the time. If somebody treats me bad, then I had a bad attitude. There's been a time or two in my life where I was miserable and had a bad attitude twenty-four hours a day, but in general, I don't have a lot to be unhappy about. I don't want to say that some of it was for show, but in order to be at the top of your game for any period of time, there has to be a difference between you and the rest of the competition… an air, so to speak. It just has to be; you cannot be at the top of your game as a professional athlete and be normal and be just like everybody else. There's an arrogance that is necessary, and that was especially true in my case. I never set out to be rude or indifferent; I just wanted to be a world champion and it brought about an air of arrogance. Period.

I think the racism definitely contributed to my "bad attitude" at times. But I wasn't out there to feel accepted; I was out there to win and I didn't need their permission. I dodged a lot of questions about it while I was in the heat of the battle because I thought it could cause me some set-backs, if you know what I mean. But it happened, it's the truth, it was always a part of my career, and I'm talking about it now. I didn't have to comply with everything that everybody wanted, but I had to get along. I got to a point where I was good enough both in the arena and in my mind so that didn't affect me as much anymore. No matter what, I was going to win.

By early February of 1991, Fred was in third place in the world standings with $12,342 in winnings in the first few months of the new season. Herbert Theriot had him by a scant $555 for first place, Troy Pruitt was second, but when the rankings were updated on Tuesday, February 19, 1991, they showed that once again Fred Whitfield was the No. 1 calf roper in the world. With significant wins already at Kansas City, Denver, Baton Rouge and Jackson, sports reporters were again calling him a phenomenon and he was again telling stories that would become very familiar over the years.

In the Feb. 17, 1991Sunday edition of the *Houston Chronicle*, Charles Carder did an extensive piece entitled "Trail-blazing Cowboy" that told of the sophomore cowboy's quest for a world title. After summarizing Fred's hugely successful rookie year, Carder added that, "He has started 1991 with the momentum that may help him achieve even more." After alluding to the prestige of the title, Carder pointed out another reason Whitfield wanted the championship badly: "He would become the first black man in the predominantly white PRCA membership to win a calf roping title." Fred responded with, "That would mean a lot to me. I think it would help me later in life. If I could become the world champion this year, there is no telling how much money I could make with endorsements and commercials and things." Described in the lengthy article as "a muscular 6-foot-3, 200 pounder," who "was not ranch born and bred," Fred told the usual story of his background: his mom worked for the Moffitts, Roy had been a father-figure since his parents divorced, Mrs. Moffitt broke her wrists, Roy went to work, Roy pays for everything, etc. etc. His long-range plans were to "…rodeo for another ten years. From rodeoing, I can buy myself a place, settle down and buy a few cows. I haven't had dreams of becoming a movie star." He admitted that there were mistakes his first year: "You can't blow money and go the way I did some last year. I flew to a lot of rodeos when I should have been in a pick-up." It sounds like he at least *had* dreams of being a movie star.

Later the same month, during the 59th year of the Houston Livestock Show & Rodeo in the Astrodome, Fred told a similar version of his story to Ray Buck of the *Houston Post* under the headline "Early Impression Helps Whitfield Lasso Rodeo Fame." After telling of his mother working for the Moffitts and Roy running the business and helping him, he spoke of his father, who usually wasn't mentioned. "My mom and dad split up when I was eight. My dad lived here and there and everywhere. We really didn't get along. It's kind of bad…but that's the way it was." The reporter went on to say, "Whitfield arguably is the best calf-roper in the world and certainly the ProRodeo Cowboy Association's fastest-rising young star in his event," and that he was "number one on the PRCA's money list." Still just twenty-three, Fred responded: "I reached all my goals – except one, if I rodeo long enough maybe I can win the world." Maybe.

I know I had a decent winter and was in the standings early in 1991, and by the time the winter was over, I had somewhere around fifteen, sixteen thousand won. That was huge back then. These days, if a guy is leading after the winter with thirty thousand, he has to make another thirty thousand in the summer months to be in good shape when he gets to Vegas. Rusty Young and I had gone to Canada together and won quite a bit of money at those winter rodeos, which was Medicine Hat, Camrose and Calgary. So, I got some money won and things were looking good.

After that, I had a pretty good spring and that summer, I rodeoed with

Rusty some of the time and went by myself some of the time, too. I had Ernie back like I liked him and he was working good, but I was still searching around for another horse. I was living over around Cypress, still with that owl-headed girlfriend of mine, and just working towards making the Finals two years in a row. It wasn't until later on that I saw I could get my first world title that year. All year long I stayed within striking distance of a world title, but my focus was on just getting to the Finals. I hit the 1991 NFR sitting about seventh in the world, about twenty thousand behind Joe Beaver. Joe was the man then, and you had to go through him to get a title. There were several other contenders, but Joe was the frontrunner.

A good friend of mine, Tee Woolman, said, "Man I think you can win the world this year, but you got to get that horse to where he pulls more for you." He said, "They're big calves and you can get them down, but if he don't help, you're going to have trouble flanking 'em."

So me and Tee Woolman, we get the deal set up to where every evening or every afternoon before the rodeo we'd take Ernie out there and put him on a bale of hay because we didn't have a log. We needed a log with a rope tied to it to make him pull it, so instead we put him on one of those big three-strand bales of alfalfa and we'd back him up right down the alley pulling that bale of hay. We'd knock him back every day and jack with him a little bit to get him on the end of that rope.

But after three rounds out there I still hadn't won nothing. My first calf kicked, my second calf strained, and I don't remember what went wrong with the third calf, but I hadn't won a penny. Then, I remember it just like it was yesterday, my good friend Stephen Perry called me at my hotel, and said, "Buddy, just don't panic." He said, "As soon as them calves start leaving and taking the tie, you're going to be a fat rat in a cheese factory." Stephen said, "Keep everything together, don't rope a lot on that horse and log Ernie every day." I told him we were already logging him.

Then I won the fourth round; fifth round rolls around and I win second in it; sixth round rolls around and I win first. All the sudden, I got this Joe Beaver worried about Fred Whitfield because I was just pennies behind him. Bob Tallman was announcing back then, and after that sixth round, he said, "We've got a serious contender here." Back then, the guy that was winning the most money at the finals roped last, so you held the key to the city. This is the best position you can be in because you know what you got to beat. So, I'm getting to rope last every night and the stage is set for some of the most exciting times of my life.

In the ninth round, Joe runs a calf and his rope comes off, so he ropes him with his second loop, his horse steps over the rope and he's got ropes going everywhere. And then he gets off the horse. Bob Tallman is hollering, "Get out of there, you're in the rope Joe, get out of there." And this fricking horse come running by him, hits the end of the rope, jerks the calf up in the air, takes off and comes down to the other end of the arena. And Jimmy Powers, I'll never forget it as long as I live, he's got a gate open about this wide and that fricking horse runs through that gate, gets through it, comes by me, hits me in the knee and rips my pants from the knee to the boot, but didn't cut me at all. Well, they're hollering at me to ride in the box to rope next and my damn pant leg is dragging the ground. I said somebody's got to cut this off because I'm going to get tangled up in it.

When it was all over, I come across there and I won fourth in the ninth round and had a clear path to the loot. I had one calf left and all I had to do is tie this calf down to be the world champion. I get chill bumps just thinking about it. We left there that night and me and Roy Moffitt was high-fiving each other and we're celebrating, and I said, we're going about this all wrong, I said I still got to catch one, and it's mine to lose now.

I backed in there the next night and I'm just licking my lips, I'm like a shark with blood in the water and loving every minute of it. I run that calf until I could see the whites of his eyes, roped his neck and tied him down. By now, I was twenty-four years old and had worked at this for a long time, but it was done and I was the fricking world champion.

Not to say that it's good or bad, but since I was a very little boy, I just love doing things that people say can't be done. When I first came on the scene, I heard what the older guys said about me, but I did not believe it, not for one minute. If you're good at something, it don't matter what color you are. And when I heard them say "He'll never win the world," I just kept it deep inside me and it just kept fueling, me, fueling me, fueling me…and here I was.

Roy reminisces about the biggest night of their lives…

> That little black boy from Cypress, Texas in the limelight was like a fish out of water. Mercy, that was wild. We was in a limo going down to the champions banquet and that big marquee out front of the MGM Grand, the one where they put David Copperfield and Elvis or whoever on it, had *Fred Whitfield* on it. I walked in the front door of the MGM and on the screens there where you check in at, every damned screen was flashing *Fred Whitfield* across it. Boy, you talk about cry? I had to put my sunglasses on…a grown man walking around crying, are you crazy? It was awesome.
>
> When he won that first one, I called my mom and she said, "How'd he do, how'd he do?" I couldn't even talk. I can't talk thinking about it right now. The most passionate time of my life was back when I was rodeoing and it was so touching to be part of Fred's success. I thought of all the people I wish would have been there to see it, like Ollie and my dad. I think I cried every time Fred won a gold buckle – and that was a lot.

When Fred Whitfield captured the 1991 Calf Roping title, with $115,040 for the year, $70, 609 of it at the Finals, he was the first African-American to ever win a timed event title and only the second to ever wear a gold buckle. Moreover, with an NFR average total of 91.7 on ten head, he also set a new NFR average record. The cover of the January1992 *Rodeo Sports News* had a picture of his winning run beneath a headline that screamed "Shattered" in reference to what he had done to the average record.

Joanne Moffitt remembers when the call came in from Vegas…

> I had my phone right there in the kitchen so I could run the business; it used to hang on that wall in there, and I was in the kitchen waiting for the call the first time he won. I don't remember the exact year, but I'll never forget that call. Both of them were crying, Roy and Moon, they were both crying, "Mamma, Mamma…" You can't imagine…I mean they were so young when all this was going on. "Mom, Mom, Mom, Mom, you're not going to believe this"…and I could hear both of them just bawling.
>
> Roy said, "Mom, he won! He won!"
>
> Moon got on and said, "Mrs. Moffitt, I won."
>
> Both of them crying like babies.

After making rodeo history, Fred was the featured speaker for the annual Black History Month program at the Richards, Texas Independent School District in February of 1992. Covering the event for the *Richards Examiner*, reporter Hank Hargrave said, "A 24-year old Cypress man recently won his event's equivalent of the Super Bowl, World Series and NBA Championship. In doing so, he became a role model for many young people, particularly blacks, armed with a message of self-confidence, hard work and setting goals." During his visit with the schoolchildren, Fred told them that "It all boils down to who wants it the most" and that success had nothing to do with the color of their skin. He threw in all the usual stuff: stay in school, stay away from drugs, make responsible choices, learn from your mistakes, and especially, enjoy your accomplishments. "I feel like I'm on top of the world. Accomplishing my goal took a lot of time and commitment. But I loved every second of it because I love to rodeo."

What the children did not get was the usual story he gave sports reporters; instead, he told of what a strong early role model his mother had been and how willing she had always been to help him succeed. "I might not be here today without her. It helps to have someone you can look up to and respect."

Although Casey had been away in the Marines for more than a year, he was back in Texas on leave just in time to celebrate with the new world champion calf roper.

> That first year he won the world I was home. When he got home from Vegas, me and Fred and his girlfriend went out and celebrated. It was a big deal. Years ago, we had dreamed this together and I would always say you're going to win the world, you're going to be the greatest…and it was really unbelievable to see him achieve those things. I don't care who wins more money or who wins more gold buckles, there's nobody that's overcome more to get it. The mental stuff that Moon dealt with and the barriers he broke, that's the true story.

Organized by the Corcoran Gallery of Art in Washington D.C. and circulated by the Smithsonian, *Songs of My People*, was a highly attended international photo exhibition that reached twenty-four cities over three years, as well as a1992 book and HBO special. In capturing African American life through the eyes of fifty prominent black photographers, organizers responded to "a crisis of identity, of image, of definition."

During the first week of June 1990, the project photographers were flown across the United States to capture various aspects of African American life. This included photojournalist Keith Williams, a Pulitzer Prize winner, who was dispatched out West to see the cowboys. Of his subjects, Williams said, "I was in a little town for a rodeo and I was in awe. I had never seen black cowboys before. But there they were, riding bulls and roping calves."

The subjects of *Songs of My People* ultimately included Colin Powell, Nelson Mandela, Muhammad Ali, Bo Diddley, Quincy Jones, Thurgood Marshall…and Fred Whitfield. [*Houston Chronicle, Feb. 23, 1992*]

I came home after the '91 Finals with seventy grand in my pocket and by now, my debt had rolled back up to right about thirty thousand with Roy. I walked into his office there one day and said it's time for Mr. Whitfield to stand on his own, and I gave him a check for thirty thousand. It had cost me seven or eight thousand to stay in Vegas for two weeks, and the rest, a little over thirty grand, I put in the bank. Paid off my Vegas tab, paid Moffitt's off completely, and had thirty grand in the bank. Here we go, let's rodeo baby. It's all me now.

Marie with newborn Fred and Tammy, 1967

Sedgwick Haynes, Roy Moffitt and Fred

Fred and Ernie, 1991

1st Time World Champion heading home, 1991

Fred & Roy Cooper, Rancho Santa Margarita, California, May 19, 1996

1996 NFR Champions Banquet

Bubba Paschal, Blair Burk, Cody Ohl, Jason Evans, Fred, Mike Beers, Kelly Wardell, Chris Lawson; 4th of July 1998

On the phone to ProCom, 1998

Fred with Moon (left) and Reno

Mr. & Mrs. Whitfield, April 29, 2000

Fred, Marie & Cassie, Texas Cowboy Hall of Fame Induction, 2003

Wayne Hawkins, Roy Moffitt, Fred, Roland Bostic, Anthony,
ProRodeo Hall of Fame Induction, 2004

Fred & Savannah

Fred & Sydney on Gator

Fred & Sydney, 2010

Fred and his dad, Father's Day, 2013

Anthony, Loretta, Denise & Fred, Father's Day, 2013

Cassie, Willie Whitfield, Anthony & grandchildren,
Whitfield Family Reunion, 2009

Savannah, Fred, Cassie & Sydney, 2012

visit www.fredwhitfield.com to see more pictures

CHAPTER 10

MADAME X

About this time, another horse came along. When I got him, his name was already Moon, like mine, and I rode that horse for so long. They'd shown him around to two or three people and then brought him over to my place one day. I'd rode the horse before and didn't really like him, but I rode him again and thought, you know, this horse has a lot of good qualities. I just didn't know if he was good enough to buy. Finally, they said just take him and ride him – if you like him, we'll work something out. That's the best way to buy one, so I took him and started getting along real good with him. We didn't have no luck at the first few rodeos, he got out run at both, then I rode him at a little pro rodeo they used to have in Fairfield and he did a lot better. Before you know it, I started winning a little bit on him.

I still had Ernie, the horse I won the world on. He was stout enough to pull a wagon, but when I first got him, Ernie wasn't broke very good and he rode like a plow horse. After several years of me riding him and working with him, he got to where he was a lot more precise and in rhythm. Ernie was temperamental and he had a mean streak in him. Moon was totally the opposite. He was a solid bay, a little over fourteen hands, weighed about twelve-hundred pounds, and was eight years old when I got him. Moon was subtle and laid back – nothing much ever bothered him. If you walked in the stall to feed him or something, he would shake his head a little bit and let you know everything was cool and go on about his business.

Cathy, the girl who owned him, wanted twenty five thousand for Moon, and I gave her ten thousand dollars down and we set the rest up on payments, which was perfect. I come back in '92 and had a decent season, ended up fourth or fifth in the world. I'd done wore that maroon truck out that I bought in '89, so I bought a new truck in '92. There ain't no telling how many miles that thing had on it. I got a new truck, got a new camper, got a new trailer and it was back to rodeoing with the new horse. One of the best things about Moon was that none of the million miles we went together ever affected him.

I think I rode Moon more at the '92 finals than I did Ernie and won a little bit on him, but we were still having issues and weren't quite in sync. Then 1993 rolled around and I won Calgary on him – won fifty-five thousand on that horse. Now I own two good horses free and clear, got my own rig, got Moffitts paid off, got a little money in the bank, everything's good. Then about '93 or '94, Moon started having some off days and I contemplated getting rid of him because he was ducking off and not working very good. I called up Jack Newton, the guy that bred and helped train Moon, and told him my problems.

He said, "Son, I'm going to tell you something about that horse…if you get rid of him, it'll be the worst mistake you ever made in your life." He told me to stop practicing on him at home, get him solid and then not rope on him except at rodeos. He said, "You cannot imagine how good that horse will be." I did some tuning on him and then left him alone at home, and this sonofagun started stopping and downing his head to where he was almost violent. The fricking horse worked.

In Moon's prime, I could go to a rodeo somewhere and if they were roping big calves, I'm talking he would just down his head to where all I had to do was run down and scoop them up. Or, I could have one a little slower, a little weaker, and I'd hold my slack and he'd just peddle along. I've always said he could size them up. I've only rode two horses in my life that could do that – Moon was one and Crisco was the other. To this day, Moon is my favorite.

Doc Currie and his wife, Sandy, knew Fred from the local rodeos he and Casey frequented, and they saw him at Butaud's every now and then. Doc recalls the day Jack Newton, a good friend of his who had business with Bill, called and asked Doc for a ride from the airport out to Butaud's place. Sandy and Doc picked Jack up at the airport and all three went to Conroe where Fred had a number of horses in various stages of training for Bill.

Later, when they got in the truck to leave, Doc says the first thing Jack asked was "Who was that black kid?" Doc said Fred Whitfield and Newton said, "You can write his name down – he's going to be a world champion." When questioned further about his prediction, Newton said that he had watched Fred ride at least six different horses in the course of their visit, and "he rode every one of them perfect." Doc and Sandy both concur that what was significant was that Jack Newton never complimented anything or anybody – ever. About him, Sandy says he is the hardest human being she knows, but, "He didn't call Fred the 'n' word; he called him the black kid." She says it was a deciding moment as there were many young men riding horses there that day, "but Fred was a standout."

Sandy Currie expands on the connection between Jack Newton, Fred and a certain horse:

> Jack Newton bred Moon and raised him until he was two when we got him. *Sonita's Wonder* was Moon's registered name, and long before Fred had anything to do with him, Jack named him Moon because he had a half moon on his face.
>
> I rode all Jack's colts in my younger days, all the two-year-old geldings he had for sale, so I rode Moon when he was two. I rode other colts that scared me and Moon was the gentlest of all of them. I was looking for a horse as a gift to our vet assistant and Moon had great big wonderful kind eyes…that was the most impressive thing

about him – his eyes. He had a beautiful head and giant eyes that said, "I'm going to be a great, great horse." I could tell you about their ability not because I am an outstanding horsewoman, but because I think I can read their minds. I'd been doing it long enough to know Moon was spectacular – he was an amazing horse even at that age. I brought him home and Doc and I presented him to Cathy. For thirty-five years, Cathy Cribbs has been our vet assistant and has been with us longer than her own family. She ropes and was looking for a head horse, so we gave her Moon as a bonus for all of her good work. She was elated.

After she got him broke good, she got him started tracking steers. Cathy would swing a rope off of him and they would piddle around and do all these things with him that made him gentle and put a foundation under him. She and Doc worked together with him and he watched her head a steer on him one day and saw how Moon stopped.

Doc said, "Oh my God…that would make a great calf horse."

Cathy looked at him and said, "He's too good to be a head horse, isn't he?"

Doc said "I think you might be right…that's a calf horse."

That's when Moon became a calf roping horse. With a calf horse, the big thing is that when you stop one, you want him to stop, you don't want him to leap forward, and a lot of people aren't smart enough to know that. But Cathy had worked in a beef yard with her mom and dad and she worked cattle on a ranch with her brother, so she knew these things.

Except Cathy needed a head horse, not a calf roping horse, so Doc tells how they changed courses with Moon.

Cathy was doing this on her own and didn't have the money to get him trained, so I said I'd take care of all that. John Rothwell, a good friend of mine, trained, showed and qualified Moon in the Senior Calf Roping at the AQHA World Show in 1990. Moon won it and was the World Champion Senior Calf Horse that year. Then Paul Tierney asked if he could ride Moon at the Timed Event Championship in Edmond, Oklahoma, and Paul won the Timed Event on him. Paul took him to some rodeos after that but they were not a good fit and he brought him back.

Then Fred tried him and took off rodeoing with him and seasoned him. Every time he won a check, he'd send Cathy twenty-five percent because that was their deal. Probably wasn't but a month went by and Fred decided he wanted to buy him, so he bought Moon.

So began a connection between Cathy and Fred and Moon that lasted until the end. Sandy says that Fred wants the best for his horses, and she should know as he has been bringing them to the Curries' vet clinic since "that poor bastard Ernie got so sick and he brought him to us that time." Sandy says it was only because of this track record that Cathy let her baby leave with a cowboy.

Cathy has a bond with every animal, but she really had a bond with Moon and she let a rodeo cowboy take off with her best friend and had no qualms with it. She knew that Fred took such good care of his horses that she consented for him to take Moon on the road. Turns out, those two fit like a hand in a glove.

Moon was an intimidating horse and he didn't want a lot of people jacking with him. He was as gentle as a lamb, but cranky at times. He loved Cathy, he loved Fred, he loved his job...beyond that, that horse didn't give a damn about anybody else. Moon just wanted to go get his job done and get in the trailer…and he never quit eating.

Ernie was a good horse, an all-business horse, but the great ones were Moon, then Reno, then Jewels. I think that is probably what Fred would say his three greatest horses were, with Moon at the top of the list. Fred bought Reno so Moon would last longer…so he could rope off another horse and not wear him out. All of us felt that Moon was our child.

While Moon was one of the most successful roping horses ever to grace the Thomas & Mack, he was never named PRCA Calf Horse of the Year, even with his track record. Doc gives his theory of the oversight:

> I've thought a lot about it and the thing with Moon is that there wasn't a lot of guys who could ride him; they just couldn't get along with him. For the PRCA to make your horse Calf Horse of the Year a lot of guys have got to ride him, and nobody but Fred could ride Moon. If other guys don't ride your horse, then you've got to politic a lot to get it done, and Fred is not a politician. Fred was never going to do that – he wasn't going to go around asking people to vote for Moon. Fred don't ask people for nothing.

While Cathy and the Curries' hearts belonged to Moon, Shawn and Wayne still cry at the mention of Ernie's name. Both agree Ernie was exceptional, Shawn saying, "He was so quick and anticipated every move Fred was going to make." Wayne adds, "He was real quick, but he didn't have enough pull for Fred, so I ended up buying Ernie from him."

> The deal was that Fred could take him and ride him any time he

wanted just like he was still his, and that's what we did. I kept Ernie and roped the best I ever roped in my life on him. Fred had gotten quicker in more and more things, but he still liked to ride Ernie when I had him because the horse was laid back and smooth. Fred looked like a million dollars on him. But we went to a rodeo one time and Fred rode him first and I couldn't ride him because he was too fast for me. That's how Fred can make animals work; that's how he changed horses and made them look so good.

Moon was more on the same page as Fred and Ernie was on the same page as me. One true thing I have to say about Fred is he expects the horse to be as intense and hard working as he is. They're expected to be at the top of their game every time and if they're not Fred is disappointed in them. He can bring all there is out of them every time and they can't do that every time like he can. They can't last as long as Fred and he needs more than one horse can give. Moon, his next horse, probably lasted longer than any of them did. Fred knew the difference between the good ones and the counterfeit ones and he loved that horse more than any of them. Moon could take that pressure, and Fred knew that and that's why he thought so much of him. Moon was a special horse, the most special horse Fred ever had. Moon was Ernie souped up on steroids… he wasn't really on steroids, but he seemed that way, you know what I mean?

Shawn agrees with Wayne about Fred's effect on his horses…and then starts to cry.

Fred is intense for a horse, but you don't see it. Fred can put the pressure on a horse to perform and you never see any outward excitement…

…Ernie was family and we had to put him down…it was so

awful. Wayne still cries like a baby over it too, but it got to where it hurt him to stand up and we didn't want to put him through the pain. This was just several years ago – we had Ernie until he was twenty-five-years old. Ernie was an awesome horse.

Not to change the subject, but whatever happened with that woman? I just knew they weren't getting along and he called me about something that happened and then she called me one time and complained about him…I was like, guys, I don't know what is happening and don't want to know.

In 1993, Edward Whitfield died days before his hundredth birthday, but his obituary listed him as one hundred years old as his funeral was on his birthday. In his late nineties with dementia and a broken hip, Big Papa was never aware of Fred's accomplishments and Roy Moffitt says Fred regretted it deeply. "He was old and sick by then, but going to Las Vegas to the NFR still wouldn't have been too high on Muggins' priority list." Anthony agrees it was a long-shot Big Papa would have ever traveled to Las Vegas.

That first time Fred was a world champ, Big Papa was still alive, but he probably never would have went to Las Vegas even if he could. My dad is like that, he won't fly either. But Big Papa was getting kind of sick there at the end, and he had to stay in bed. Fred took it hard when Big Papa got old and sick and died. It was hard for Fred to watch.

He got Alzheimer's and he would see squirrels out in the yard. I used to go over there every day and sit and talk to him and there was always a shotgun laying right there by the door at his place. One day he was talking to me and he said "Boy, go shoot those squirrels out there…them rascals just out there playing in them trees." Well, I got that gun and I put a bullet in it. He left the window open and

I went over there and shot up in the air out that window at nothing. Man, Big Papa almost got up out of that bed. "Did you get him?" I said yeah, I got him. I'll never forget that.

In July of 1993, I won fifty-five thousand at the Calgary Stampede and opened me a bank account in Canada and put that money in the bank and left it up there. Then around November, I used it to buy the land I still live on today. Since about late '91, early '92, that woman and I had lived in an apartment over at the edge of Houston, south of Cypress, and I was getting pretty tired of it. I thought I'm going to call up a realtor and find me some land. So I called up Freddie Wirt and he told me about six and a half acres out there in Hockley, just off 290 there a couple a miles.

I wanted to look at it right away, but he said a lady had some earnest money down on it and had until Friday to close. I said I'd go by and look at it and if I like it, I'd be interested in buying it if she don't. I also told him I'd be paying cash and he said I could get it a little cheaper if I paid with cash. We drove out here and looked at it, and oh hell yeah, it was a perfect little spot. We was fixing to have to sign another six month lease and we thought we'd put us a little singlewide out there on that land and get out of that damn apartment when our lease was up.

Freddie called me on Saturday. This was before cell phones and we had those bag phones where you plug them into your truck and the horn honked when the phone rang. Man, I had me one right off, so Freddie called and said the lady had defaulted on their deal and I could buy that place. He said that if I could get him a check right quick, he could get everything drawed up and we could close on the property Monday or Tuesday. Just right. Now, my dumb ass has got to call Canada and get my money wired here from my bank account. I called Roy and said, look, this is what I want to do and Roy said he'd just call down to the bank and I'd be covered until my money from Canada got here. I wrote them a check for forty-two thousand and paid for it right on the spot – there you go.

The stupidest thing I ever done in my life was not buying forty or fifty acres, instead of six and a half. The guy that owned my place and a bunch of other land around mine had died and his kids were breaking it up and selling it. I think the guy next door to me bought forty acres, which is what I should have done. Anyway, we move out here and it's the perfect little spot. Other than two nice big old oak trees and some cattle, there was nothing here, so we found us a little singlewide, I bought like a sixteen-by-eighty, for twenty-something thousand, and we got out of that apartment. We ain't got no barn, but we got some property and got a gate up. All this happened in like thirty days. So I take off rodeoing again, back on the road. I had that girlfriend, but she could fly around and see me, so back then, I'd leave and stay gone two or three months.

I had a pretty good Finals in '93, didn't win the world, but ended up sixth with $86,214. I come back home for a while and started the winter of '94 and everything was good. That year I bought another horse named Hurricane, and I still had Ernie and Moon, so I had three good horses and am loaded for bear. I missed winning the world by just over $20,000 in '94, but I did win Cheyenne again that year.

By now, things hadn't been going good at home for a long time. I messed around and got in a real bad relationship with that woman and just didn't apply myself for a couple of years. We was feuding and thinking about splitting, and that took away from my rodeoing because I wanted to stay close to home so I could watch her. Roy was mad at me because I was focused on a female instead of roping, so we weren't on the best of terms. God, I was so stupid back then. I stayed with that girl for years, way longer than I should have. I wish I'd have known I was in love with a whore.

It finally ended in the winter months of the '95 season. We'd been arguing and getting along terrible. That's all we did towards the end, fight and argue like idiots. I was at the Houston rodeo and she was supposed to be in

Houston with me, but had told me to go on by myself and she'd come later with her girlfriends. I'd already roped and done good and was just waiting for her to get there so we could clash some more. I checked my phone and she had left me a long, drawn-out message about, "I'm not coming to the rodeo, don't try to find me…I'm leaving, I got a cousin down in Austin…" Well hell, she been down here since 1991 and never had a cousin in Austin, and all the sudden this cousin appears in Austin? I was pretty disappointed to hear it on the phone, but if she ain't got enough guts to tell me to my face she's leaving, then see you later. She stayed gone for a couple of weeks, but then she showed back up.

She was sleeping with a guy I certainly wouldn't call a good friend, but a friend that I'd been helping since his rookie year. I don't know who's heard the story, but it was Cody Ohl and it was in my own house. The thing is, he's not a bad guy and it wasn't all his fault. He was young and I'm almost sure she initiated it. I had sensed it; I suspected something was up, but when I knew for sure, man, I was devastated.

I was talking to Roy about it and he hooked me up with this private investigator. He said, "Man, if you want to know, there's ways to know…all he needs is a license plate number and he'll have the goods." In the back of my mind I already knew the truth, but I wanted to know for sure because I'd done bought her a ring. As a last resort, I went by the guy's office and gave him a thousand bucks and left town, still battling that nonsense in the back of my mind. That investigator got the goods…I mean he got the goods.

I come back home and called him, and he told me to come by, so I did. Before he showed me the pictures, he said, "Are you sure?" I said damn right I'm sure. I done paid for it, I want to know. So he flipped out a little envelope with a series of forty, fifty pictures in it and I picked it up and started looking at them. The more I saw, the madder I got.

It wasn't only Cody; it was the brother of a guy she'd been working for. She'd start her evenings with him laying out by the pool, having fancy drinks with him and her girlfriend. She always had somebody with her, an alibi, so whenever I asked what was going on, she was just hanging out with friends. She was pretty slick. Then, about two in the morning, she'd drive her friend home, make a u-turn and then go back over there to that guy's house alone. That investigator had pictures of all of it and let's just say she didn't spend a lot of time alone when I was gone. I'm boiling inside when I come back home, but I didn't say too much to her. Three days later, I confronted her.

I was coming home in the middle of the night from a rodeo and she came loping up the road here at the same time. I said where you been, and she told me she had been down at that guy's place "with him and his girlfriend." So, I went to his house where he was supposed to be with his girlfriend, but he didn't have no girlfriend…other than mine. I'd had enough, I just had enough. We were there in our little singlewide trailer house and I sat down on the bed in there and I said it's time to talk. She asked me what my problem was and I put that envelope of pictures down on the bed and told her to open them. She blew up and I blew up, and it was sheer pandemonium around here.

She said, "You sorry sonofabitch, I can't believe you had me followed." She was insulted. I was pretty insulted myself and told her that if she wanted out, there's the door. See you. That night still wasn't the end of it – it was back and forth and here and there. She took off for a couple of weeks, and then I took off rodeoing and come back to a house with nothing in it but a couch, two lampshades and the box of black plastic bags she used to bag up all my stuff. I had about twenty thousand dollars worth of antiques I'd bought the last few years and I guess they went in plastic bags too because this sucker didn't have nothing in it.

The fight was on again and I called her up and asked her what in the hell she thought she was doing and she told me she was going to file a common-law divorce and take more of my belongings. I said for all the screwing around you did, you already got way more than you deserved. She was pretty free with my money the whole time we were together and I stayed in the red with her. By the end of March 1995, we were really done. Good riddance. Hell, I couldn't help you anyway – you needed too much of it.

God only knows who else and for how long she'd been cheating on me. It might have been the whole time, I don't know. I'd been hearing rumors for a long time that she might be slipping around, but I didn't want to hear it. I was too stupid. We ended up together for almost five years and it turned out to be a horrible little breakup. I actually thought I was going crazy. I lost a lot of weight, saw a shrink, had a pity party and just didn't care much about roping anymore. I was a sad, sad case and looked it. I was walking the halls and every time a car would come by, I was hoping it was her.

In early June, a reporter called me from the PRCA office and said they heard I was thinking about retiring. I said I been going through a few things, but as soon as I get over them, I'll be back at the Finals. I'll call you myself when I get ready to retire. It was a terrible winter – I went to two pro rodeos and won about five thousand the winter of '95. I wasn't the least bit interested in roping and didn't even have any calves on the place.

It just took time to get over it, but Sandy Currie talked me into a shrink. It helped, but after a while all that shrink was doing was pacifying the problem. Not that it don't work for some people, but I was going around in circles like a cat chasing a ball of yarn. I've always had a lot of willpower, and finally, I thought you know what, get off your ass and quit feeling sorry for yourself. At this point, I was like fiftieth in the world and things were a little delayed that year.

Roy says she was a beautiful girl and when Fred first brought her around, he razzed him about being able to get prettier woman with gold buckles. Roy also says that there was always a lot of tension between Fred and the woman, lots of fighting, a stalled career, and misery on all fronts – and Fred was so sad to see it end.

When that white girl left him, boy…he lost it. He come to my house one day and I don't know how much weight he lost. He was gone by then and had gotten really skinny and was wearing some kind of bullshit jeans, I don't even know what kind of jeans they were, one of them designer-type jeans. He took that one hard and at the time, I was very worried about him. He was moping bad, but I told him that wasn't the only woman in the damned world. Give me a break buddy, you're young. I'd never seen him like that, but that was his first love and it cut deep, very deep.

There was some infidelity in that relationship with some pretty close friends of his. Fred never did slap the hell out of Cody Ohl for that, but there was nobody to blame but that damn woman.

Casey describes the woman as "good and bad," with the good part being how much she loved Fred. Then, as you might expect, Casey goes a little deeper…

He's not like this as much today, but I'm going to tell you, Moon was jealous and sort of controlling with her. He was just funny about stuff, but he's grown out of it…a little bit. Back then, he would just stay at them and always pick, pick, pick. Any woman who's ever had a husband or a boyfriend like that, knows it sort of takes a toll on them after a while. They had troubles and they had a lot of drama until finally they just went their own ways. That was his first real love and I don't think he was ready for a permanent relationship.

It took losing her to learn how to love his wife like he does and make their relationship work. Him and his wife don't have all the drama and they're more stable and more secure. And he's won more and done more in the latter part of his career so his wife has certainly been better for his career. I think he probably could have ruined this relationship if he hadn't had the loss of that relationship. He learns good is what I'm saying. When he makes mistakes, Moon is one of those people who doesn't do them again. That woman hurt him in a lot of ways, but he was still tough enough to do what was best for him and he went on without her. Then, when he met his wife, he made a whole lot less of those mistakes, and when he did, he went back and made it right.

As Fred said, his mother and Madame X were like peas and carrots, but it doesn't sound like she had Marie snowed as bad as Fred thought. In fact, Marie seems real clear about what went on when the sun went down.

I loved her, yes I did. She was all right in my book. We would meet and have lunch and she would buy me stuff and was real nice. Fred said, "Yeah, you like her because she's giving you all my money." That wasn't it – we were just real close. But she broke his heart good, that's what she did. Where he made his mistake was putting her on his account – she cleaned him out. She took everything he had – all he had was that couch.

I went up there to see about him, because I knew he was sad and depressed. When I got there, I'm telling you, he was a mess and so sad. I had never seen him cry, but he was crying and it hurt a piece of my heart to see him cry. I came straight on over to Roy's house and I said, Roy, you got to go see about him, he's in a bad way. Roy went up there and he spent time with him and helped him to get back on his feet. Yeah, he was in bad shape because that was the first woman he ever loved like that. He really did love her.

Fred probably didn't tell you that Cody Ohl stole his woman. That's right, but Fred had a problem and I let him know it. He'd get friendly with guys and help them in the rodeo and then they'd be going with his women. He was naïve about it, you know? He doesn't know it, but a lot of times he'd be out of town and I'd go by his house and check things out. Yes, I would. I knew she was messing around.

Chapter 11

A Full Recovery

In June of 1995, I finally decided I had moped around enough and it was time for a rebound. With everything that had been going on in my love life for the last few years, I had been a little complacent, instead of working my tail off like I had done previously. If I went to practice, I wouldn't stay for the whole thing, I'd run a few calves and then quit so I could get back to seeing what she was up to. I had not been doing the things I had to do to stay at the top of my game and that had to change. I hadn't been 100% in and now I was – it was time to rodeo again.

Me and Ernie just didn't click no more and Wayne wanted him, so I got me a quick twenty grand and stuck the money in the bank. I bought a new truck and me and a couple of my buddies take off rodeoing in mid-June. I hired Justin Miller from Pasadena to drive for us and we loaded up and took off to Reno. I remember it just like it was yesterday – I left home and left that relationship behind for good. I didn't do no good in Reno, but then I went to Delta, Utah and Grand Junction, Colorado and won me four or five thousand the first week I was gone. I won twenty thousand in June and went from being barely in the top fifty to being in the top ten. The Fourth of July rolled around and I won about fifteen thousand over the Fourth; shortly after that, I won another eleven or twelve thousand at Cheyenne. Before long, the PRCA calls me again and says, "You sure been having a good summer." So much for retirement rumors.

It just snowballed and I ended up winning thirty-one thousand in July;

another thirty thousand in August; and by October, I was number one in the world. When I left home in June, I wasn't in the top fifty and by October, I had Joe Beaver by five or six thousand.

I went to the 1995 NFR in first place with over a hundred thousand in winnings and had a good feeling going into the Finals. I rode Moon that year, and I'd had him a few years now and knew he was ready for the challenge; I just needed to do my part. I won the first round and didn't do much good again until I won the ninth round, so it come right down to the last round. When it was all over, I had a second world title and won third in the average. I had $146,760 for the year and Joe Beaver was behind me with $122,598.

I was twenty-seven years old and really, really tickled about this second world title. Some said the first time I won, it might have been an accident, but I validated being a world champion by having that second gold buckle. To go from being fiftieth in the world to being number one in the world made for a pretty spectacular year. Life still wasn't great, and I was still a sad sonofagun, but it was starting to get a little bit better. I was heart broke real bad, and if you've ever been in love, you've felt that emptiness. It hurt for a long time, and I had a lot of good friends that were behind me and I got through it and managed to win the world the same year. It was a personal redemption for me.

I wasted several years after that first world championship, and I wasn't guaranteed to ever win it again. But I was almost a cinch to make the NFR every year – that was easy as long as I went to forty or fifty rodeos. It was an early career goal of mine to qualify for the NFR twenty times and I was confident I could do it. There was always the urgency to qualify early so I was never one of those guys that squeak in at the last minute. Every year I made plans to be in Vegas in December, but anything could have happened – I could have gotten hurt, the horses could have gotten hurt, but such things never entered my mind. The success I've had rodeoing was kind of crazy and the most fun I ever had in my life. I doubt it would have been much fun if I'd been out there losing.

Then, they started calling me the Michael Jordon of rodeo. I didn't like that. I honestly didn't, because of the money. Michael Jordon is worth hundreds of millions; Fred Whitfield is not. I like comparing apples to apples, not apples to grapes. Rodeo ain't near what other professional sports are financially. I've won three million, but it took me twenty-two years and a lot of cash out of my pocket to do it. There are similarities as far as me having success in my field, but that comparison always made me uneasy.

Anthony missed being at the Finals in 1991 for his brother's first world title, but he and his wife went to the NFR regularly after that. However, it was a tour finale rodeo that stands out most in his memories of Fred's career. The calf got up and Fred was flagged out, but Anthony said that was only after it had been down for a long time, what felt like longer than anyone else's was down. Anthony recalls that Fred had been back on his horse for some time when he was disqualified. To both brothers, the discrepancy was obvious.

> That's when I saw firsthand the prejudice that was going on. Man, Fred was burning up. He came back there and threw his roping can down and he said, "Man I'm tired of these rascals cheating me." They just cheated him out of I don't know how much money and he was so mad. He told me to go back to Houston and get him a lawyer. I thought about it and I said Bro, this is your livelihood, you know? You get to jacking with lawyers and stuff and they liable to find a reason to kick you out and this is how you take care of your family. If you do it, you do it on your own. He was still mad, but he knew it was the truth.
>
> Fred was the only black cowboy at that level. Back then, there

wasn't no black cowboys that made it to the Finals. Over all that prejudice, Fred accomplished what he did and he don't have nothing to hang his head about. I have to say it was a blessing…nobody we was close to ever did anything like that. To me, he's the Michael Jordon of rodeo.

Over the years, I've taken other black guys with me around the PRCA circuit and people just love them and there's no problems. But they'll walk right past me and not even say hello. Since I was a kid, it's always been a whole different deal with me – and I used to thrive on it. See, when you're black and you get to where you can kick their ass every time, it's a different story. I'm dead serious. In rodeo, those guys are fine with a black cowboy as long as he don't take *all* their money *all* the time. If you don't like it, then you don't like it, but it's the truth.

I was at a roping around 1996 and there was this guy there that had taunted me from my rookie year until I finally put an end to it one day. Hell, he was one of the guys from that roping in Sudan that I match roped for five thousand. I was winning the jackpot in Clifton, Texas and we were all sitting around on our rope cans waiting for the short round. I was way out in the lead and this sonofabitch come by, stepped on my foot right before the short round, and said, "You think you can catch another one?"

I missed in the short round to win a horse trailer and he come out there to my trailer afterwards and started to say something else to me. I got right up in that dude's face and I said I'm tired of you f-ing with me. If you ever say another word to me, I swear to God, I'll blow your brains out. I decided I'm done with this and had to stand up to him. Ever since then, him and me been on the straight and narrow.

Another time, I was at the Texas' Best and was dating one girl and brought another one to the rodeo and them counterfeit cowboys got together and went and told both of them. It was just a particular group that had it out for me – that just did not want to see me succeed. They used to say, "If he wasn't black, he'd be just another face in the crowd." It built up anger from within me and I used to fight a lot because of it. Now I'm way mellow.

Roy says that Fred hadn't been in a lot of fights until he turned pro, but that a group of them gave him a very hard time in the early days. He remembers it was always upsetting to hear about Fred being tormented when he was far away and could do nothing about it…which is how the only cowboy that was black became the only cowboy that had bodyguards.

> He learned how to fight when he got to the pros and finally knocked the right guy on their ass and then he had their attention and their respect. You beat the hell out of the right person, you don't have to fight a hundred…whip the right one and you're done. Fred called me crying one time from the road, crying tears because it was at the point he had to fight…he got to where he had to whip some folks to get them to leave him alone. I knew they were trying to mess with his mental game and I wasn't going to let it happen, so I hired him a bodyguard. I was that concerned.
>
> Fred got in a fight in Calgary, a bar fight over a pool game or something and he whopped the tar out of them boys. I mean Fred mopped the bar with them guys. He's fast as lightning and he's strong and he just beat the hell out of them. They were bull riders and it turns out that somebody from Vegas was backing them and the word was that Fred Whitfield would never run his first calf at the National Finals that year. Some big wig from Las Vegas supposedly put out a hit on Fred…old money from Vegas. It didn't surprise me coming from the bull riders and their connections to the other players…it didn't shock me one bit because I've heard stories about them deals.

My brother knew somebody who had done some work for some of them big casinos out there in Vegas and he said they would do that kind of stuff. That's another world to me and I didn't have any idea...could they put a hit on somebody that easy? Vegas is the home of the mob, where it all started, and I'm sure there's some stragglers left. I don't know if I believed it or didn't believe it, but I wasn't taking no chances.

I sent word back that not only would Fred Whitfield run his first one, he would run his last one. I said no matter what you do, old Fred will be roping calves at the National Finals. Then we hired a bodyguard. Fred run his first calf at the Finals and Fred run his tenth one, and Fred won the world that year. Take that, gangster man.

His name was Big Ron and he was huge. I had a truck with a boot between the cab and the camper and he got stuck in it and couldn't use it because it wasn't big enough. That boot was as big as a back pick-up windshield, and he didn't fit through it. I didn't dodge those bull riders and we would see them, but we never had any more problems with them. With that crazy-ass Roy in charge of bodyguards, there were six of them by the time we got to the Finals in '96. They went everywhere with me, Roy would have some with him whenever he was in Vegas, and it was a long time before I ever went to the bathroom alone again. There ain't no telling how much money we spent, and it was a waste of money really, but Roy and me didn't think we better take any chances.

This all started in June of 1996 in a bar in Reno. It was getting late and me and some guys were shooting pool and a couple of girls were rolling around there, too. One of them guys come up to me and said "Hey, which one of them bitches are you with because we're going to do the other one." I said, man, that's probably not the right approach. He was real drunk and he said, "Did you hear what I said?" I said no I really didn't and the best thing you could do is go on home before you get your midget ass kicked, because you don't want no part of me. I just brushed it off and that was the end of it for then.

Not quite thirty days later, we get up to Calgary in July and we're in a bar shooting pool together. I probably should have stayed away from them after what happened, but we get to gambling, and I'd done won four or five hundred off of them shooting pool. They get to running their mouths again and I thought, here we go. A guy with them walks over and says, "You don't want to mess with those two guys, I back them and I'm from Las Vegas and I'm this and I'm that…and I can make one phone call tonight and have you done." I said if you can't get that guy on the phone up here right now, the best thing you could do is get out of my face because he can't help you if he's in Vegas and you're here.

One of them tried to hit me upside the head with a beer bottle, but I hit him first then turned around and jabbed that other one and then here comes homeboy and somebody cracked him over the head with a pool stick. From there, I just went to work on them, do you hear me? I mean, I just went to work on them and laid all three of them out. One was laying there on the floor moaning and I walked by and kicked him in the ribs and I was done with them. They threw all of them out and told me I could stay, because I hadn't started any of it.

Well the next morning Roy Cooper calls and says, "Hey, you made a mistake last night." I said how's that? He said, "I got a phone call that said to tell you that you need to be careful from here on out." I said that's fine, ain't no big deal. I was spooked, but I didn't want him to know that. I called up Roy Moffitt and explained the situation to him and we decided to call Big Ron, a guy from Vegas. I called him up and I told him the deal and he knew the guy I was talking about, and said I should take it seriously. Ron said he'd be on a plane as soon as he could and told me to lay low until he got there. He flew in and we took off rodeoing.

After 1995, I was really confident. I knew that if I prepared myself in the winter and had a few decent wins, that I would have the chance to win another world championship in 1996 and the year started out real good. That winter I won eighteen thousand, which was a great start when it took sixty thousand to make it to the Finals. I felt good about 1996, and this was the first time I actually *planned* to win a world title. I had already won two gold buckles and if I maintained my focus, I hoped things would go my way again.

By now, Moon was really coming into his own. That horse had showed me some things at the '94 Finals, I was even more confident with him in '95, and it just snowballed into '96. I won or placed at all the major rodeos and had a real strong season. I won Reno, won Salt Lake, Pendleton and a bunch of other big ones, and I won the Texas Circuit title. Things fell into place just right and I went to the Finals number one in the world.

Calf roping was real competitive back then and there were five guys that had a chance to win the world all the time. It wasn't just me at the top by myself. In Roy Cooper's day, he had been dominant over everyone else, but there was a crop of competitors during these years that kept the world title in the air until the last minute, and '96 was no different. It come right down to the last round between me and Joe Beaver and Cody Ohl, but I managed to come back and win my third world title in '96. Back to back world titles – just like I planned.

To beat the best guys in the world two years in a row was the ultimate high. It told the competition I was for real and it validated that in my mind too. I was confident I had a future here and I belonged here. I'm sure I was arrogant back in the day, I won't deny it, I'm sure I've rubbed a few people wrong. That's just the way life is. When I screw up, it takes time for me to cool off. I've gotten better over the years, but when it's my fault and I know I've wasted an opportunity to put money in the bank, food on the table,

I'm pissed off about it. I've always been a winner, and when I don't win, I don't cry and throw a fit, but I need a few moments. When you're at the top of your game, and you can screw up and smile about it, there's something missing.

At the time, I was in a contract with a major clothing line and at the end of '96, they decided they weren't going to re-sign me because they didn't like something I wore at the NFR. I said that's fine, pay me what you owe me and I'll go on my way. I had got to be friends with the vice president of Cinch and in the spring of '97, he came to me and said he was going to get me a deal with Cinch and about halfway through the summer, he did. He said they were a start-up company and didn't have a lot of money, the same thing I always hear from people who want me to endorse something. But I had a good feeling about Cinch and I liked their clothes because they were fresh and different. Even back then, Cinch was waking up the western wear world and I thought it would be a good opportunity for both of us. It wasn't a very big deal at first, but he told me I could grow with the company and it would get better, and that is exactly what happened.

I am one of their original endorsees and our first contract was a verbal agreement in the fall of '97. The next year we moved up to a small handwritten contract and I still have that first handwritten deal I signed with them. Of course, they're huge now, and it's the smartest business decision I ever made. There isn't a lot about being a cowboy that is secure, but Cinch has been a consistent part of my life and a big part of my success for the last sixteen years. We've had a great relationship, personal and professional.

There are people who won't admit it, but I've drawn a lot of people to the sport of professional rodeo. I have a lot of fans and I can't say enough about every one of them. Being loved the way I've been for the last twenty years, means the world to me. Everywhere I go, from Canada to Brazil, it's just crazy the people who recognize me. There ain't a rodeo I can go to that people don't start gathering around me and that motivates me to this day.

From the smallest country rodeo to the largest rodeo in the world, I back into that box and everybody is yelling "Get 'em Fred…go get 'em Fred" and it makes me feel good inside. I think it has a little bit to do with me being African American – people can spot me. I'm different than the others, but I'm good at what I do and it might even have something to do with a little bit of charisma.

My signature "raise the roof" deal started in about 1994 and I don't really know where it come from, but it caught fire. I didn't win the world that year, but I just missed it and had a great NFR. I was making great runs at the Finals, so I started raising the roof and it caught on quick. Every time I did it, it was like striking a match and the people started getting into it. To this day, I can be driving down the road and people will drive up beside me and be raising the roof going down the road. It's crazy.

The '96 NFR was the first one without a good friend of mine, Shawn McMullan. We had been good friends since 1992, Shawn's rookie year, when we split winning San Antone that year. By '95, he was in the mix for a world title; it come right down to the wire between me and him and Joe Beaver, and '96 was looking pretty good for him, too. Shawn was a great guy and I thought a lot of him.

In August of 1996, we were at a rodeo in Canby, Oregon, my first one back since I had gone home for a few weeks after Cheyenne. Me and Shawn had agreed to team rope together, and we had roped together that night at Canby. Afterwards, we went to some little old bar and had some girls come meet us there. I'd been hanging out with a girl from over there at Wilsonville, which was right near Canby, and she had some girlfriends coming home from college that night. I said, I got a buddy; maybe they'll hit it off. Shawn had a driver and Stran Smith with him, so two drivers, and I had Big Ron with me to drive, so we met at the bar and had a few drinks. It was starting to get late and we were up at a rodeo just south of Pendleton the next morning, four-and-a-half hours away from where we were at, and hell, we shut the bar down. But we had drivers, so it was no big deal.

Me and Big Ron leave the bar and we stopped and filled-up, and Shawn and them kept going and said they'd see us in Pendleton. After we gassed up, we got out of there about three in the morning and don't go thirty miles, not too far outside of Portland, and they had traffic stopped. I had crawled back in the camper to sleep a few hours, and I never woke up until daybreak. A guy come walking back there after I woke up and he said, "Man it's going to be a little bit, some hay haulers hit a car head-on up on the interstate and it's bad." When he said hay haulers, it never clicked that it might be Shawn. They had a bunch of hay on a hay pod on their trailer, and when they wrecked that hay went all over the road.

The sun was just coming up when Stran came walking out of the fog. We were only the third vehicle in line from the accident and Stran hollered at me "Man, there's something wrong… you better get up, this ain't good." Stran had blood all over a white t-shirt he had on and he came back there to the camper door and told me they'd had a bad wreck and Shawn didn't make it. He said, "He's dead, dude." A cop came walking back there and said we're about to cover him up if you guys want to come and say your goodbyes. I walked up there and seen him and he was sitting up in the passenger seat with his seatbelt on – it was just like he was asleep.

Another car had got turned around leaving a rest stop and was going the wrong way. They had hit that car head on going seventy miles an hour and it just run up on them, and when they hit, it moved his seat from where it was to the back seat. It didn't kill the driver, Stran was in the trailer asleep and it didn't kill him, but I guess it broke Shawn's neck. I was devastated and went back to Texas for his funeral. It hit me pretty hard and I thought about staying at home for a few weeks, but I ended up going back on the road with the other guys who were tore up over Shawn like I was. He was a good man and a good friend and I still think about him to this day.

Reno, another great horse, came into my life in '96. Tom Epperson owned Reno and he'd haul him around and I'd get on him, and I had him brought to the NFR in '96 as a back-up horse. I rode him a little there, and then rode him a little in '97 and a little in '98. Oh God, the first time I got on him was like the first time I got on that buckskin Ernie. The connection was instant from the first time I rode him. This sonofagun stood flatfooted, and I'd back him in the box and he would not move. Reno was a little over fifteen hands and he probably weighed just over twelve hundred pounds and was so athletic he could flat fly. Horses get wise to you over the years, they figure out what you're doing, and you want them to have that consistent pattern. Reno had that from day one. Now I had Moon, Hurricane and access to Reno, so the horsepower was there. All of the sudden, they're having hell trying to figure out a way to beat me. Then we went to the Calgary Stampede in July of '97 and Moon got hurt – bad.

At the time, Calgary counted towards the world standings and I won some money up there but didn't win the whole thing. It's an outdoor arena and the ground was muddy and slick and it was kind of raining. I ran out there on him and roped and when he stopped, he really slid into the ground and the ground gave way. He hung up and tore his stifle. I had a driver, I don't know who it was, but Sunday afternoon we jumped in the truck and took off for Nampa, Idaho where I roped the next morning. I can remember leaving Calgary that night and thinking, man, what in the hell am I going to do? I had those other horses at the time, but I didn't have the confidence in any of them that I had in Moon.

We drove to a little town in Montana, probably eight hours or so from Calgary, and I went to unload Moon out of the trailer and he couldn't even walk. I stood there on the side of the trailer in front of whoever was with me and I just broke down in tears. I said I can't fricking believe this; I ruined my horse up there. I gave him some hay and water and a bunch of drugs to kind of ease the pain of hauling and we took off driving. By nine the next morning, I had him at a vet in Idaho and we tried to get him out of the trailer and walk him around a little, but he was just holding his back leg and couldn't even pick it up. I told my vet what happened and before we even unloaded him, he said his stifle is tore bad. Moon's leg done swelled real good and the vet said he needed to lacerate it so the blood could drain, then go in there and scrape the stifle so it'd have a chance to heal.

I asked him what I needed to do, and he said, "Well, there's nothing more you can do. He's done for a while." Moon stayed in Idaho at the vet's for about thirty days and I checked on him regularly and then found a ride for him back to Texas. Some people picked him up and took him back home to Doc Currie and he stayed there for about two more months. Doc done some other stuff to him and put a tube in so it could drain. Six months later, I was able to ride him and I could just tell he wasn't the same.

Chapter 12

Once Upon a Time...

So 1997, here comes Cody Ohl – hungry and thirsty – just like I was when I first jumped in the ocean. This was his second year in the pros and I mean this dude is the real deal and all the sudden he's my biggest threat. Joe Beaver was still around, but it was Cody I had to worry about. Every rodeo we went to, he'd win first at one, then I'd win first at the next one, and it went back and forth all winter and all summer. Well, he got me by four thousand in '97 and won the world by a nose, but I set a new average record that still stands today. [*84.0 seconds on 10 head; considered "one of the greatest performances in the history of the NFR."* PRCA bio]

By now, I'm about two-and-a-half years removed from that traumatic relationship, and I was not the least bit interested in another one. I'm not going to lie, I was bad – I was real rude and I'd rather not get into it too much. I run across some pretty decent girls and it was a lot about me and not a lot about them. They were there for a purpose and one purpose only. I didn't want a relationship, I didn't want a woman, I was pissed off at ya'll. I was very bitter, very angry. When they started acting like they liked me, I didn't call them no more. I was so mad and so negative. I was a freaking three-time world champion by now and I didn't deserve such heartache and misery. I deserved the best and if you ain't all about me, I ain't interested in you. That's just the way it was for a couple of years.

You could probably name the black women I dated on one hand. That's a touchy subject really, but that's just how it turned out. I never found one that understood what I was trying to do. I don't know...I guess love shouldn't really have a color

I came home after the Finals in '97 and everything was great. I had set the average record, won over sixty thousand and got money in the bank, so me and a bunch of my buddies decided to celebrate. We load up and we take off to the bar one night, a place in Houston called Tumbleweed, and before long we get to talking to these average-at-best girls we had just stumbled onto. About then, in walks Cassie – soaking wet.

I said what in the hell happened to you?

She said, "My eyes are up here."

I was attracted to Cassie immediately, and she was with two or three other girls, so I just hung out with her and her friends, not expecting nothing. We visited and danced and probably had the best time I'd had with a woman in a long time. I thought man, this chick's pretty cool. There's just something about her that I was always drawn to.

Cassie Loegel was working for her father who owned a computer network in Nebraska, introducing a new program to his customers in the Houston area. She was also in Houston trying to escape a short-lived marriage to a crazy meth-head in Alabama and was right in the middle of a situation she calls "a matter of life and death." While trying to survive the hardest time of her life, friends insisted that a night out on the town would do Cassie a world of good. Turns out, they were right...eventually.

> A lot of people don't know the details, but it's never been a secret that I was married when I met Fred, but that marriage was doomed before it ever started. I was there with friends and had offered to take everyone's coats outside to the truck as an excuse to get out of that bar for a while. The truck was way across the parking lot and it started raining hard while I was out there so by the time I made it

> back inside, I was soaking wet. While I was walking around looking for my friends, I saw Fred Whitfield talking to them. He caught my eye, I caught his, and we started talking.
>
> He introduced himself to me as Brad, and I just went along with it and said, it's nice to meet you, Brad. I had watched the Finals on TV just a week earlier and saw him set a new average record, so I knew exactly who he was. Before long, I could tell he was getting a little antsy wanting me to know who he really was, so I finally said, "You did a good job at the Finals last week…Brad." At that moment he realized I knew who he was and had just been going along with the Brad thing. So that's our joke now. People will ask, "Are you Fred Whitfield," and he'll say, "No, my name's Brad."
>
> I remember I had my rodeo queen buckle on and it was kind of flashy, and of course he had on a gold buckle, so we talked about our belt buckles. Then he started getting a little too flirty and he was kind of arrogant. I was wearing a t-shirt and jeans and he said something inappropriate, so I let him know I was not going to put up with that and I just walked off into the crowd. I could see he was looking for me above the other people, so after a while I came back and he apologized for what he had said to me. After that we hung out and danced and had a good time, just making the most of the moment. It was a sweet, unexpected meeting. I was just enjoying myself for the night, trying to get through a rough patch in my life.

After the bar closed, everybody ended up at Cassie's friend's house where she was staying while in Texas. By then the storm had knocked the electricity out, so they lit candles, drank all the wine the women had in the house and had a good time. Fred says he "tried to smooch on her, but she wasn't having none of it." When the night was over, he asked for her number, and she was reluctant, saying, "You've probably got a girl in every town."

She gave me her number and two days later, I called her up and asked her to go with me to pick-up a new trailer I had coming. She said yes, so I go load her up and we take off to Denton to pick up a horse trailer a new sponsor had got me. I didn't have too many sponsors at the time, and they asked me if I wanted them to put anything on it. I said yeah, put "Sponsored by Raw Talent" on the hayrack, and they did. God, that pissed some people off.

We spent nine or ten hours together that day, and I'm thinking I really like this chick. She was genuine. It was after dark when we got back and I took her to a nice restaurant for dinner. We talked a lot about her situation and she assured me she was getting a divorce, so I thought, if she's leaving, then its fine. This situation is what it is, and there ain't nothing I can do about it. Just before Christmas, my crazy ass goes down to some jewelry store and bought her a fancy tennis bracelet. I'm not saying I was in love that quick, but I done a lot of stuff early on with Cassie that I hadn't done in other relationships. I wasn't trying to impress her with that diamond bracelet, but she was a nice person and very laid back, and she wasn't too hard to look at either. It was expensive, but I liked it and I liked her, so I just bought it.

To this day, the tennis bracelet story still touches Cassie. They had known each other only days and it was Christmas morning after another chaste slumber party, when what he did was almost as sweet as what he said.

> The next morning Fred said, "I don't know you that well, but I can see this going somewhere. I know you're going through a hard time and I'm sorry. You deserve this, so don't try giving it back to me because I want you to have it and I hope you'll give me a chance." He handed me a long box and I opened it and saw a diamond and gold tennis bracelet and I remember my mouth dropped open. I

thought so little of myself at the time because of what I was going through and I couldn't believe such an incredible gift was for me. He was very sincere and sweet and because of what he had said, I didn't even try giving it back. They say love comes when you're not looking and a relationship was the last thing I wanted at the time, but at that moment, I thought I'll give this guy a chance. He was sweet and funny and made me laugh.

He also had a very large black book, but anytime anyone called, he would tell them about me. I would hear him on the phone, and he would tell the girls who called that he had found "the one." So in February, I moved to Texas, which was quite an adventure.

The thing that really hooked me was she held out for a long time. I'm thinking, you got to be kidding me…I've done everything just right and I deserve it…but she didn't budge for a long time. But we're rolling right along by the first part of January, been dating a couple of weeks, and I asked her to go to the Texas Circuit Finals with me. She couldn't go until Saturday night, but she came out there and I won the whole damn thing in '98. A lot of them at the rodeo didn't like me with this beautiful new woman and had plenty to say about it, but I knew they were going to say something, no matter who I showed up with. Jealous female friends of mine told me Cassie looked like the last one, and then turned around and said that she didn't look like my "usual type." She wasn't my usual type and that's what I liked about her. If she'd have looked like a mud bone, they'd a said, "Can you believe he's with that ugly old rag?"

Cassie had moved out of her husband's home and into an apartment in Alabama, "just trying to figure out what I was going to do," and then left on her trip to Houston several weeks later. After meeting Fred and deciding to extend her stay, Cassie's friend in Texas invited her to stay with her and her husband, so she moved into their extra room. But Cassie couldn't shut the door on her old life until she went back to Alabama and moved out for good.

> My plan was to go back to Alabama, pack up my stuff and get back to Texas as quickly as possible. I was scared to death. That guy really wanted to get back together and I had been down that road and knew where it led. He was a big meth user, there was major infidelity, and he had already pulled a shotgun on me. It was like dealing with the devil. The minute I got back in town, he started calling me and calling me, trying hard to get back together.
>
> That night Fred called to check on me and asked if there was anything he could do. I said you can come get me, and he was on a plane the next day. He flew into Nashville and a friend and I drove to the airport and picked him up. It was night when we got back to the apartment, and went right to bed so we could get up early the next morning, load up and get out of there. But neither of us could sleep all night. We were so nervous because we didn't know if he was going to come knocking at the door. Thank God, he never had a clue Fred was there with me. He was a total redneck and I didn't know what he might do.
>
> By early the next morning, we had all of my stuff packed into a U-Haul truck and loaded my pick-up on a trailer that we were pulling. We were done and gone in less than twelve hours from when Fred got there. Of course, this is Fred; so on our way back to Texas, we had to stop at a few rodeos…in a U-Haul. Things for me were back on track and after everything, I felt safe again. This was all within the first month or so after I met Fred, and it was really sweet…at first.

★

She'll tell you I loaded her up and brought her back to Texas. Homeboy was calling that apartment all night, I mean, calling all night long and I'm wondering if he was going to come by and kill me. He's just a little ways away from where we were and was leaving Cassie crazy messages until finally she just turned her phone off. I slept next to none and come morning we got loaded and got the hell out of there.

I fixed it so I could go to Jackson, Mississippi and another rodeo on my way back. Tom Epperson took Reno over there for me; I was still paying him to haul him around and let me ride him. Of course, as soon as everybody saw me driving that U-Haul, they made fun of me. I told them I was moving a girl back to Texas, but Joe Beaver and them gave me a hard time. I roped in the slack that morning and I'm 9.1 on the first time and come back with a 7.2. When I left the arena I told them they all ought to be driving U-Hauls to the rodeo, then they might be tying them in 7.2. So there you go.

When she very first moved down here, we didn't even live together. She lived in Spring with her girlfriend, and we were just dating. She hardly stayed here when we first met, she wouldn't do it, just would not do it. I was getting out of my old routine of going and doing whatever I wanted. When you get into a relationship, things have to change. You can't continue to go out every night and run the bars and go out with single buddies, so things in both of our lives changed a lot. It was a miracle I met Cassie; it was no accident. She was just the right kind. I knew from the minute I talked to her that she was different and it blossomed from the start. After four or five months, I said this is the one. She really is.

I come back in '98 and had a decent winter, but Cody ended up in the lead going into the Finals and it went right down to the wire, but he ended up winning the world again. So I'm pissed off because I can beat this dude. He got me in '97 and he ends up winning it again in '98. I let my guard down and he won it two years in a row.

There's a star born every day and I want to beat the best guys. If it's easy, I just as soon not rope; if I'm not going up against the best there is, I don't perform to the best of my abilities. Sometimes I get so mad at people because it's like you haven't won enough, you haven't done enough, for some of them. At Houston last year [2012], an old guy said to me, "Well, you still gotta get by all them youngsters." I said, man, I don't give a damn about them. I want Tuf Cooper in there, I want Cory Solomon in there, I want Cody Ohl in there, I want Trevor Brazile in there - put them all in there. I don't want nobody saying they gave me nothing, I want them all in there. I fear no man with a rope, and I want to go through the competition, not around the competition. Without the best guys there, I don't perform to the best of my abilities. I start doing stupid stuff and start second guessing myself.

In '95, '96 and '97, I intentionally went solo to Vegas, so I'd spent a couple NFRs footloose and fancy free. In 1998, Bubba Paschal and me and Cassie rodeoed together. Cody Ohl even went with us for a while, and we all rodeoed quite a bit together. Bubba made the Finals that year and he was single and we just got out there and got to running around and things transpired and Cassie just wasn't having none of it. I was running around like I was single, acting like them other guys and it didn't bode well for Cassie, which I can't blame her. I was most definitely still tender from that last one, but we'd been together almost a year and I don't know quite what I was thinking. After a few nights of this, she flew home from Vegas and stayed gone a few rounds.

By the time the '98 Finals rolled around, Cassie had already noticed some changes in Fred. She was working a fulltime job and was often gone evenings, so she didn't know if it was that or just part of his NFR preparations, but something was different. Once they got to Vegas, things got worse and whatever his problem was, Fred wasn't talking about it.

> Everybody always wants a Cinderella story and I thought that's what I had with Fred. That whole first year was wonderful, until De-

cember of '98 when we went to the NFR and I saw a whole other side of Fred Whitfield. It got a little rocky before we even left and I didn't know what was going on with him. He had been down to earth and cool until now, but then the arrogance hit. Fred is very competitive, obviously, and the NFR is up and down. One night it's good and one night it sucks and you have to wait for the next round before you know what his mood would be for the next twenty-four hours. That's how it is…that's just rodeo. When it's good, it's good, but when it's bad, it's really bad.

Back then, they used to do the buckle presentations at the Gold Coast after each round and I didn't even know what a buckle presentation was because I'd never been to one. He won the round one night and I remember the announcers talking about the round and how well he did. Then Fred went up on stage and kind of reminisced about when he was younger and told stories of him and Roy Cooper and I just saw him in a different light. Then he took off and left me at the Gold Coast.

I was scared to death and a girlfriend of mine was there, thank God, and she kept me company, but Fred was long gone. I was completely lost in Las Vegas; it was his world and he completely shut me out of it. Before me, he had been quite a ladies' man and he got out to Vegas and wanted to be a ladies' man again. I knew Fred had women before me and I was never going to hold that against him. What mattered was who he was with now, not who he had been with before. But as soon as we got there, I was in his way and my heart was absolutely broken. So I ran. I didn't want to, but I left.

He was very egotistical and had a hard edge to him; Fred enjoyed the adoration and attention of lots of women. I didn't see it at first, but when we were dating I can remember going to bars and him trying to pick a fight with me over other girls and I wasn't going to go there. I am not about the drama. If that's the situation, if he's flirting with another girl or something, then I'll just leave…I'm out, I'm done. And he wasn't used to that and I think he wanted us to pull hair. He liked to see the catfights over him and was pretty good at making that happen. Then I came around and said no, I'm not a catfighter. Sorry.

So, I flew back home before the NFR was even over. Some of our friends were flying out there for the second weekend and they convinced me to go back and I did, but he was still being standoffish. Because of what I had gone through before, I felt like life was too short to be treated like this. I loved Fred, but I was not going to be treated badly again.

We reconnected before the NFR ended and came home from Vegas and had Christmas together. Things were fine, but he never apologized or talked about what happened out there. After Christmas, he thought everything was back to normal, but it was time to put my foot down and ask for an explanation about what happened in Vegas. He thought it was all in the past and got defensive and started to argue.

I was in the kitchen doing dishes, he was sitting across the bar, and I said do you even want me here?

He said, "I'm so tired of this."

I said do you want me to leave.

He said, "Maybe you should."

I said do you really want me to leave.

He said "Yes."

I said fine; consider it done. And that was the end of the conversation and I went and got my clothes on and went to town and rented a U-Haul and started packing. I called my dad and said you need to wire me some money; I need to get out of here. He told me to just take a few days and chill out and see if he cools down. I said, Dad, I don't want to stay if he doesn't want me to; I need to get out of here right now.

I had boxes all over the place and he stayed gone all day trying to avoid me. When he came home that night, he said, "Wow, I guess you're really leaving." He started to see this was real. We went to bed and Fred held on to me all night long. He was going to the Mike Johnson Roping in Tulsa, a huge jackpot roping they have after the Finals, and when he woke up the next morning, I said I'm getting ready to leave out today. He said good-bye in a soft voice and walked out the door. I looked out the window as he was loading the horses and I jumped out of bed and ran out there and hugged him one last time and wished him luck for the upcoming season. Even though I wasn't going to be a part of it, I just knew '99 was going to be a good year for him.

He left and I finished packing my U-Haul. Later, his friend came by and saw what was going on and called Fred and told him I was loaded up and really leaving, but he never called. I was going to drive out that night, but two couples we were close to invited me to dinner and one of them talked me into coming and staying at their house and leaving out the next morning so I could get some sleep.

By that next morning, Fred called their house to talk to me. He was quiet and I could tell he'd been crying. I wanted to hear from him why he was crying, and I asked if it was because I am leaving and he said yes. I asked what do you want me to do, Fred? He sort of waited a minute and said, "Maybe you should go and I just need to figure things out." I drove all day and night, twenty-four hours straight through, and went back to California where I'm from originally, but I never wanted to go back there. I moved in with my mom, registered for college and got my old job back at the restaurant where

I used to work.

I knew very shortly after meeting Cassie that she was the one for me. When she said she was leaving, I was disappointed, but I had to go to that roping in Tulsa. When I got home, I was shocked that she really left. I didn't think she was going to leave, I honestly didn't…and then she did. I'll just level with you –I wasn't cheating on Cassie, but I was still being a little scandalous out there in Vegas. I don't know where my head was at.

I honestly didn't want Cassie to leave but I apparently didn't say the right things and she left and was in California twenty-four hours later. I ended up winning sixteen or seventeen thousand at that roping in Tulsa, but I came home to an empty house and realized what had happened.

Fred called Cassie every day and checked on her, and made small talk. Then one day he called and said. "I made a mistake. I realize now that I let the best thing in my life go." He asked Cassie to come back to Hockley and come home.

> Before I would move back, I met him at the rodeo in Denver at the end of January 1999, so we could just meet up face to face and make sure we both wanted to try this again. And the sparks were still there. I had been in California for exactly a month and then Fred flew out to California to get me. I told him, if you want me to come back to Texas, you're going to have to come get me. He came out on a Friday and stayed the weekend and he met my mother. He had just broke my heart and had to prove himself before he left with me again, and my mother absolutely fell in love with him. There were no hard feelings and we went to a San Diego Charger football party and met more family members and friends and they all loved him. We loaded

yet another U-Haul trailer and brought it and my truck back out here to Texas. And Fred did a one-eighty and became a whole different man.

The whole next year was about building our relationship and the relationship got to be great. He was a whole new man, he was my dream man, and I knew marriage was seriously on his mind now. This was the man I wanted and saw myself with.

To debut the 1999 rodeo season, Roy Moffitt bought a bunch of steers and some team roping horses and announced that Fred was now going to win an all-around title because "…it will be easy." Fred replied, "That's just you talking."

Let me start by saying that Fred can do anything he wants to do. He's got enough heart and determination and ability to do whatever he wants to do. He's so focused. People said Fred was arrogant, and Fred was this and Fred was that… Fred wasn't arrogant; Fred was so focused on winning gold buckles, he didn't care about anything else. From the time he was eight, nine, ten years old, he didn't care about nothing else but being the world champion. Once he won that, he felt like he needed to prove it over and over again.

I used to get mad at him because he never took a shot at winning the all-around. There was a lot of years he would have won the all-around if he just would have competed in another event – a lot of years. So he come home, I think it was '98, and I said I'm going to bring you up here and we're going to team rope. He said, "Man, I don't need to team rope." I said come on, let's go. I bought five horses, a hundred head of steers, and we went to roping steers and he was pretty damned good at it. I knew it'd be easy.

CHAPTER 13

THE ALL-AROUND

Casey Butaud shares more theories and reactions regarding the color of Fred's skin:

Trevor Brazile is considered to be the biggest deal in rodeo, but from the stands he's not distinctively different from the other cowboys. Most rodeo fans, just the mainstream rodeo fans, can't tell Trevor Brazile from anybody else. But they can always identify Fred. I think Fred has more fans than anyone else because the color of his skin helped fans recognize him. At rodeos, the cowboys are very far away from the fans, and who are we kidding, at that distance all those cowboys look the exact same. Fred was the only guy in that elite winner's circle at the top that was black and, in my opinion, that's one of the reasons his fan base grew like it did...they could locate him.

I been with him at airports and restaurants and different places and with that gold buckle and a cowboy hat on, people say "Hey, you're Fred Whitfield." There's been lots of times when people walk up to him and say "You're the rodeo guy in the calf roping...you're Fred Whitfield, right?" Or, "Hey, you're that rodeo guy on ESPN that's great at calf roping." Hotel lobbies, airports, everywhere we go, he gets recognized. Sometimes these people are in suits and ties and business attire and you can tell they're not die-hard rodeo fans

> – but they still know which one is Fred. I been with Sylvester before and people would ask him if he was Fred Whitfield. He would laugh it off, and say, "No, Fred's not here…he'll be here in an hour," or something like that. They see Fred as the only black cowboy on a national level.
>
> But mainly Fred's recognized for being the best of the best and a true champion of rodeo. They love him because he's been winning for so long. And he's a nice looking man, he's always dressed real nice, he's professional. A lot of those guys behind the scenes are not professional and I can honestly say Fred has always stood to the highest professional standard in that sport. He's the epitome of what a world champion cowboy should be. Fans and celebrities alike see that and gravitate towards him because of it.

Tom Epperson was making money hand over fist with me paying him twenty-five percent of everything I won on Reno, because everywhere we went I won money on him. Reno could run so fast that there was times I would miss the barrier a foot, foot and a half, on purpose just to toy with them. Then I'd reach just a little bit and catch them calves the same spot everybody else was catching them.

In '91, Jim Fuller rode Reno at the Finals that year and won second in the average. That horse was six years old at the time and he won second in the average on him at the National Finals. I don't know if that's the youngest horse that's been there in the calf roping, but it's close. So he took him to the Finals in '91 and then nobody rode Reno at the Finals again until I rode him in '97 and set the average record. In '98 I rode him a little bit, but then Tom leased him to Stran Smith that year. I told him, man, you're going to make the most money with me, and I think it ticked him off a little bit. He said, "Hell, I'll just lease the horse to somebody, who'll pay me a bunch of money up front."

I finally bought Reno in 1999 when Tom and the other people who owned him decided they were going to sell him. Tom let Bubba Paschal ride him in '98 and he missed a calf and the horse run off and got tangled up in the rope. After that the people that owned him seen what was going on and came and told me they were going to sell Reno. Really?

I asked them if they had anybody interested and they didn't. I said when you do, tell them not to bother getting their loan approved because I'm going to own him. I never asked what they wanted for him – just spouted off at the mouth like a dumb ass. Hell, I'd won a couple hundred thousand on him, so I had to buy that horse. A couple of days later Kenna Squires calls me and says JD Yates seems to think he's worth about seventy-five thousand. I was at my house sitting on one of them bar stools and I just about fell off in the floor. I said you got to be fricking kidding me. She says, "No…and by the way, Rusty Seawalt wants to try him." I said okay, just consider all offers and when you decide you really want to get rid of him, just let me know.

They called me a couple of weeks later and asked me if I wanted to try him, and I said no, I don't need to try him. I just need to know how much cash you need and when I can pay the rest. And they said oh really, so you want to be put on a payment plan? I said no, I don't need to be put on no payment plan. I can give you half the money today and I need thirty days or so to give you the other half. They said that'll be fine. So I give them forty thousand cash up front and then another thirty-five thousand a month later and finally took Reno home with me.

In July of the same year, 1999, I passed the one million dollar mark in winnings and the media made a big deal of it. Those things probably weren't as big a deal for me then as they are now, because I cherish the things I've done when I look back on them now. The achievements and accomplishments are always in the back of my mind; the thing I worry about most is getting to the next rodeo, winning some more money. The only thing I kind of regret about rodeoing is that financial planning didn't really come into play until I met Cassie. I was bad, but she got me out of all that nonsense. When I split up with that girl, I didn't file taxes for the next three years. To hell with the IRS, they ain't never going to come bother me. I was in bad shape for a couple of years, but just didn't worry about it. When I very first got in the PRCA, Roy's company did all my taxes, and then that woman decided she would do it. Well hell, I ain't never done taxes, so when I split up with her, the last thing I was worried about was my taxes.

When they did come calling, they wanted a hundred thousand dollars out of me. Cassie spent I don't know how much time going through duffle bags of receipts and she got them all organized into each year and added up everything and then she hired a good CPA and gave him all the figures she had. I ended up giving them like twenty thousand cash and got out of it. Cassie was a nervous wreck for a while.

So 1999, here we go, chasing that all-around. I bought two good head horses and a practice horse that was good enough to take down the road, and hell, we just went to entering. I roped with several different guys. The very first guy I team roped with at a pro rodeo was Arles Pearce, a kid from Hempstead. The winter of '99, we placed at Denver, we placed at Houston, placed at San Antone, and were in the top five in the world in team roping after the winter rodeos in '99. I'm thinking woo hoo, but them team ropers ain't liking it at all. Here's a guy in the top five who ain't never team roped on the circuit and I could sense them guys were jealous and didn't think it would last. So we got all this money won and Arles calls and tells me he broke his leg. We're entered at Austin and he breaks his fricking leg. I'd heard he was wrestling around, playing grab ass in the fricking parking lot, so I was mad. A few days later I went and seen him and he's says, man I'm sorry. I said hell dude, ain't nothing you can do now.

So in April we load up Arles and went to a couple of rodeos out there in California and spent the whole month of May on the west coast. Cassie and I hauled him around, saddled his horse, helped him up on his horse and he roped a leg damn near everywhere we went. I'm turning steers to win money, and he's just legging them because he couldn't squeeze his leg to dally. I'm finally fed up and said Arles this ain't working. I said go home until you're ready. This is the end of spring and it's going to take him about eight weeks to be ready to go again.

Well hell, here comes slick ass Trevor Brazile and he says we ought to rope together, and the pressure got me because I'm in a free-fall in the standings because I hadn't been team roping. So I got hooked up with Trevor and we went to Canada to a rodeo, we placed there, we went to a few more and placed at all of them. Fourth of July rolls around and we show up at Oakley, Utah, and I told him we're up in the calf roping this day and the team roping that day. Well, we go over there and we're not up. I guess I wrote it down wrong or the people at the entry office read it back wrong, but he just loads up and goes home and throws this dude in the dirt. Now I ain't got a team roping partner.

Then I get tied in with Mike Beers who's a world champion. The first week we rope together, we win eight thousand, so I'm back inside the top ten, top eight. Good. Everything's perfect. I got twenty-something thousand won, I'm not a cinch to make the Finals, but if I just rope along, I'll get there. So, I go along there with Mike and we're entering all these rodeos, going to Idaho Falls, to Seattle, Washington, going here to there. Before long, the horses are worn out, Mike's riding my good calf horse, things ain't going good for me…and we're not winning team ropings. I buy steers and put them at his house so we can practice and we're basically living in Oregon, plugging along another five or six more weeks trying to make the Finals in the team roping. Then, in late August, Mike comes to me in Lovington, New Mexico and says this will be our last steer together. Are you kidding? He said, "I got to do something different, I'm running out of time." We were well inside the top ten, and I said I'll tell you what, maybe yesterday ought to be our last steer and I turned out my steer at Lovington. Man, who am I going to rope with now?

I had roped with three different guys already and next I roped with Nick Rowland, a kid from Oklahoma. I roped with him a couple a weeks, no luck, roped with another guy for a week, no luck and I mean I'm falling fast in the team roping standings. Everything started out good with Arles, so I went back with him after his leg healed and roped with him a week or two but we didn't win nothing. I wanted to make the Finals in the team roping, but they were crowding me big time and I'm feeling the pressure.

Fred's PRCA cowboy bio, says, "Always cool under pressure, Whitfield has made a name for himself in ProRodeo by consistently coming through in clutch situations. His signature "raise the roof" salute caught on with fans across the country who have become accustomed to his dramatic victories."

In July 1999, Fred became a million-dollar cowboy, having earned $1,014,426 since joining the PRCA. Over the Fourth of July, he competed in five rodeos to set a record for earning $100,000 faster than anyone else in a regular season. Other 1999 wins included San Antonio, Tucson, San Angelo and Medicine Hat, as well as the Texas Circuit all-around and tie-down roping titles. Cassie says it was a busy year, indeed.

> I remember people around us were asking, "Why don't you get married?" But that year we were both focused only on the all-around and we were in it together. I drove as much as I could that year, I saddled horses, I did everything I could to help him and was devoted to him winning that title.
>
> At some point that summer, we were at Casper, Wyoming and he had an accident coming out of the chute. He was on Moon and Moon jumped forward as they opened the chute and Fred's ankle got caught on it and he fell off in the arena. It was very dramatic and very scary. We went to the hospital and the doctor looked at it and

said it was sprained really badly. He couldn't even walk on it and we were both just devastated about what this might do to him in the all-around standings. We had to buy a different pair of boots that he could fit his foot in with a brace on it to support his ankle. He couldn't get off his horse and land on his feet, so he couldn't rope calves for two or three weeks. He went to every rodeo he was entered in, he just team roped and turned out his calves. After a few weeks, he was back in the saddle and continued roping calves and steers. Then we got to the NFR...again.

In his whole career that I've been with him, that was the one year that words can't describe how we were feeling. The Finals start with how you get there; what you have to endure to get to that point, and once you finally get there, you never know what's going to happen from one round to the next. I remember some time after the halfway point, I don't remember exactly what was going on, but he was getting closer and closer.

I was in the top fifteen of the team roping all year until late August when I dropped out and didn't make the Finals in the team roping that year. But I was leading both the all-around and the calf roping when I hit the '99 NFR. I was hauling Moon and Reno and rode them both. Reno was gaining a lot more confidence and that same year I bought him, I won San Antone and placed at Houston and Ft. Worth on him.

I can remember the 1999 NFR just like it was yesterday. I placed in the first round and then missed a couple of rounds, then got on track and started winning and ended up winning the average and winning the calf roping title. I won over sixty thousand in the calf roping at the NFR, which was enough to win the 1999 All-Around title, too. Ty Murray had won it for the last few years, but that year it was mine. To beat Ty and Joe and be the man that year, it was a once in a lifetime experience. Not to say that I couldn't have won it more than I did, but that year I set out to win the all-around and actually accomplished it...and won the world in the calf roping, too. To me, that ranks just behind having my children. It doesn't get any better than that, to be *the* guy in your field of expertise. It was getting to the point where the competition was getting tougher and tougher. It wasn't just one or two guys you had to beat; by now it was five or six guys I had to keep my eye on all the time. It was amazing to be part of an organization with more than ten-thousand members, and then come out on top of all of them and be the best in the world. I'm still the only black man to win an all-around title, and I know it is cliché, but it was the ultimate high.

We went to the awards banquet and we were all just on cloud nine. Then we went out and had several drinks and gambled a little bit, too. That night was a celebration with all the people who had been around me and watched the whole process and it was so exciting. My close friends have been my family. I've had to weed a few of them out here and there, but being able to grow up around somebody and then celebrate your success with them, it means as much as the title, honestly.

That night in the casino, Roy won $70,000 and I had $30,000 of it on me, $15,000 in each pocket. I took this sonofabuck back up to the room because he was drunk, really drunk, and I said I'm going to take this money and give it to your wife. Trisha was up there in her robe and I give her $30,000. But Roy took off again and he lost the $40,000 he had. That dude would always win big or lose a lot in Vegas and always had a good time. He came almost every year and those casinos catered to him.

Fred told announcer Bob Tallman that with Roy Moffitt in his corner they couldn't beat him. Roy says, "Fred was a black man in a white man's world and he needed somebody in his corner." Roy was there in good times and in bad and right now it was nothing but good after Fred precisely followed his instructions to win the all-around.

We were loud and proud at the Finals. Fred was winning and making money and I was working and making money, and we thought we were somebody. I've spent so damn much money out there in Vegas that I could have spent a month in Europe or something... could have gone on a cruise around the world. Instead, I gave it to a blackjack dealer. I was so damned drunk I don't remember much about being in Vegas...just that we had fun.

Still stinging from the 1998 National Finals, Cassie didn't get to Vegas with as much confidence as Fred did.

I remember thinking he was getting all weird like he did in '98 because he gets pissy when it gets tense. He's very competitive and has a horrible game face and I was just trying to lay low. I just remember the final round, after he roped and won it, he came and found me in the stands and sat with me and held my hand and was so excited. We hugged and he whispered in my ear with tears in his voice, and said, "We did it, hon."

We were all business that entire season and it was all business at the NFR that year, but in the end, it was all worth it. I remember we got dressed and went to the champion's banquet. We dressed up – we always dressed up. That's what distinguishes Fred from the other cowboys and you just know that he's somebody because he has that classy look about him. We were always very formal and I always felt a red-carpet status with him back in the day.

We were at the MGM Grand in a big, dark, beautiful banquet room. I remember being at the table with everybody – Roy and Trisha were there, Anthony and his wife were there, they were always at the NFR, and we all had dinner and celebrated. We had a fun table.

The PRCA did away with the champion's banquet after the final round and now they just do it on a stage in the arena after the rodeo in order to include the fans. I think it sucks that they do it like that, because they used to announce each world champion winner at the banquet and they came up and gave an acceptance speech. When Fred walked up on stage, everybody at our table turned to see him. I remember in his speech he talked about the two events that year, the ups and downs, how he'd had to switch partners several times in team roping. He thanked all of us at the table, me and Roy and Wendy, his manager at the time, and whoever else was involved that year. He made us stand up one at a time and he talked about us. It was very emotional for him and he got a little choked up.

Most people would be bullshitting you if they told you this, but the honest to God truth is that if I could have got on a computer and made a woman just for me, I couldn't have made a better one than the one I got. When we got home after the Finals in '99, I was working on buying a ring, I just hadn't told her. I had a friend that owned a jewelry store down there in town and I went by there and I said man, you need to get me a nice diamond. Cassie told me she wanted a pear shaped diamond and the jeweler said that's one of the most elegant. I learned about diamonds, learned what was a good quality, but I hadn't found anything I liked yet. Finally, I found a pear shaped diamond I wanted, so I went down there to the bank where I'd been saving up some money and said I need to take all my money out...and the lady said you can't do that.

I said, wait a minute, are you kidding me? The guy had made me a hell of a deal on the diamond if I paid him cash, and they wouldn't give me my money. Then I started cussing. I used to be a hot-head and I said what the hell do you mean I can't have my money?

She told me to calm down.

I said I put this money in here and I need it; I got a man waiting on me with a big old diamond I'm fixing to buy. We got things figured out and I got my money and I got my ring and I come home.

I'm always fricking excited; I can't hold ice water if it's something I want to do. Cassie had just got out of the shower and was sitting on the bed with her hair still wet; looking just like she did the night I met her. I pulled out the ring and said will you marry me? She's started crying and said yes. So then I got to call her dad and ask for her hand and I think that's the most nervous I ever been in my life. I'd met him, but didn't really know him, so I called him up and he said you got my blessing, get after it. It was official – we were engaged.

Then her mom came and stayed with us for Christmas and I had a feeling those two were up to something. On Christmas morning I got my stocking from over the fireplace and dug a couple a CD's out and whatever else was in there, and all the sudden I find a baby rattle wrapped with this EPT test. My dumb ass is like, what the hell is this? About that time, her mom just happened to go outside and leave us alone for a few minutes. Cassie started crying and said, "I'm pregnant."

We got married in April. Ray, that's Cassie's dad, rented a fricking condo down there in California and he had the whole one side of it, so all our rooms were adjoining, like a horse shoe. We'd had the rehearsal dinner and after dinner me and some of my buddies went out for a little bachelor party. Trisha made Roy go back to the room. We got lit up and had the time of our life. The next morning I got all of my stuff laid out and I knew I had set my shoes on the bed, but I went back in there and my shoes are gone. I said Ray, man, don't start this…we're too far into this deal to start having hitches and glitches now. So I search around there and finally said, which one of you hid my shoes? He just stared at me. I said Ray, bring my shoes back in here. I knew all along he hid them and was pulling a prank on me. He kind of slapped me in the face and said, "Son I ain't got your shoes." I said Mr. Ray, you got your one free slap; don't ever do that again. I finally found them, and

I knew he had hid them.

All of my in-laws are good as gold. That's the coolest family I've ever met and they never had a problem with me. I don't want to make race an issue and I never have because I've been through enough of it. I have faced prejudice for years, but they've never had a problem with me being black. If anything, I think my own mom was kind of leery of it at first, but she's learned to accept it over the years. The more people are educated, the more they don't have a problem with it. It's them sonofabitches that are less educated that cause problems.

After her contributions to his roping success, especially assisting with the all-around, it's no surprise that Roy approves of Fred's final selection.

> When he first told us he had a new girl, we met her and they seemed to be a good match. I was his best man and it was a beautiful wedding and we had a lot of fun. For the wedding, we flew to San Diego and went to El Cajon to a golf resort. We got in late and I didn't go to the bachelor party the night before; I was running in and running out to get back to work. I remember there was a zoo and the wedding and the reception. It was pretty and nice; it just was strange for Fred to be getting married at a golf resort, a country club…I mean that's how damned white he is.

Saying, "I'm not a wedding or a funeral guy; never have been and never will be," Casey missed Fred and Cassie's wedding and says he never apologized and it still bothers him to this day. He still has plenty to say on the subject.

> My opinion again, but I think Moon has a hard time showing

love because of the way he was raised. I have dealt with that myself, so I can look at him and see it. But when he married Cassie, the aura around him changed. That would be a good way to describe it. He was more settled and peaceful with himself and his situation. I know he loves Cassie a lot and cherishes his family as much, if not more, than rodeo.

All he knows is rodeo, that's all he knows...horses and rodeo, and I know Cassie is very understanding of him. It's better now, but he used to be gone so much and when he did come home, he'd go to a jackpot or an amateur rodeo three or four nights a week. He might leave at five or six in the afternoon and not get home until midnight or one in the morning. Then he gets up early and the girls go to school and then that afternoon he might be going to another jackpot or rodeo. He don't come home from rodeoing and then hang around the house.

Happily ever after for Mr. and Mrs. Whitfield began on April 29, 2000 in San Diego where the springtime weather was beautiful. Even so, Cassie says Fred hates California and yet here he was, marrying a girl *from* California *in* California.

I'm from California, but he hates California because he says every time he goes there something happens. Back in his earlier days, way before me, he got that scar across his face from a knife fight over a girl. He doesn't tell people that very often. The night I met him, I asked him if it was from a rope and he said no, but didn't elaborate. I later learned what the story was.

My friend that I was staying with when I first came to Texas, she and I started planning the wedding in February, but Fred is so hard to plan stuff with. I wanted to wait until after I had the baby so I could have a waistline, but he was like no, I want to do it now. I didn't have much of a guest list from his side and because it was so far from Texas, a lot of friends didn't come. His immediate family was there and Roy and Tricia Moffitt. We did give invitations to some rodeo friends, but Fred was no help with that. I think Shada and Trevor Brazile, who were dating at the time, were the only rodeo people who came out – mostly just my family & friends were there.

Then, on August 14, 2000, our oldest daughter Savannah came. She's a Leo, like her daddy. My mom was here already because we knew the baby would be coming soon and Fred came home just after he won the Cheyenne rodeo. He brought home his winning calf and I remember him getting her out of the trailer when he got home. We went out to dinner and that night we were home in bed when my water broke, so Fred got here in the nick of time. And the next day we had the most perfect baby, our daughter Savannah. But unfortunately, we don't have the trophy calf from Cheyenne anymore. Fred had her somewhere on pasture and a couple of years ago she accidently went to the sale barn. I don't think the guy that bought her knew they were eating Fred's winning calf from Cheyenne.

When we were dating and first married, Fred was never home, but I traveled with him most of the time. We were gone from home a lot and I remember one spring we stayed out on the west coast for months. When Savannah came, it worked fine when she was a baby. But after she got a little older, and especially after Sydney came, it was just too much for all of us. The kids would get tired and grumpy, then Fred would get tired and grumpy, and it wasn't worth the effort anymore.

Cassie calls Savannah, "my easy baby," who kept herself entertained both on the road and at home. Knowing a little girl was on the way, Cassie wanted to name her Hannah, Fred wanted Nicole, and they were at a stand-off until the night Fred signed an autograph for a little girl named Savannah. He loved the name and came home and sold Cassie on it being close enough to Hannah, so Savannah Nicole Whitfield it would be.

Now an accomplished young woman of twelve [2012], Savannah wants the world to know that, "My dad is very kind, he's really down to earth and he doesn't lie a lot." She says that it wasn't until she was older that she knew her daddy was a famous cowboy, she only knew he was gone most of the time.

> He isn't home much because he's always on the road. But Daddy loves what he's doing and you don't want to take that away from him. Whenever he's in the middle of signing autographs and everyone wants to take pictures with him, I kind of worry about the poor guy - they really swarm him. We like to sit by him and see how much everyone adores him and how he's just "it."
>
> It will maybe calm down a little pretty soon, but it probably won't change much. I hope he will be around more and we will get to do more stuff with him like go to the movies, get ice cream, go to dinner. My dad takes just me and my sister for smoothies whenever my mom is at Pilates and we go to dinner a lot, but not all the time because he's gone. We haven't been on the road with him in the last couple of years because we have school and we have to focus a lot on that and make sure our grades are good. He wants us to be successful, to be athletic and in shape because he wants us to have a good future. Daddy never wants us to rodeo; he lets us ride, he just doesn't want us to get too involved with the rodeo.
>
> Since his surgery [neck and shoulder], he's been home more and we get to hang out with him. He likes to spend time with us and he misses that and wishes he could do it more. That's why he's slowing

things down - he wants to spend more time with his family. He's usually not here for my birthday because it's in August. Last year, he wasn't home for my birthday and he called but acted surprised when I reminded him. I started crying because I thought he had forgotten, but he was just messing with me. He had really nice flowers delivered to me at school and everyone got to see them. He likes to joke around with us.

Sometimes when we're at home, we play outside in a big tree we have that has a little swing. He will come and push us and we'll go really high and it's fun because we almost wrap around the tree. Sunday is his steak night when he likes to cook us steaks. He loves making us steaks and we have baked potatoes and corn on the cob and green beans. He says that when he settles down and is done rodeoing that maybe he should open his own steak house.

At my school, we have this day just before the Houston Rodeo that's dedicated to cowboys; it's Western Day and one year he got his dummy calf and his horse and he brought them up to the school. Everyone got to see him rope it and my friends thought it was really cool. I was like "That's my dad…he's my dad."

He took me and my sister to lunch a while back and we were driving home with him in his truck. We went by a new interstate they're building near our house that Mom said wouldn't be done for probably ten years. I started thinking and I made a comment to Daddy, I said I'll be out of here by the time that's done. My dad was like uh oh, and he said "Don't say that." I told him that by then I'll almost be done with college and I think that scares my dad.

Chapter 14

Moon's Last Run

Doc Currie is not only Fred's trusted veterinarian, but a close friend as well who sometimes travels with him. He recalls the day in Hill City, Kansas when Fred blew the transmission out of his truck just as they drove into the rodeo grounds. "He just goes ballistic," says Doc, "but there wasn't nothing he could do about it." A wrecker came and hauled the truck to Hays to get fixed, but that wasn't happening anytime soon, and Fred had rodeos to go to as soon as this one was over. Doc recalls how this seeming disaster turned around for them.

> After the rodeo, we're sitting there at the trailer with no truck in front of it, just stranded. A lady with two little boys came up and asked Fred to sign autographs for them. He brought out his little tablet and asked their names and gave her two boys an autograph. The lady asked where we were headed and Fred told her his truck was broke down, but we needed to get to Dodge City. This total stranger said "You can borrow our truck," and she left to get her husband.
>
> Fred looks at me, and that's the only time we ever talked about race or whatever, but he looks at me and says, "What white person is going to let a black man she's never met take her truck?" I said I don't know, but it beats sitting here. Fifteen minutes later, her and her husband show up with a truck for us to borrow. We used it to

pull this big old living quarters to a few rodeos north of there, then came back a few days later and picked up Fred's truck and gave them their truck back. We were on our way out of town, when Fred said we had to go back by those people's house. When I asked him why, he said that woman was going to cook us dinner. Really?

Turns out it was Fred's birthday and I guess that lady knew it, so we went back to their house, this little bitty farmhouse, and she made us dinner. Her and her husband had three little boys, but the youngest one had misbehaved and didn't get to go to the rodeo the day we met the rest of the family. After dinner, those kids wanted Fred to teach them how to tie a calf. They had a tying dummy but it didn't work very good, so Fred said, "Ya'll don't have a calf that we could practice on?" They had a little milk calf they were feeding a bottle to, so they got him out and Fred showed them boys how to tie calves. I didn't know he could teach that good, but it ended up all three boys learned to tie the calf. The lady made him a birthday cake too, so after they tied calves, we had birthday cake and then we left.

The lady brought the boys by to see Fred at the Finals a time or two after that. Two of them made the high school finals and Fred saw them there in Rock Springs, Wyoming a few years ago. It was the damndest thing I ever saw.

Even with the all-around in 1999, I was still disappointed I didn't make the Finals in the team roping, so I decided to regroup in 2000 and go at them again. The next year, 2000, I get lined up to team rope with Marty Becker, who I'd been friends with for quite a while. We roped a little bit together, but didn't have much success, then I roped with Nick Rowland again, and I'm just bouncing back and forth. This went on for a while, until about 2004, when I told Cassie I'm sick of this – I'm done with team roping. I think I give twenty-one thousand for that one head horse and fifteen or twenty for the other and five thousand for the practice horse. Hell, I got forty thousand tied up in a few horses, so I sold them and was done with team roping by '04. A couple of years back, I filled in for a guy in Canada on one steer just to help him out, but that's all the team roping I've done in years.

I come back in 2000 and had another really good year and won the calf roping that year – back-to-back world titles again. I won some big rodeos in 2000 - Cheyenne, San Antonio, Reno...and, believe it or not, Houston. That was the first year I ever won Houston – my hometown rodeo – and, for thirteen years, I thought it would be my last. After that sixth gold buckle, other than Houston, I just had that silent confidence within myself that I could go get it done. That's not saying that the competition wasn't there, but I've always believed in myself and, in my opinion, that's brought on a lot of success.

Riding Moon was a big factor too because I had as much faith in him as I did in myself. It's a shame that horse never got recognized for how great he was, but that's not on me or him, it's on the people of that era who didn't think he was good enough. Not a lot of people could ride him; that wasn't his fault, he's still as great as there has ever been. They talk about this one and that one, but Moon was just as good or better than any of them and I knew that in my heart and in my mind. The only reason Moon was never calf horse of the year was that I don't go around kissing everybody's ass, asking will you vote for my horse. For as many years as he was in the PRCA and as much money as I won on him, there's just no reason. Moon won third one year and that's as close as he ever got. To hell with them – a trophy wasn't going to make Moon any better than he already was. He was one of the greats.

The next year, 2001, I didn't win the world but I still had a good year. I won Austin, Abilene, San Antonio and San Angelo, among others; won $50,000 at Calgary and won the Texas Circuit title. I didn't ride Moon very much at the 2001 NFR, just three rounds. I rode him two rounds and he didn't do anything wrong, but I could tell he just wasn't the same. The third round I rode him in, they blared the music real loud right there by us, and he circled me – just forgot what he was doing and run a circle around me. That horse had never done anything like that before. I roped a calf right there and I'm talking about this sonofabuck stopped like he always did, but about the time I got my hands on that calf, Moon just took off. That was him telling me he had had enough and it was the last time I ever rode him.

Casey Butaud, like everyone who knew the horse, says that the similarities between Fred and Moon went well beyond their shared names.

> Moon was his favorite horse ever. That horse had a personality like Moon himself and they liked each other and nobody else. Moon wouldn't really work for anybody but Moon – I don't care if you were Roy Cooper, nobody else could ride him. He wouldn't buck them off or do anything crazy; he just wasn't the same horse, he was sort of lazy. Moon would get on him and he would be great. He was consistently great and that's what Moon was looking for when he got him. That horse was special. Moon the horse gave Moon the man the confidence to be as great as he was. If Moon would have been a horse, he would have been Moon.

Cassie calls Moon "a robot," that didn't acknowledge anybody else and didn't need anything from anyone but Fred. Then she tells of the detour Fred made on the way home from the 2001 NFR:

> Fred had an actual relationship with Moon. That horse loved him and did whatever Fred wanted him to do. Fred would pet him like a dog and he used to wrap Moon's legs with this concoction that he made himself. It was some sort of cooling stuff to make his legs

feel good and then he'd wrap them just right so his legs didn't take any stress when he hauled him. They were quite a pair.

Moon was a push button horse designed only for Fred, and at the 2001 NFR, he just wasn't a hundred percent. Fred always had the utmost respect for that horse and he could have kept riding him, but he didn't want to push him. He roped that last calf and Moon was off in his own little world and he just kind of ran off. It wasn't pretty. I don't know if he was sore somewhere or if the blaring music and screaming fans finally got to him, but it was just out of that horse's character.

That was Fred's last ride on him because he would never let Moon be remembered as being anything less than great – Fred would never let that happen. On his way home after the Finals, Fred stopped at Doc's and handed him back to Cathy Cribbs, where he came from. He came home that year without Moon and that's possibly the closest relationship Fred has ever had with anything.

Once that horse was out of the picture, I was searching for the next Moon. I was looking for a certain feel and I'd use the same bits and the same saddles and ride every horse like I rode Moon. Every time I roped, I did the same stuff on them that I did on Moon. It took me three years to realize that he was gone. I just woke up one day and said you know what; you're being a dumb ass. It was time to see other horses for what they are instead of wanting them to be Moon.

The year after I retired him, 2002, I won my seventh gold buckle, but it was bittersweet without Moon being there. That year, I had $151,856 already won in the calf roping before I even got to Vegas, and I won the average and was third in the all-around. I rode Reno and another horse that doesn't merit mentioning at the 2002 NFR. When I bought Reno, he was sixteen and had already been to the Finals seven times, so by that time, he was twenty-years-old. I rode him sparingly in '02 and '03. Then in '04, I did the same thing with Reno that I did with Moon, and gave him back to Tom Epperson while he was still in decent shape. Those two horses there, they pretty much defined my career. They didn't owe me anything and I wasn't going to ride them into the ground. In 2003, I bought Gator and he was a pretty good one, but it took me a couple of years to get him in the Whitfield frame of mind. When I got that horse, everybody said I'd never win the world on him and I said we'll see.

During the 2003 season, I won the Dodge National Circuit Finals Rodeo in Idaho, the Winter Tour Finale and the Pace Picante ProRodeo Tour Finale, both of them in Vegas, and crossed the two million mark in career earnings. I didn't win the world that year, but at the Finals, I won the second round with a 7.7 second run and the eighth round with a 6.9 and finished second in the world with $200,656. I also became a daddy for the second time.

With Fred on the road so much, Cassie says she has become an accomplished do-it-yourselfer. "I love that man to death, but he's not the best handyman. He's used to me taking care of things." Through the years, Cassie has handled anything with "some assembly required," including furniture and toys, as well as a memorable car seat installation that her mother captured on video lest anyone ever forget.

> It is such a big deal to plan anything with Fred, especially a vacation, and we had a Hawaiian vacation planned for the spring of 2003, the objective being to get to work on a second baby. We planned this baby around the rodeo schedule, but we jumped the gun and I went to Hawaii already four months pregnant, which changed my vacation plans quite a bit.
>
> When we were at the hospital having Savannah, Fred saw the

name Sydney on somebody else's door and we agreed then that if we had another girl that would be her name. Sydney Marie Whitfield, our second daughter, arrived on November 6, 2003. Fred had been home when she was born, but had to leave for a big rodeo the next day. It was the Dallas Stampede, which at the time was a tour finale rodeo, so he had to check in the day before or else he would get fined, even though he just had a newborn baby come into the world. My mom and dad were here by the time he left, but Fred didn't get to bring us home and I think it's important for a dad to get to do that. He was bummed when he left with both of us still in the hospital.

Sydney came two weeks before my due date so I wasn't really prepared. I didn't have my bag packed for the hospital and I didn't have the new car seat put in the car. I asked my parents to bring me clothes to go home in and I asked Fred to make sure he put the car seat in the car before he left. On the day I went home it was lovely Texas weather – hot and humid as hell. After just having a baby, I wanted to look good, look trendy, but they brought me a leather jacket and thick pants, instead of the outfit I had asked for. My mom is recording everything as we leave the hospital and the nurse pushes me to the car and I open the door. Fred had "put the car seat in the car" just as I had asked, except that's all he did, just took it out of the box and set it in the car. And if you've ever installed a car seat…

Naturally, my mom and dad didn't know how it worked, so I am squatting in the car trying to get this car seat hooked up – and my mom is getting it all on video. I finally said, turn the damn camera off…just turn it off. I was so upset with Fred; my hormones were making me crazy, but mostly it was just Fred. I definitely brought it up to him later, and he said, "You know, I thought about that after I left...maybe she wanted me to do more with the car seat."

I was there when both of them were born, you damn right I was there. It changes your whole perspective on life and after you witness childbirth, you have a whole new respect for woman – I promise you, to this day I still do. With Savannah, I didn't know what to expect and when she popped out, oh my goodness – there was another little Fred. She was white as snow and had that film all over her and the doctor tapped her on the butt and she goes to crying. You got to experience it and feel it to understand it. I put the birth of both kids being born over the world championships – my girls come first and then the titles. Hell yeah, I was there for both of them and nothing or nobody can ever take none of that away.

With Sydney, our second one, I was knocked out in bed, sound asleep. It was about nine at night and we just got home from dinner and I went to bed. Before long, Cassie started poking me and saying it was time to go and she was already up and running around. I was still half-asleep when we got in the car and we hauled ass to the hospital about ten miles away. We had Dr. Montgomery and the whole pre-natal deal set up, so they were expecting us. They brought her a wheelchair and wheeled her in there and she was probably in labor for seven hours...then there were two.

Sydney was born in November of 2003, and it was earlier that same year, in January, that I was inducted into my first hall of fame, the Texas Cowboy Hall of Fame. Because you're elected by your peers, it speaks to the magnitude of what you've done over your career and it's hard to describe what that means to me.

Then in 2004, I was honored to be put in the Cheyenne Hall of Fame and that same year I got the call from the ProRodeo Hall of Fame. Back then, you could go in while you were still active in your career, unlike other sports where there's a time period that you have to be away from the game before you can even be on the ballot.

I got the phone call from Steve Hatchell, who was the commissioner at the time, and he says "You think you're ready to be put in the ProRodeo Hall of Fame?"

I said man, that's not my call, that's up to whoever puts the ballot together.

He said, "I think you're going to be on the ballot this year."

I said you're kidding me.

I was only in my mid-thirties, and it was crazy, totally crazy. I'm not the youngest guy to ever be inducted, and I'm not the first that was still competing, but I was still overwhelmed at it. All my family and friends were there, Roy and his wife, Doc and Sandy, and all of Cassie's family and her friends were there, and I got up and spoke at the ceremony. It was quite the gathering.

Roy Moffitt was at all of Fred's inductions and at the Texas Cowboy Hall of Fame at the Ft. Worth Stockyards he introduced Fred. "I had to follow George Strait…you think that ain't a tough act to follow." He says he tried to prepare something, but in the end, he just went with whatever rolled off of his tongue.

> I said something like I am often given credit for teaching Fred Whitfield how to rope. That's like saying Lance Armstrong's daddy taught him how to ride a bicycle. I might have taught him how to rope but I didn't teach him how to win world championships. I taught him the basics, the fundamentals of roping.
>
> Lance Armstrong's daddy might have taught him to ride a bicycle, but he didn't teach him how to win the Tour de France…them steroids did. Just kidding. It was a very big deal and I was so proud to be at all of them.

It was during the 1995 NFR that Miss Marie met and spent the evening with a very special friend of hers, a man she now calls simply, "George."

> I was at the MGM Grand in the casino with Fred, and George Strait sat at our table and I got my picture taken with him and talked to him all night.
>
> Fred said, "Mother, leave that man alone."
>
> George said, "She's alright man, she's telling me about her good cookies…let her talk to me."
>
> I was up 'til two or three in the morning just talking to George Strait and then he sang a song for me, *All My Exes Live in Texas.* I was telling jokes and talking loud, oh, I had a blast with him. Fred know I don't drink, but he said, "Mother if I didn't know better, I'd swear you were drunk."
>
> George was there when they put Fred in at the Texas Cowboy Hall of Fame in 2003, but he took off right after he spoke. I didn't see him again until 2008 when I was in Vegas with Fred. They had George in one of the booths up in the air at the rodeo, but he had bodyguards and Roy Cooper was one of the guys guarding George's door. I brought him some cookies, so I went up there to take George them cookies and Roy Cooper wouldn't let me in. George heard me arguing with Roy Cooper and asked him who it was and Roy told him it was Fred's mama. George said for him to let me in. George had me come on in and he ate my cookies and he said, "Thank you Mrs. Whitfield, I really enjoyed them cookies."
>
> Sometimes I have to show people my autograph and the picture I got of me and George because they don't believe me that I know George Strait.

The first time I rode Gator at the Finals was '03, but it took two years for us to come together. For ten years, the calf roping title went back and forth between me and Cody Ohl, but in 2004, Monty Lewis got by both of us by just a little to win it. I ended up third in the world with $158,000 and was fifth in the average. When I bought that horse, I thought he worked good and by '04 he was a lot better. In '05 he peaked and I went to the Finals in the lead and won my eighth gold buckle. I placed in five of ten rounds and won a total of $168,782. The naysayers said it couldn't be done on that horse, but it just took a couple of years for me and Gator to gel. I had several big wins that year riding him. I won Albuquerque, the Winter Tour Finale and led the pack most of the season in '05. I said the competition in the mid-nineties was tough, but hell, it just got tougher every day. It was always a battle between me and Cody and Trevor, maybe Blair [Burk] and Stran [Smith], but I managed to hold off all them guys and win the world again. Anytime I made the National Finals I felt like I was competing against the field, because at that point, everybody was trying to beat me and it's hard to stay on top when you got everybody just clawing at you.

I was thirty-seven-years-old, and I left Vegas in '05 consumed with the thought of an eighth calf roping title. I felt like it could be done and it was the only thing on my mind. Dean Oliver has eight calf roping titles and three all-arounds, and I had seven calf roping titles and one all-around, and I wanted to tie his calf roping title. I left Vegas, basking in that eighth gold buckle and thinking ahead to trying to tie Dean's calf roping record. There was no back-up plan. My health was good, I had good horses, endorsements were good, money was coming in and I wasn't worried about anything outside that world. It was back to rodeoing fulltime and in 2006 I qualified for my sixteenth National Finals Rodeo with $87,647.

Just before the 2006 NFR, we were down in Athens, Texas tying the NFR calves, getting them ready for Vegas. I took about five horses and a guy with me and we had been there roping for about two days. I was riding some guy's practice horse and roped one, but that horse just kept running. I picked the reins up with my left hand and used my right hand to try and hold the rope up so he wouldn't go over it and get us in a bind. Then he stopped and when he did, that rope come tight in my hand and just jerked me off his back and I hit the ground. It kind of dazed me for a while, but I got up and got everything collected. Hell, I didn't think it was that bad.

The next morning I couldn't get out of bed. My shoulder didn't hurt that bad, but two fingers on my right hand were numb. I guess when it jerked me, it jarred something here in my neck, just pinched something. Then that Joe Beaver come over there and offered to pop my back and my dumb ass let him. He puts his arms around me, picks me up and drops me, and you just hear things crunching. I was like ah, that wasn't it. Then my fricking shoulder starts hurting, and I thought what the hell have I done to myself. I said man; I better take my ass home and go to the doctor.

On Wednesday, I come home, Thursday I was no better and by Friday, I was lying on the floor and crying like a baby. I'm leaving the next day to go to Vegas and finally, on Friday, I thought I can't take this no more and I go get an MRI. They did the MRI and got it off to Tandy [Dr. Tandy Freeman, Justin Sports Medicine team physician] so he can look at it when he gets to Vegas. I take off on Saturday driving to Vegas, even though I knew I couldn't rope, but I got out there Sunday night and they gave me some pain pills and stuff, so I'm feeling somewhat better. On Monday, Tandy looks at the MRI and says there is no way I can rope. He says, "There's a level three tear in your rotator cuff." They had also taken a few laterals of my spine and he said "There's some… blah, blah, blah…spinal something…blah, blah, blah." I'm ignorant to all these terms he's using, so I said what does that mean. Tandy says, "Well, you're in need of some surgeries." Then he said we may be able to inject it and I'd be okay until after the Finals. All right, let's inject it. So he pulls out a needle about that long and injects it right there on the spot.

I wait around there a few days and it feels a little better, but I told Cassie,

I ain't going to be able to rope. Friday rolls around and I had to at least try, but the first round starts and I come across there and rope this calf and I'm like molasses. I have hell flanking because I've got no feeling in these two fingers, it's like I'm tying backwards.

I made it through the whole Finals and they injected my arm probably four or five times before Doc saw what was going on. I took Doc down there with me one night, and he said, "Fred, that's the end of that, don't let them inject it anymore." He said that with everybody in and out of that locker room, it was unsanitary. Doc told me, "You're going to jack around and get an infection and it's going to kill your ass." I had to go through the rest of the Finals like I was.

I won second one night and placed in another two rounds, finished fourteenth in the average, won $19,381 on those three rounds and finished the season ranked eleventh in the world with $107,028 for the year. It was about the halfway point that Clint Robinson called and asked if he could ride Gator. I charged him twenty-five percent of anything he won and he won sixty thousand riding my horse at the Finals, so I made fifteen thousand on that deal. Clint asked me if I'd sell him Gator, and I said hell yeah, I'll sell that horse…for a hundred and twenty thousand. He'd already won sixty thousand on him on five calves. He said I don't want him for that and I said that's fine, I'll take him home with me. It ain't no big deal because I didn't bring him out here to sell him.

At the end of the rodeo, Clint came by Del Frisco's where my wife and I and a bunch of my family are there eating a steak and he come by there and wrote me a check for fifteen thousand. I only won nineteen, but I left Vegas with thirty-four thousand. It wasn't the best NFR I ever had, but it wasn't all for naught.

Sandy Currie recalls the day Fred arrived at their clinic with Moon after the 2001 Finals and said he needed to talk to her, Doc and Cathy. He told them all "That horse has been good to me and I want to let him enjoy the rest of his life," and he gave him back to Cathy. Moon took it easy from then until December of 2006, when he was playing in the pasture and fell and broke his hip. Doc had to put him down and Sandy had to tell Fred.

> It was during the 2006 Finals that Moon died. Fred was already having such hell being hurt, and I swore to everybody on this place, including the man that buried him, that if any one of them told Fred Whitfield, I would kill them and bury them next to that horse. So no one knew and that Monday after the Finals ended, I called Fred and asked him where he was at and he said he was in a PRCA meeting. I started crying and told him to call me back because I needed to talk to him. When he called back, I told him and we both just cried. For a very long time, Cathy and Fred could not look at each other without falling apart and I think it may have been a year before they could even talk about Moon.
>
> Not very many men have as much love and respect for their horses as Fred and he gets more out of them because of it. They go all the way for him because they know he will go all the way for them. There are horses that Fred has gotten on that his beating heart is too much for them. They can't take his intensity. The weak horses pee their pants, but the strong horses get it on for him – they raise the roof. Fred is electric and when he throws his leg over a horse, mister, this is the real deal…this ain't no hay ride. It's blood and guts every pull.

When Sandy called the first time, I knew something was up because she was already choked up. I called her back and asked her what in the hell is going on? She told me that they had to put Moon down about halfway through the Finals, and man, I didn't know what to think. I said I'll call you back and I hung up the phone. It took me a long time to get over it, but in my mind, he had lived the best possible life. I have seen people ride horses until they just fall over dead and he deserved better than that and he got better than that. Moon was single-handedly the best horse that I have ever been on. I had him a real long time and I loved him.

Moon never had a better home than what he had with Fred. He took excellent care of Moon, as he does all of his horses. Fred's horses aren't just tools with which he performs a job. They are his livelihood. Fred never rode any of his horses into the ground. Fred's horses were allowed to retire as a winner who was still at the top of their game. I admire Fred for a lot of things, but that is probably the biggest. He's a good friend.

Cathy Cribbs

Chapter 15

A Lion in the Winter

Once we got home from the '06 NFR, I went and saw Tandy and he said I needed to get into surgery as soon as possible. I didn't want my arm in a sling during the holidays and put it off until after Christmas and went home with a bunch of pain pills. January rolled around and I headed to Dallas for surgery. Another doctor did the vertebrae surgery, the spinal stenosis where he went in there and scrapped the spinal canal and I stayed the night in the hospital and came home the next morning. I went back and seen him in a month for a check-up, and had the other surgery to repair my labrum and rotator cuff scheduled for the next day, February 7, 2007.

I told Tandy that I needed to be roping by the first of July and he said there was no way. I said watch me. He said it takes six months to recover. I said I need to be ready in five. Three days after I had my second surgery, I started therapy. Man let me tell you something, oh, my God…I always thought I was tough, but there ain't no pain like that in the world. I promise you, it was rank. I spent the first couple of weeks with my arm in a sling taped to my belly and had to sleep sitting up in a chair in my room. It was very frustrating to have to go through that whole process, but all I thought about was being ready to rope at Calgary in July.

In February, I went to Houston and announced a little bit at the rodeo, but it was a long time until July and I had to find something to do or I was going to go crazy. Roy said hell, since you're going to be out of commission for five or six months, why don't you come to work over here. He said I could ride around with his best salesman, take a few notes, and maybe start doing some outside sales. By late March, I was getting around better and my arm was out of the sling, and since I didn't have any serious money coming in other than endorsements, I tried it out. I'm about half-assed depressed, but excited too because I was going to get to do something else. I visited some customers and made some sales and I gave it a good honest try. Cassie was so proud of me. I had me a little book and appointments and was getting some deals done. For me, the hardest part of being in sales is being a good bullshitter, and I've never been good at it because I'm straight to the point. Here's what I'm selling, if you want to buy it, get after it. Honestly, that don't work in the business world. The other thing I didn't like about it was that people want to socialize and hang out. They want to meet after work for drinks and do that type of selling – show and tell selling – you show up and I'll tell everybody I know you.

That would lead to one drink and another drink and I was getting pretty hefty. Roy would call me and say I need you to come over here this evening and we would meet friends here and have a couple of drinks there and we'd be drinking somewhere else with some more friends and it just got to where it was less work and more drinking. I didn't mind the working part of it because I had my own schedule and as long as I went and seen the right customers and kept them happy, then there wasn't a problem. But it got to be where it was social hour every evening and people sitting around talking and drinking just ain't my cup of tea. I can go out with friends and have a good time and drink a little and there's nothing wrong with that, but this got to be where it was every night.

The only thing I was getting accomplished was developing a drinking habit, and it got to wearing on me pretty good. I come home one day and told Cassie we're doing more drinking than working and I don't want to wake up at forty years old being a freaking alcoholic. I didn't walk in there one day and tell Roy, hey, I'm not going to work for you anymore; I just said man, I'm not a hundred percent sure this is what I want to do, so I'm going to back away. Don't hesitate to call me if you need me to go see some customers or whatever, I don't mind, but I'm not going to get up every morning and drive all over Houston and come home at ten or eleven at night half sauced up. I started there in late March in '07 and I think I quit going over there to the office about two months later. I hate working anyway, I thought I'm fixing to rope.

I had started physical therapy just a few days after the surgery and I'd go just a little bit at first. Then I started going five days a week and I guarantee you it was less than two months and I was pretty free-wheeling with my arm from doing all those exercises. A little over three months after the first surgery I went back for a check-up and Tandy said things are looking pretty good. So I made sure I was at that therapy five days a week in March, April and May and about the middle of May, I went to Dallas to see Tandy. The doctor went back in there and did a little scope test and he said everything's anchored in there just right and it was coming right along. Tandy said it looks good and feels strong, and he asked me if I had been riding. I said I'd maybe been on a horse once or twice in the last few weeks. He asked me if I roped any, and I said no, but I been swinging a rope a little bit, playing with it. He said I could just slowly start beefing it up a little bit.

I went five months and never picked up a rope, never done nothing with a horse, but I started riding a little bit and I wasn't supposed to, so I didn't say anything to anybody. Then one day, I was out jacking around on a horse and fell off and landed on my shoulder. I just knew I tore something up. I called Tandy and I told him, man, I busted my ass yesterday. He asked me a bunch of questions and told me it sounded like everything was still okay and he thought I'd be fine.

By now, May's just about over, and I think man, I need to get me a horse. Gator was still around and was doing good, but I wanted a weapon. So I been going to some jackpots, not roping, just hanging around, and I see Jewels, this mare that I got now. I thought baby, where you been all my life? This guy made some runs on her and I don't think he caught a single calf. Then, I saw another guy ride her and man did she work. I wanted to buy that horse.

I didn't want them to know it was me that wanted her, so I called one of my buddies, Rod Hardesty, and said why don't you call that guy up and tell him you want to buy that mare from him. So he called him and never heard back from him. About a week, ten days, go by and I call up Rod and say man did you call that guy about that horse? He said hell, I called him, but he never would call me back. I said call him again. He called him again, but the guy said he didn't really want to sell her. I said call him back and tell him you got a guy interested in that horse and he'll pay just about whatever. I said better yet, I'll just call him. I hung up the phone with Rod and dialed up the guy who had Jewels.

I said man, I'm interested in that horse you got.

He said, "Nah, we don't want to sell her."

I said no, seriously, I'm interested in that horse.

He said, "She'd be high…"

I said what's high?

He said, "Around fifty thousand."

I said that's fine, when can I ride her?

This was the first or second weekend in June and I'm up at Reno on the twentieth. I'd done started entering again and ain't told nobody nothing. I'm thinking, man, I got to get ready to go. I went out one day and I get a calf on the end of a rope and I'm jacking around and I can't even step across this sucker. I said, I'm done…done, done, done. I mean I can't even string him, my muscles are so tight. Cassie gets me going to this 24-hour fitness place and I have this quack-ass guy work on me, stretching and stuff. Then at home, Cassie put me on this Pilates reformer, a machine that stretched me from all different angles, and hell, it wasn't but another two weeks and I was limber enough to step on them. I called that dude back up and I said hey, I want to ride that horse. He said he was entered in Crosby on Saturday night. I said me too.

In the middle of June, I went back and saw Tandy and said what do you think? He said it looked good, but I was still a month away. We're about four-and-a-half months out of surgery and I told Tandy I fricking want to try and rope some calves. He said don't tie none down, just breakaway a few. A buddy of mine had been riding my horses for me, keeping them legged up, and I go out there and get on a horse and run a couple. I came across that first calf and don't even hit him; I threw my rope and my rope's over here and the calf's over there. I come riding back up there and everything hurt. I tried flanking a little bit and my arm was pretty sore, but I thought man, it'll be alright.

So I'm entered at the rodeo in Crosby on Saturday night, but I want to try Jewels first, so I go to this guy's house on Thursday. He's got some big old sorry ass calves, and I back in there on this mare and I run one down through there and I'm telling you what, she stopped and I run down there and I pick this big sonofagun up and I flank him and tie him. Oh yeah, I ain't missed a beat. So I run another one and another one, I run about five, and every calf this mare gets better. Boy howdy, here we go. I go to Crosby on Saturday night, first rodeo since the NFR, and …boogedy, boogedy, boogedy, bam. I won second and come home that night and told Cassie I wanted to buy that mare. She said we didn't t have fifty thousand in the bank. I said that's all right, we'll get it.

I called the guy up the next morning and told him to bring that mare over to Doc's for a vet check because I definitely wanted to buy her. I had a check coming in about two weeks, so if she vet checked today, I told him I'd give him thirty-five cash tomorrow and the other fifteen in two weeks. She was sound and the next day I paid him the thirty-five thousand and we signed an agreement that if I didn't give him the other fifteen in two weeks he could have the horse back. I've had her almost six years now and I think

I've made her the same way I had Moon. She's a great horse, but nobody else likes to ride her because they don't have no horsemanship. I know that horse inside out and I know what she's going to do before she does it – ain't no different than quarterbacks reading a play.

The very next week, I called Tandy and told him I'd been roping. He said I'm probably not supposed to do this, but I'm going to release you, but be easy and don't get hurt. Calgary is less than three weeks away. I bought a new truck, picked up a new trailer from P&P, loaded up Jewels and off to the races we go. I get to Reno and Jewels runs smooth off with me. I said you have got to be kidding me. So I go for about two weeks and I don't win one dime on my brand new fifty-thousand-dollar horse. Everybody talks about how good she looks and how beautiful she is, but I'd back that horse in the box and she'd prance and jump and move around and I'm thinking, man oh man, what have I done?

I'd been gone about two weeks and I called Cassie and I said honey, you ain't going to believe this, but there ain't nothing I like about this fricking horse. She's like Fred, are you kidding me? I said no; I may have made a mistake here but I'll just ride her a little while and then I'll sell her. So I call up the dude I bought her from and I said man is there any secrets to this horse? He said no; just ride her, she takes a lot of riding. I backed off of Jewels at rodeos and started riding Gator again, and hell, I went to winning right away. I didn't have nothing won when I left home and before you know it, I got thirty thousand won and ain't been gone no time. I thought, I can still make the Finals. Boy howdy, here we go, and next I went to Calgary. I didn't ride Jewels at Calgary; I was on Gator the whole time.

I'd won eighteen thousand before the hundred thousand dollar round, so everything's pretty good already. I called Cassie on my cell phone and I'm giving her a play by play of what's happening. I had a 6.7 and Blair Burk was the last roper so he's got to be under that to beat me and he comes across there and figure-eights the calf's tail and I fall off the fence. I said honey, you ain't going to believe this, I just won a hundred and eighteen thousand dollars. Next I called up the doctor on the phone and said Doc, guess what? I just stole a hundred grand and I did it with a 6.7, the best of my career so far. Except Calgary doesn't count towards the world standings and I had missed other rodeos in the states to go to Canada.

I won quite a bit of money at Cheyenne and it put me back inside the top fifteen. But after Cheyenne, I didn't win nothing and the rodeo season is winding down and I'm fricking panicked. Cassie planned a big family trip to Jamaica in August for my fortieth birthday, but I had missed that so I could keep working towards the Finals. I made eight thousand, but didn't make anything after that, and my family went on my birthday trip without me. At the time I had maybe thirty-five thousand won and I'm thinking if I can get to fifty, I got a chance. I was just grinding and pressing and the more I thought about it, the more it weighed on me. I needed to be winning, but I was drawing bad and nothing was happening and I was pressing too much. I finally just went home and said to hell with it. I gave them a six month head start and damn near caught them, and I'm just not going to worry about it. I came home in that mind set, but once I got there, I was just disgusted. It was so stupid.

I missed the 2007 Finals for the first time in seventeen years, and finished the season 36th in the world standings with $30,111 in earnings. I would have made it, but I had been so fricking stupid. All that money I won in Calgary sure was nice, but I should have skipped that rodeo and went to seven or eight more that counted for the Finals. To this day, I kick myself in the ass because of it. That hundred and eighteen thousand cost me another NFR. It damn sure did, because I was roping good enough.

When them doctors did that surgery on me, they said there was no way I could rope in July. I made Calgary my target date because it was in July and I wanted to prove them wrong. I said I'm going to buy me a new horse, I'm going to rope in Calgary and I'm going to win it – just so I could prove the doctors wrong. And it cost me an NFR.

When I first decided to go home, in a sense I was really happy, but once I got home, reality set in that I missed the Finals for the first time in my entire career. I'd never been so mad in my life. This was the first time I ever been depressed in my life over roping and it took me forever to get over it. It did. I never really showed it, but it was heartbreaking and I would be less of a man if I said it wasn't. I was bitter and angry and pissed off inside and I stayed that way, way too long. I come home, I didn't rope, I didn't freaking want to rope, I thought about quitting, and I was just hurting. It still pisses me off today, if you can't tell. God, it made me sick, but I learned a lot and it made me tougher, it really honestly did.

To make things worse, I still had to go to Vegas that year because I made a deal with Houston Hutto to ride my mare at the Finals. Oh, it was terrible. I went to one of those performances and they announced, "Ladies and gentlemen, we have eight time world champion…" and I had to stand up and tip my hat…from the stands. I told my wife I would never go back to Vegas and watch ever again until I was done rodeoing. It's just an uneasy feeling when those other guys rope. It looks so easy sitting there in the stands, but until you're down there with them, you don't know how hot the fire is. After seventeen NFRs, I didn't think they could have it without me, and there I was, sitting in the stands. It was a very uneasy feeling.

In a 2010 article, Fred told a reporter, "It takes an unbelievable woman to put up with a rodeo man. Cassie and the kids are the best things that ever happened to me. It's hard to be away from them when I'm on the road, but it makes it that much sweeter when I'm home." Cassie tells how things have changed in the last few years.

> We knew, and everybody else knew, that Fred would make the NFR every year, and by the first half of the season, he was usually

already qualified. Since I met him, we planned on it every year and right after Thanksgiving, we were always on our way to Vegas.

When he didn't make it in '07, I only went with him for a weekend. He hated that he had to go out there anyway, but there was only one night of the entire ten that they gave him a VIP pass. I've always been surprised that they didn't ask Fred to be a guest commentator during the NFR, and I've asked him why he doesn't pursue it. He says, "I'm not going to kiss anybody's ass," which is how he sees any self-promotion. He would be great to commentate any of those events, but there are people out there who don't like that Fred tells it like it is. I am talking about the rodeo establishment, not fans, because fans love him. When he performs, he always gets the biggest, loudest screams.

Back in the day, he'd call me after every rodeo if he either placed or won a round, but in the last five years, the calls are not as consistent as they used to be. Since I met him everywhere Fred would go, he would win. Fred is known for winning, but without that consistency, rodeo has brought a lot of frustration for the past several years and I sometimes wonder if it's worth it. The stress of knowing that you've got to go to the next rodeo and win something so you can come home and pay some bills, and still have money for rodeo expenses…it's a vicious cycle, but that's the life. You look at other people that are successful in rodeo, and they have family money backing them and that's not the case with Fred. Family money didn't get him here and family money isn't waiting for him when he's done.

He bought this place in '93 or '94, when he won fifty-thousand at Calgary, and here we sit still. Nowadays when we get that kind of money we set it aside because I know he's going to need it. I don't want him to be out on the road and be out of money; I don't want him to have that stress. A lot of these people, especially because they're younger, they just never go home. Fred wants to be home more now, so that's another frustration rodeo brings.

Casey says that Fred's family thinks he wins a million dollars a year, "and it ain't like that." He says that over the years, he has seen Fred help family members financially, but with the end of his professional career looming, he doesn't see much of that anymore. Casey reports that Fred's money now goes strictly to his wife and children, and extended family members are on their own.

Not that long ago, Moon said to me "If I had your money, I would win five more gold buckles," and I knew exactly what he meant. When I would rodeo, I'd be broke and I hated it… it was really hard for me to be broke. In rodeo, you have to learn to lose as much as you win, and I didn't do well mentally with that.

The same things that motivated Moon to be successful in rodeo motivated me to become successful and I applied a lot of what I learned from him to make my own business succeed. When I went back to rodeo in 2009, I spent like three or four hundred thousand dollars and bought a bus, bought a trailer, had a driver, bought some good horses and me and Moon loaded up and went to Canada. We're up there in Ponoka and its raining and snowing and it's about thirty degrees and we been up all night and we drive in there and all I want to do is sleep. Moon's up saddling horses, getting draws, getting ropes ready… I'm thinking he's been at it for twenty plus years. I been out here for a few weeks like I'm on vacation and I don't even care anymore.

I knew it wasn't just the money for him, he had enough money to go to the next one, it's that drive and determination Moon has that keeps him going. I took a lot away that day about perseverance.

I made the Finals again in '08 and had a decent season and pretty decent Finals. I placed in five rounds, was fourth in the average and finished the year ranked eighth in the world with right around a hundred and thirty thousand.

In 2009, I sold Gator to Bubba Paschal because I felt like I'd gotten all the good out of him. I gave thirty thousand for him in '03, kept him six years and got thirty five thousand for him. Gator was eleven when I bought him and seventeen when I sold him, so I mean he served his purpose with me. I didn't want to let him stand around here and get to be thirty years old and watch him die, so I sold him when he was still of some value. I had Jewels a couple of years by now and had more confidence in her, but 2009 was another horrible fricking year and it had nothing to do with my horses. I didn't qualify for the NFR and ended up in twentieth position with just under fifty-five thousand.

When I missed the Finals in 2009, it wasn't because of injury or anything else; I just didn't rope good enough and I'll be the first to tell you that. I've told a few people that and I don't know if they thought I was trying to be a smart ass or what, but that was the bottom line. I wasn't in the top fifteen and everybody was asking me, were you hurt last year? I said no, I wasn't hurt; I just didn't rope good enough to make the Finals. After swearing I'd never do it again, I had to go to Vegas anyway and do some personal appearances for my sponsors. It was just like in '07, I'd go watch the calf roping and it was sure a bad feeling.

After I missed the Finals in 2009, I come home and Cassie and I had a long talk about it. I told her that I didn't feel like I wasn't good enough by any means, so I was just going to work at it a little harder. I would get my ass out in that arena and practice every day and expect to win. I expect the best of myself at any age. I know that if I get out there and I apply myself and am still as dedicated as I used to be, my age will be less of a factor. Of course, I'm not as dominant as I was in 1995 when I could show up at a rodeo and people was scared to death. But I've always labeled myself as a big game player – the higher the stakes, the better I play, and I think there's still a little fear left in them today.

Where my age bothers me most is getting in that truck, driving a thousand miles, hopping out and tying one in seven and having the same bounce in your step that you had twenty years ago when those miles didn't matter as much. The last few years I've had a driver in the summer time and that takes a lot of the stress off of you. But I've also rodeoed all by myself and drove everywhere I was entered…just me and Jewels. The mental toughness, the drive, the strong will, the fortitude – it's all still there. But as much as you think you can still do it, there comes a time when your bones say you can't.

I'll tell you what, after missing the Finals in '07, at the '08 Finals I cherished every moment. I was tickled freaking pink to be there and I'm not taking it for granted anymore. I'm getting a little older and it's getting a little complicated. There's guys coming up that rope good and I started to consider that every NFR I make is possibly my last. This might not last forever. In 2010, I had a phenomenal NFR and had them set up to possibly win the world again, until the ninth and tenth round. I was winning the average with a pretty commanding lead on eight head, and then I had two calves in the last two rounds that were just horrible. I'm not going to sit here and say they cost me a world championship, but they damn sure cost me a chance at it. So that's just the way it was.

Chapter 16

Last Words

Casey Butaud:

Now that Moon is a world champion with all the accolades he's got, those old guys, the ones that called him "nigger" and treated him bad back when Moon was amateuring, and even in the pros, they want to be his friend. They wonder why he won't talk to them, but Moon just doesn't forget. He's real distant with them and rarely does he have any kind of relationship with those people. Only now is Moon starting to let go.

We were talking about life one day and he said, "If I could go back, I wouldn't hold grudges. Some of those grudges have been in me so long...I haven't let them all go."

I said I think a lot of those grudges helped your drive in some ways.

He said, "Yeah," and that was the end of the conversation.

He could have made the Finals every now and then, drove a second-class truck, rode a common horse, and not dated white girls and they'd have been okay with him. If he had been just reasonably successful, they might have left him alone, but he was head and shoulders above them all for so long and it made them mad. He beat them bad and he beat them for a long time and they were hateful...just sort of redneck ignorant about it. It didn't ever make him quit; I know it made him be better.

It wasn't like he was a running back for the Dallas Cowboys. Moon was an individual with no coach and no team and he still reached the highest rewards that his sport has to offer. Rodeo is a tough mental game anyway and then to have everything that people put him through made it just five times harder. Moon's got the dedication, he's got the killer instinct, he's got the drive and the perseverance to overcome any obstacle that comes between him and where he wants to go.

I am a kid to Moon, but there have been mentors and parental figures who've played a big part in his life. They've been instrumental in Moon's success and he's appreciative of them and he's respectful of them. People like Roy Moffitt and Joanne Moffitt and Stephen Perry and Sandy and Doc Currie. But Moon has never given my dad any credit, never mentioned him in any articles, never said anything good or bad about my dad. I think that's good for Moon - that's his revenge.

It was probably around 2000 when he started saying, "I'm done with rodeo…one more year and I'm done." I've heard it every so often from him since he was thirty-two, thirty-three years old, but when he got hurt in 2006, he really started with it. The only advice I've given him is before you retire, consider that this is something you're great at – not something you're just kind of good at. I don't know when he'll be done – I'll believe it when I see it. It doesn't matter if he's forty-five, if he's still tying calves in 6.4 like he did last summer [2012] in Calgary. I don't think being forty-six next year is a good enough reason to retire.

People got to know that he's a compassionate person. A lot of people in rodeo don't know that because Moon's always got his guard up and comes across as a world champ who is bigger and better and has been there longer than anyone else. He's got some stigma because he's a straight shooter, but in reality Moon is a kind person who likes people. He's got a big heart; he just ain't real expressive – verbally or physically. In all my life, I bet I never hugged Moon but one or two times. We had a few tiffs and I probably haven't always been the best person either, but I've always admired Moon so much for so many reasons. He's special, he really is. I call him once a week and see how he's doing. He might be short answering my five or ten questions, but that's just him and I'm used to it.

Miss Marie:

Fred's got so many fans that at the rodeo you can't hardly get to him. One time at the rodeo, Fred was busy and these people was around his trailer waiting for him because they know he carries papers to autograph, so I signed autographs that day. They thought he was inside the trailer and I would take his paper inside, sign it, and take it back and tell them Fred signed it. When he came to the trailer, he says, "Mother, what are you doing?" I said I'm signing autographs. I had copied his signature, copied his *W* just right, and I was giving lots of them away. Boy, he looked at me and he said, "Mother, don't do that here." Yeah, I did that, and I got me some extra sheets and I used to autograph them and give them to people. He don't know that, but I did, because I felt so special knowing that I got a son like that.

I got him to go to my church one Sunday, and he said, "Mother, ya'll hold church too long." I said boy, be patient. My pastor love him, he do, he love him. He watches him on TV and he got a big picture of him in his office. Everybody loves him. I went to the beauty shop in Tomball and these people swarmed me and said, "Oh, I saw your son on TV, I saw your son at the rodeo, oh I'm so happy just to even meet his mamma..." and they all hugged me. Tomball had been a prejudice town, but they just begin to hug me, the only black person there. Oh my God, it was something. Now I take them cookies because they are very nice to me.

In June [2010], all the kids got together and surprised me for my sixtieth birthday at my house. I live on Moffitt Oil property and they all hid at my house. I used to live in with Mrs. Moffitt's mamma until she died in '94. Miss Dorothy was Roy's grandmother and his mother, Mrs. Moffitt, it's her property and I stay across the walk from her. I had been living with one of Tammy's daughters, the mother of that little grandbaby that live with me, but me and her had a big falling out, so I moved. When I did, I told Mrs. Moffitt, is your mother's house available? She said why, you need a place to stay? I said yeah and she let me have it. I been there two years now and see Mrs. Moffitt all the time now. Every Christmas I've gotten a gift from her and I used to bake something for her every week, but she's losing weight so I don't guess she's eating.

Anthony and Fred have kind of drifted apart. Anthony…he's smart too, and he owed his own trucking company at one time, he really did. I remember in '03 he had three eighteen-wheelers, he had six drivers and he was making like forty-thousand a month. He built his family a brand new home from the ground up and was doing great. They used to come over and he helped Fred rope and we had get-togethers all the time. But they don't see eye-to-eye anymore and so now we don't get together because of that rift between them. It is because of some things that happened which I cannot say.

For one thing, Fred holds onto stuff too long instead of letting it out and talking about it, you know, family-wise. I try and talk to Fred about what happened because I know he loves his brother, but for some reason, Fred won't let go, he just won't let go. With Fred, you either going to make something out of yourself or you going to be worthless. Because of drinking, Anthony lost everything, but I tell Fred, your brother's getting back on his feet now and he's doing better.

One of the bullets that was in Willie's butt came out last year. He called me and said, "I was sitting on the commode and went to get up and a bullet fell out'a my butt." When I shot him that second time in 1978, the doctor told him that in a few years it would come out and it did. We friends now, me and Willie. He said, "You think we could ever be anything, because I would marry you." I told him I don't need to marry you.

I don't know if Fred remember the first time he won, but I do. I remember everything about it. He was nine years old, his time was nineteen seconds and he won twenty dollars. I still get real nervous to see him rope. When I went to Vegas, I thought my heart was going to stop. I was shaking and going on because I was so afraid they was going to give him a big calf and he couldn't flip it. I still watch movies of some of the old times, where he done roped and won, and I get nervous about it because you see so much happening. But he loves it. Truly, Fred's done great for what he's been through. He been through a lot and he made something out of himself and people look up to him. With his father being an alcoholic, he could have went that way, but he made something out of himself and I'm very proud of him.

I have a picture of him when he turned seven and I made him a chocolate cake. I love to bake and Fred loves my baking. I went to his house one Christmas after my stove went out and I couldn't do my usual Christmas baking. Fred said "Mother, that's all the sweets you brought?" I said my stove went out, and he had me a new one there in less than a week. One time I tricked him and brought him a sweet potato pie over here and I told him it was pumpkin. Cassie said he ate it by hisself and said it was so good.

Cassie Whitfield:

I don't know much about Fred's childhood, but I've heard things and maybe there's some shame there, some embarrassment. He didn't want to be from the stereotypical poor black family, but he is. It's how he was raised; it's where he came from. His dad was abusive and he doesn't really care for his dad. His mom and his brother have told me that his dad picked on Fred the most, and I think that is why he attached himself to Roy Moffitt like he did when he was young. The Moffitt family played a big part in his childhood.

Christmas is where I notice his past the most. He just gets normal gifts – underwear, socks – but he's so excited when he opens presents, just like a little boy. He's like a little kid when there's something under the tree for him. I got him a coffee maker one year and he was so happy when he opened it and thought it was the best gift ever. Fred will get unbelievable gifts for me, but throws a fit when I go overboard for the kids. My family tradition was that Santa always brought big extravagant gifts, and I have to remember that we're from two different worlds when it comes to this. I've told the girls that all Daddy got for Christmas one time was a jacket he already had; that his mom washed and wrapped a coat he had worn for several months just so he would have something to open on Christmas. We didn't know any of this and he needs to talk to his daughters about his life.

He has a typical story that he always tells in magazines and articles, but there is so much more to it than the same stuff that always comes out of his mouth. There's a lot about his family that I found out later on, and I don't know why he didn't tell me. He has two full-blooded sisters that Marie gave to somebody else to raise, and I found out about them from his brother's wife. I see Denise and Loretta occasionally when his mom has gatherings, but he never told me about them. His mom raised Tammy's two kids after she died, and they're adults now and have their own kids. Honestly, Fred doesn't talk about these things because Fred lives in the present; he doesn't look back. I hope now that he's going to be home more, that maybe someday he will talk to us more about his childhood.

You either love Fred or you hate him. He's very aggressive, he's very competitive, he's very stern and he's very outspoken. There are no curves around Fred, no trying to paint a pretty picture. Fred is a perfectionist who expects 110% of himself and others, and if you cross the line, he's done with you forever. Still, he's very much a people person once you get to know him. He's smart and it's great to just sit and listen to him. He surprises me with some of the words he uses…uh, let me go look that up, Fred. He can keep his composure, but he has gotten into fights and he's not proud of it. Other than the girls and me, Fred doesn't put much thought into anything on an emotional level, so it builds and builds and gets released all at once. He holds stuff in until he explodes. He'll warn you. He'll say get out of my face or I'm going to punch you, and if you don't, he will. Still, at this point in his life, he lets a lot more roll off his back and he's not as hot headed as he used to be.

The highs are very high, but the lows are so low and our life is very much a roller coaster. In my previous relationship, I only saw the sleazy side of rodeo and I thought it was disgusting. Then when I met Fred, I saw the professional side and it was like night and day. I have a lot of respect for what he does and how he does it. Fred still gets up every day and takes care of his horses; he feeds them, he saddles them, he grooms them, he exercises them and he doctors them all himself. Because he expects the best from them, he gives them the best hands on care that he can. It's a whole different ball game with Fred, that's why he is a world champion. Cody Ohl won his first world championship in '97 and he had rodeoed with Fred that year and Fred helped him. He sent Fred a letter thanking him for everything he had taught him; it was a thank you note from Cody Ohl. Their relationship has been interesting over the years.

Fred attracts a lot of people, and he can't walk around without a trail of people behind him. I stay in the background and let him have his moment and let the people have their moment. We were outside at the Finals one year and people started to catch on to who he was and grown women were pushing my girls aside to get to him. I had Savannah by the hand and he had to pick up Sydney and we ran. Fred was always the favorite cowboy of the fans, but he never won the Coors Fan's Favorite Award and Fred would almost expect it because we knew how the fans reacted to him. All those years at the NFR and he never received it. There were years that you'd see the cowboy who won it, and be like what? I think African Americans deal with that sort of thing all the time – it's the way racism works and they just kind of expect it from our society. I think there's a piece of him that still doesn't feel fulfilled in his career because of it and that makes me sad.

There's a lot of things I feel and have seen through the years, but haven't talked about. I think it was '99 when they put him on the cover of the NFR program and used a popular photo of Fred, but they painted it instead of using the actual photo for his cover. Here he is making history for African Americans and they put a painted photo of him on the magazine, not the actual photo. I thought that really took away from what he had done. We've been there with other cowboys who have won the all-around and there was a clear difference in the treatment they got and what Fred got.

I see less of the racism now, but maybe it's because I don't go to as many, or maybe it's because there's a whole new generation of cowboys out there. During the Cody Ohl/Fred Whitfield era, it was intense, but I don't notice it as much as I did ten years ago. I remember San Angelo Roping Fiesta was probably the most blatant. I still have to be careful where I sit with my kids because I don't want them to hear the hecklers. Before we had kids, I used to sit down in the bleachers closest to the roping box in San Angelo; now we sit all the way at the other end where it's not as busy. They know I'm listening, and someone will say, "I think that's Fred's family," nudging their husband or whoever to be careful of what they say. When they see the kids, I think they have respect and they're careful, but it's still out there. You can tell who the rednecks are at rodeos by the way they cheer and the things they say about other cowboys. There's competitiveness, but there's racism too.

During the short round of a jackpot a few years ago, Fred roped his calf in what I knew was a great time and I knew he was winning. After watching him for so long, you have this internal time clock and I was like oh yeah, he's winning it. The next guy comes out, ran further, swung his loop more times than Fred did, ran half-way down the arena, caught the calf and tied him and I almost jumped up and screamed because I knew we'd won it. That kid had to be a second and a half longer than Fred was, but they shouted it out as two-tenths less of a second than Fred. It was such a sinking feeling trying to figure out what just happened. They just took it away from him when he totally deserved it. Fred told me stuff like that happened and this was just one of the times I saw it with my own eyes.

There was another jackpot Fred used to go to and the exact same scenario happened with another well-known roper, and they gave it to the other guy. Fred's never gone back to that jackpot, even though he gets an invite every year. They started sending him a certified invitation that we had to sign for at the post office so they knew he got it, but they screwed him so bad he never went back.

None of that really matters with the fan support Fred gets, and it doesn't take away from the athlete that he is, the champion that he is, and his professionalism. When I first saw him, I knew he was somebody. When I realized it was Fred Whitfield, the first thing I noticed was how well he was dressed and how good he looked. He's got a look about him. There are other good-looking cowboys, but they do not stand up to Fred at all, not at all. He'll look in the mirror and put his hat on and tell me, "You are one lucky girl."

He has that hard exterior that he puts on for people, but the best thing about him is his tenderness with me and the girls. I was reminded of that when the girls and I left on vacation last year [2012]. We go visit my mom in California and my dad in Nebraska every summer while Fred is on the road and this time we left home before he did and Fred teared up. I could tell he was hiding tears behind the sunglasses and as the girls and I drove out, I looked in my rear-view and Sydney was bawling. Before, we were used to it and sometimes even knew it was time for Daddy to get back on the road because he was antsy at home. Last year he had been at home more and didn't go to some of the big rodeos and he didn't go out on the west coast, so he was around a lot during the winter and spring and we felt like a regular family. Then summer comes, and all the sudden it was time to say good-bye. We knew it was going to be a long summer and then to see him be so emotional made it that much harder to say goodbye. I know what's really in his heart – us.

Until recently, if it didn't pertain to roping, it wasn't on Fred's radar, but he's finally shifting his priorities. There's been many times I didn't feel we were a priority – it was always rodeo; it was always about his career because that is what pays the bills. I would point out that there's more to life, that his kids are growing up, that it's going to pass him by, that it's time to chill out and pay attention. I would try to make him see that there were memories he was missing out on that he was never going to get back. I think he sees that now. He's a good dad and in the last year, there has been a bond between him and the girls that's a lot different than in the past. He's more involved and has definite plans for the girl's future, especially their education. During his entire career, he always set such high expectations for himself and now his expectations are to be at home with his family watching his kids grow up. He knows that and I think that's why he's ready to slow down.

When he comes through the door, he's expecting us to jump up and be excited, and we are. I always make him a special meal, but my cooking is a sore subject. His mom is the best cook ever and he calls me a California prunie because I like baked and grilled foods like chicken. Fred's a beef and potatoes guy who prefers the kind of food his mom makes him. When we married, he wanted me to be a rodeo wife and we agreed that I would not work; he wanted someone who was going to be there to support him. Then we had the girls and I love that I've been home with them. The girls are my world, especially with Fred being gone so much. I'm a typical housewife and we have our ups and downs, but that's marriage. I had two working parents, but I want my kids to do better than I did. I want them to have more, and I'm fortunate as a mother to be present constantly. I know my husband appreciates me as a wife and a mother, and that's a very good feeling. I'm blessed to have a man like Fred.

Roy Moffitt:

Willie got hit by a car and lost his leg, so now he's got a wooden leg. I threw him in the pool one day and his wooden leg got waterlogged, and he said he was going to go in the house and get a gun and shoot my ass. I said I ain't worried about you shooting me, then I remembered who I was talking to. He's been shot a few times, stabbed a few times, run over by cars, lost a leg, gone to prison, you name it…and he's had to mellow a little bit in his old age. Willie is not a young man any more. He still calls me looking for money every few months and I tell him to come on over.

One look at his daddy and it's clear that Fred defied the odds. He was just a dumbass kid like all those other kids that come out of Cypress, Texas. Fred came from a broken home, his daddy was in prison, his mamma lived in another town while he lived with his ninety-year-old grandpa, and it's hard for a kid to overcome all that. Anybody else would use that as a crutch; Fred used it as a stepping-stone – he knew what he did and did not want. We all played games like kids do, and it was so much fun, but I think it was different for Fred. I truly believe that when he was seven or eight years old and roping calves at my house off that black pony, in his mind he was in the tenth round at the National Finals about to tie a calf to win the world.

I heard an ESPN guy say one time that Fred's been a great ambassador to the sport, and I believe that a million percent. Fred carried himself so well and he brought a lot of fans to rodeo. He's got the best work ethic I've ever seen and there isn't a black mark against him in the sport that I know of. I think he represents his sponsors well, every one of them. You didn't hear about him getting drunk and getting stupid – Fred took care of business. I got my money's worth out of him and I love him like I love my kids. That's a fact.

I've always known that it would come to an end. It's not a matter of if; it's a matter of when. It will happen when Fred wants it to happen and Fred's not going to weaken. He's stayed healthy, he's never been overweight, he doesn't drink excessively, and he doesn't smoke, so he will have a career in rodeo as long as he wants a career in rodeo. It might not be at the same level, but he can make as much money amateuring as he can in the pros and stay home every night with his family. I haven't discussed team roping with him in years, but I don't see that happening.

I don't know what efforts they've put into it, but I've always wished the PRCA would come up with something to help these guys post career. If they took ten percent or fifteen percent of their earnings and contributed it to a fund, them guys would have something when they were done. Especially the guys like Fred that stood the test of time through the years. To my knowledge, the PRCA has made few attempts at anything like that, but when you're young and rodeoing like that, you need every penny you can get. Them cowboys would probably have a fit if they got a check they had taken fifteen percent out of. God knows rodeo hasn't made him a millionaire. I mean he's won gold buckles, broke a lot of records and Fred will go down in history as one of the greatest calf ropers that ever lived, there's no doubt. But you can't eat that.

After Moffitt Oil, I had my own gig and was president of *Roy Moffitt Customized Fueling Systems* – but mostly I was the salesman. I was always selling, I was always doing something with my business, I always worked out, I was always healthy…and I always drank. Everybody likes to drink – big deal. Back then, there wasn't no hangovers – I would tell people there might be a hangover but it won't be today as I opened my morning beer. Then I lost nine million dollars in '09 on a business deal and my drinking escalated to a whole other level – Vicodin, beer, whiskey – I didn't give a damn. I used to do crazy stuff, get drunk and lose a hundred thousand on a bet, charter a private jet for thirty thousand, just crazy stuff. Now I manage my money to where I have enough to live the rest of my life, but money is secondary. To hell with money. I used to live in a double wide with my wife and kids, and we was fine.

I sold the company May 4, 2011 and did have a little bit of an identity crisis after that. I told somebody, man, me and Patricia going to party for the first year and do what the hell we want to do. We have a goal here – to see how wasted we can get. A year later, I was in bad health…I wouldn't have made it another week. I was puking every morning, couldn't eat, I was drinking a quart of Crown Royal a day along with about thirty beers and a few Vicodin to help really get that buzz going. Yeah – I'd gotten bad. I had been to AA, I'd been to rehab, I'd been to detox, I been to all of that the few times I thought maybe I had a drinking problem. Hell, I couldn't spell drinking problem until this last round. I'd sleep to noon, wake up and get me a Vicodin and a shot of whiskey and a beer and a cigarette all at the same time.

Last spring [2012] I woke up to find Fred sitting on my deck. He drove from Oklahoma to my place in Matagorda, dropped his trailer, pulled his horses out and put them in the field across the street, and come and sat out on the porch with tears in his eyes, waiting for me to wake up. When I got up, he told me to grab a six-pack and we jumped in the truck and went for a little ride and did some talking. I was still drinking when he left here, but I quit a couple of weeks later on June 22, 2012. Fred helped the lights come on, but I didn't do it for anybody but Roy. Not long after his visit, we was coming home from the bar one night and I was wasted. I said I'm done. I didn't make a big deal about it, I just quit drinking. It's over – history.

I was so messed up mentally and physically, I was blowed up and red-faced…I was sick. I kind of wear the label of addict now. I thought I ain't no alcoholic, I just like to drink and have fun, but I was spiraling rapidly. I weighed thirty pounds more, my face was as red as a damned tomato, I was bloated like you wouldn't believe and couldn't even make it up and down the steps I was so sick. I still smoke, but I drink a lot of water now and I've lost the weight, I've lost the red in my face, and I feel better. I'm happier than I've ever been in my life and I have zero desire to drink. I quit drinking in

Matagorda, Texas, a party town, and somebody said if you can quit drinking here you can quit anywhere in the world. I won't be drunk this year during the Finals, which should probably save me a lot of money.

Chapter 17

2012

His boys called me and told me Roy was in bad shape. Me and the oldest one, Roy Jr., are closest, but I've got a good relationship with the two younger ones, Rusty and Ryan, too. Roy would always pour me and my work ethic all over them, and they tried to rope as kids but just never took to it. I had already heard Roy was taking all kinds of pills, but after the boys called, I left Oklahoma and headed to Matagorda. I stopped by my house on the way and got enough clothes packed to be gone a day or be gone a week, it didn't matter. I had other stuff to do, but everything had to wait, I needed to go see Roy.

I didn't call him to tell him I was coming; I showed up unannounced because I wanted to see exactly what was going on. I got there about 10:00 in the morning and there was always a lot of people around there, so I waited outside on his deck. I hadn't seen him in three months because they'd been living down on the coast, but I talked to him periodically. Finally, he got out of bed and come out there and I'm telling you what… his hair was long, he had big old sideburns, his face was red and puffy and I said damn man, you all right? He said, "Bro, you won't even believe it."

Pretty soon a couple of his wife's friends showed up, and the first thing you know, hell, they're popping the tops and it couldn't have been 10:30 in the morning. Roy got a beer and come out there where I was and we made small talk for a while and he kept drinking. We didn't get to talk about anything serious because of the other people so I said get you a six-pack, let's go for a ride. We cruised down to the beach and I said tell me what's wrong. He said, "Fred, I don't know…" Roy was always real smart when it came to business; now he's smart when it comes to his life.

He didn't miss too many NFRs over the years, but the last time Roy was there was in 2010. I bet out of the twenty times I've been there, he hasn't missed three, but this past year [2012] he couldn't find anybody to go with him that didn't drink so he didn't go. I totally understood, but I still wished he would have went, so I called him and told him I was disappointed. I guess I didn't have to do that, but I did. I wouldn't want to be in that type of environment if I just quit drinking six months ago. Not too long after the 2012 NFR, Roy took off to Puerto Vallarta and is living down there in Mexico. He's there by himself and he's still sober.

On July 29, 2011, Fred won second place in the first round at Cheyenne with a time of 11.2 and winnings of $6088, just enough to put him over the three million mark in PRCA career earnings. Trevor Brazile and Billy Etbauer were the only other cowboys to cross that line before him. Fred picked up another $3701 in Deadwood, South Dakota, $1095 in Burlington, Colorado and $1220 in Rock Springs, Wyoming for a total of $12,104 for the final weekend in July, which moved him from outside the top 50, into 28th place. The August 8, 2011 edition of the ProRodeo Sports News, reported that Whitfield was looking for his 20th trip to the Wrangler National Finals Rodeo. About that subject, Fred told them, "These last few weeks have really been clicking for me and I'm entered in nine or ten rodeos in the next couple of weeks, so we'll just see how it goes. I'm not giving up yet on another trip to Las Vegas in December."

I missed it again in 2011, but went to Vegas anyway, sat in the stands, they introduced me, it was terrible…stop me if you've heard this one before.

I just never got on a roll in 2011, never had any big wins and sat there on the outside looking in once again. Through it all, I kept telling myself I could go to twenty NFRs, and I kept trying to make myself believe it. I been around some guys over the years that rope great and have never been there, and I never took it for granted again after I missed it the first time.

The next year, 2012, the one thing I was so conscious of was seizing every opportunity I had to make money. When I got the chance to win, I had to make it happen at all costs if I was going to make my goal. I think I only missed one or two calves out of the whole season, and at every rodeo that had a final round, I made almost every short. But then I would get to the short round, have a bad calf; get to the short round, break the barrier; get to the short round, get kicked, and before long all this starts to add up. It was frustrating, but I didn't have to win first everywhere I went, I just had to maintain. I'd get me four or five thousand here and go to the next one and do it again. All went well and I stayed in or around the top ten all year long, and I never let any doubt ever creep in that I could do it.

The highlight of the year was making the fastest run of my entire career, a 6.4, at the 2012 Calgary Stampede. Forty-five years old with a 6.4 second run…huh? Everything just came together for the best one I ever made in my life and I picked up forty-six thousand there. But again, Calgary doesn't count towards the standings.

In September, I won the first round at Puyallup, Washington, come back in the short and didn't do very good, but that first round win was still enough to send me to my twentieth NFR. I'd been through highs and lows and had just shy of seventy thousand and I thought I'm good. There was guys that had a chance to get me but they were out of rodeos and had been to too many, Blair Burk being one of them. I had squeaked in, so I hauled ass to Hockley; drove twenty-three hundred miles to the house all by myself. I left Saturday night, stopped in Hermiston, Oregon, stopped in Evanston, Wyoming, stopped in Raton, New Mexico, and on Tuesday, September 11, I pulled into my driveway. Except for two more little trips later in September, the 2012 rodeo season was over for me. I had mixed emotions when I started looking back over the season, but I believe that things are the way they were meant to be. I was just tired, tired of the rat race, tired of putting up with all the nonsense, tired of driving and so glad to be home. I was going to take a month off and just do nothing and then get ready to go to Vegas. Hell, I got the Finals made all day long.

I came home in September with three weeks of the season left and seventy thousand won, when all the sudden four guys, Matt Shiozawa, Adam Gray, Houston Hutto and Ryan Jarrett, all went on a terror those last three weeks. At one point, I had a ten thousand dollar lead on all of them, and then Ryan and Houston each win themselves around ten thousand at Pendleton and Adam won seven thousand in a week. I'm sitting eighth in the world on September 9, 2012 with just twenty-one days left in the season and got moved to twelfth place in three weeks. I did make a quick run to Albuquerque and broke the barrier, then went to Omaha and won a few hundred dollars, but I basically watched those guy's rampage from my house.

This shows how important the season is from start to finish, from the first rodeo you enter to the last rodeo. A guy told me one time, he said "If you're not entered, you don't have a chance to win." And I wasn't entered anywhere so there was nothing I could do at this point. You think this black stomach ain't turning inside out and upside down? In the end, it all worked out and I squeezed in by three thousand, so I'm tickled to death – I had made my twentieth NFR.

Before I came home in early September, I had roped in Puyallup, Washington and fell backwards flanking a calf and hurt my neck. Then, about a month later, Rod Hardesty had just bought a hundred head of pretty strong calves and we started breaking them, getting them ready for a couple of jackpots in early October. I went to the first jackpot and I think I won a couple thousand and I was tying calves getting ready for the jackpot the next day. We were in the alleyway when this big calf hit me, knocked me down, half-hitched a rope around my leg and started dragging me. It took four or five guys to catch him and get me loose. I roped in the jackpot the next day and ended up winning four thousand that night, so I got about six thousand gathered up and everything's good.

I was leaving on Sunday or Monday of the next week to the Heartland (All-American) Finals, when about Thursday my left arm started hurting. I told Cassie, man I think something's not right with me. I went ahead and left on Sunday morning and went to Waco and roped Sunday night and again Monday. My first one was no good, but then I won the second round and it paid a couple thousand there, so I won eight thousand in a week's time and am feeling pretty good about things. Except my arm was hurting like hell by now and two fingers on my left hand were totally numb. I knew something was way wrong with me.

I got home Monday night late and kept telling Cassie, man, something ain't right with me. I tried lying on the floor and I tried lying in the bed, but I couldn't get comfortable and couldn't sleep. I just couldn't get away from the pain. Tuesday I started calling doctors. I called Tandy's office, but he was busy doing stuff, so I called Sandy Currie. She's got an acupuncture doctor in Brenham whose husband is a neurosurgeon in Houston, so I go in there on Wednesday and that doctor is going to inject me – shoot it with a little local anesthetic and see if we can't dissipate the pain in my shoulder.

I'm in there with my shirt off and she's injected me before, so it's no big deal, but then she started doing these little tests. She told me to stand up, so I stood up, she said put your hands out, so I put my hands out, and she put pressure on my left hand and it just dropped. Are you kidding me? She said don't worry about it. Don't worry about it? The NFR is in eight weeks, what do you mean don't worry about it? She put in a call to her husband to see if he could get me in today and told him it was urgent. He could get me in at two-thirty that afternoon, so she told me I needed to head to Houston. I called Cassie to line somebody up to pick the girls up from school, and picked her up and we take off to Methodist in Houston.

I saw her husband, the neurosurgeon, that afternoon and he said the same thing, this ain't good. Well hell, they schedule an MRI for seven that night and we got two kids at home and can't hang around there, so we re-scheduled it for ten the next morning. We get up at six the next morning, which was Thursday, and we go back to Houston and they do an MRI at ten that morning. We hadn't heard nothing by Friday afternoon, so Cassie called the doctor for the results and he said the MRI was "inconclusive." I said what now? He said I needed a myelogram where they half-way knock you out and shoot that dye in your spine and turn you upside down on the table so that dye goes all the way down. They scheduled it for Monday and I still have to get through the weekend. The doctor had given me some steroids and pain pills and I'm all pilled up and still can't hardly stand it the pain was so bad. I'm getting like two or three hours of sleep a night, walking around in circles and talking to myself. I know I'm hurt and I know the Finals are seven weeks away.

So on Monday morning we go back to Methodist for the myelogram, and as soon as it was done they sent me to the doctor's office to get the results. The neurosurgeon says I have to have surgery. I said man, we're less than two months from the Finals and you're talking about surgery, but he said there was no way around it. Cassie and I said we need to talk about this; I really don't want to be cut on if there's not a chance that I can rope at the Finals.

He said if you wait seven weeks, your body is going to be exhausted from all the pain meds and the steroids anyway and there could be some permanent damage. So they scheduled surgery for Tuesday morning, and the next morning we're right back down there. Three and a half hours later, I'm in recovery. It was seven weeks until the NFR

They did a cervical laminectomy, where they went in and relieved the pressure between C-5 and C-6. Right away my fingers started tingling, and I thought something went wrong. Now they're fine, but they tingled a little for a while. When I had this same surgery on the right side, the minute he done the surgery the feeling was back in my fingers, but this time it took some time. It's hard to tie calves when your fingers are numb.

So we leave the hospital that afternoon and head to the house. By then the Morphine started wearing off and I was in pain…my word, I hurt so bad. So I still got some of the pain meds he prescribed me at the start and the doctor said to double up on them to get through the weekend and see how it goes. I did, but I just couldn't get away from the pain. I didn't do nothing for the first two weeks, and it hurt like that for about seven days and then I was able to quit taking the pain meds. Now the Finals are five weeks away.

I had to start doing something, so pretty soon I ventured out away from the house and saddled a few horses up. I wasn't supposed to pick-up a saddle, but I took it easy and just tried to do a little more each day. The whole time I'm thinking we got a month left…we got three weeks left… The clock ticked a little louder every day.

Two weeks before the Finals, that surgeon's wife did all the post-op tests. She said, "Well, it's not looking very good," and told me there was a fifty percent chance that I could re-herniate the disk in my neck. I said it only pays twenty-thousand a night out there – I wish I'd a known all this prior to the surgery, I would have took my chances. She said, "Well, you weren't any good the way you were." I was there for maybe thirty minutes and when I left I was a mad sonofagun, I tell you what.

I thought if I'm not going to be able to go to the National Finals, I want to know today, so I went home and started saddling horses. I run me three or four calves and there was a little bit of pain but I could stand it. On the fourth calf I run down there to flank him and he leaned away from me. Instead of throwing in the towel and waiting for a better one, I reached across him and dug him up out of the ground. I'm telling you what…I was hurting like you can't imagine. I told Cassie, we're in a bind. I said I don't think I can go.

A week before I was supposed to leave, I started feeling a little better and tried again. I never run a practice calf until a week before the Finals and then I started cramming. I'd string them and tie them a little bit and oh, my shoulder was killing me. But I was headed to my twentieth NFR, so I never told nobody about the pain.

When Fred arrived in Las Vegas in December for the 2012 National Finals Rodeo, few people knew of his condition. Both he and Cassie intentionally kept it on the down low, and the biggest leak was Joe Beaver talking about it when he was commentating the calf roping, saying, "Fred had neck surgery, but he's doing good." Only seven weeks since the surgery, the neurosurgeon said it would be a three-month recovery and had not released Fred for anything, let alone the NFR. Calf roping requires more endurance, stamina and coordination than most healthy people have, and Fred was far from healthy. But he hadn't made a goal of being healthy at twenty NFRs, the goal was simply to make twenty NFRs, so technically, he was right on track.

December 12, 2012, Las Vegas, Nevada:

I was coming here, regardless of how hurt I was. I would have run the first one, then I would have turned the next two out, then I would have run the fourth one, then I would have turned five and six out, I would have run the seventh, turned eight and nine out and run the tenth. I'd a run five head out here if nothing else. Not to take anything away from the sixteenth guy, but it was my name that was in the top fifteen, I'm the one that got an invitation to come here and compete. I just wished things would have been a little different the last two months.

So far, my twentieth NFR isn't going so great. I haven't drawn very good, but I'm roping pretty decent for no more than I've practiced. I rode a borrowed horse the first couple of rounds, and it's a proven horse and I would never say anything bad about him, but I didn't ride him enough beforehand. I just showed up out here and run two or three calves on him and we didn't click. Now that I'm back on my mare, I placed in one round and had a damn runaway calf last night. But I think I've roped well this week and still got an outside chance to win or place in the average and maybe place in a few of these rounds.

The thing about it is that in the past, I've run four or five hundred calves before the NFR and my body can't take that kind of practice anymore. Hell, I am forty-five years old and that's how I've done it my whole life. I feel like if I spend the time in the practice pen, I minimize the mistakes when I get to the rodeo. It's going to carry over, there's no doubt in my mind. The problem is I didn't get that practice time this year, but if I show up and I got the best calf on them, I'm still going to win some money. I may not win first, but I'm damn sure going to place. It's knowledge and wisdom meeting opportunity.

It goes without saying I got mixed emotions. I teared up the other day and I will again, but it's just that something so great is coming to an end. Twenty-three years at this level is enough for any man and it's gone by so fricking quick, I mean it seems like it's just been yesterday that I was here as a rookie. But I've gotten older, I've got young kids and a good wife and it's just time. I'm not tired of rodeoing, I'm tired of all the other crap that comes along with it.

I told them on that stage last night that I would rodeo until I was sixty if the money was right. Look at golfers – them boys play up until their sixties, but they go win tenth place in a tournament and win two hundred and fifty thousand. We come out here to this rodeo and eighteen thousand a night is nothing to sneeze at, but it's nothing like other professional sports. When I got my card in 1990 and made the Finals my rookie year, I'm pretty sure that the rounds here in Las Vegas paid a little over eight thousand and twenty three years later, they pay eighteen, so that's a ten thousand dollar increase. Except I ordered a new pick-up the other day and that sonofagun cost sixty thousand dollars, so I got to win more than three rounds to pay for that truck. And back when the rounds paid eight thousand, my brand new pick up cost me sixteen thousand and I only had to win two rounds to buy that new truck.

I won eighty-seven thousand this summer, between Calgary and the PRCA, but I spent over forty thousand to stay out there for three months. It cost me half of what I made in expenses. Hell, if I didn't win that forty-six thousand at Calgary, I'm working for free. You got to give up so much to be out here and the profit is just not there. It don't make sense.

Rodeo needs to come to a point where a guy can profit out here. The more you profit, the more you can afford the sacrifices…but it's never going to come to that and old Fred's done realized that. It's time to get some other things going to where I can make some money. Hell, if I was at home working a job making sixty thousand a year, I could put that money in the bank. But I'm out here up and down the road winning eighty and spending fifty and that stuff takes a toll on you…it really, honestly does.

I want to win me a couple of these fricking go-rounds before I get out of here, I know that. The thing about it is you can't be intimidated, whether it's me or a twenty-two year old rookie, you can't be intimidated. You qualified for the National Finals Rodeo, so hold your head up high and be proud of what you're trying to accomplish. In the rodeo world you can never show weakness. You missed three in a row? Keep your chin up. You walk by somebody and look down, they're liable to kick you on the way down…it's brutal, it honestly is. Rodeo is a pretty cutthroat deal. They make it out like there's all this camaraderie and everybody gets along, and that ain't exactly how it is. There's guys you've been buddies with all year and you come out here to the Finals and most of them won't even talk to you once they get here. That's always been the case and it's no big deal to me – you don't have to speak to me for us to co-exist.

Truth is, there ain't no guarantees I'm going to win anything this year; I'm hurt and I ain't hardly practiced. I'm out four grand in expenses before I ever run the first calf – and back in the old days I showed up here and had thirty thousand in bonuses coming and it was no big deal. Now that ain't the case and I got bills to pay – know what I mean?

On December 15, 2012, Fred Whitfield prepared to rope his two-hundredth calf in the Thomas & Mack arena, knowing it would most likely be his last NFR run. Cassie says there was nothing different about him that morning, but after he and Savannah returned from an autograph session that afternoon, he was more emotional as it got closer to time to go. While relaxing before the final performance, Fred told Cassie about the fan's reaction to him for the entire ten days of the NFR and how honored it made him feel. She says she wished he could have gone out with a better NFR, but the fans support helped a lot. "I want the fans to be supportive and I want them to love him forever. I told him the other night that people aren't going to remember what happened or didn't happen this NFR. They're going to remember Fred Whitfield, the legend – they're going to remember his charisma, his character and his personality, not statistics."

Cassie was prepared for an emotional night and had tried to convey to Savannah and Sydney the magnitude of what was about to happen, but says, "They were just glad to be in Vegas and I don't think they get it."

Around five that afternoon, from his spectacular SkyLoft at the MGM Grand in Las Vegas, Fred talked about his last run at his last NFR, which would take place within hours. It had been a grueling ten days – horses not just right, soggy calves, bad draws, a still tender neck and not much money made. Earlier in the week, Fred had cried while talking about his last run, and tonight he spoke softly, frequently choked back tears and several times had to walk off and compose himself. Fred was sorely disappointed in how his NFR had panned out and after tonight, it would all be over.

To be honest, if I'd had a better NFR, I'd probably be a little bit more content, but it is what it is. It started off kind of shaky and never got much better. I placed there a couple of times, which weren't really highs, but I hoped maybe I'd get a little momentum going…it just hadn't worked out for whatever reason. It's just been pretty tough, period.

I've had a lot of fun doing it, but I don't know that I will be back at this level again. There's going to be life and there's going to be rodeo after the NFR but I'm going to miss it. I've never been one to make excuses, but had I not had this surgery and I would have practiced like I needed to, things would have been different. Practicing roping for a week prior to the NFR and then coming out here and thinking you can beat the best guys in the world…it's not that easy. It's going to take a little while to get over this one.

Next month, I'll enter Ft. Worth and San Antone, but I'm not running forty calves before I go. I'll jerk my mare up, break-away a few on her, and go there with the expectation to just rope. If I draw good, I might have a chance to win some money. Next, I'm going to piddle around with them colts I got in training and decide if I want to take them to a few rodeos around the house. If not, I'm going to stay home and pursue some other opportunities and start…I don't want to say the real life, because to me, nothing I have done in the rodeo world is considered phony.

I've met some of the nicest people in the world and we've got true friends all over the United States and Canada. When I say a true friend, I mean somebody you can call when you're down and out and not just somebody who was there for the limelight. Glory fades sooner or later…no matter how bright you shined at one time, it's going to fade.

It's just crazy to me in the last ten days to realize the impact I've had on people's lives. I've got an older generation, a middle generation and the younger generation of fans. It's carried a ways and twenty years is a long time to be competitive at anything. There's a lady came up to me today and she was literally bawling, and I said ma'am you have to stop. She had them big old tears and was truly hurt by the fact I may not compete at the NFR again. That line for autographs today was a mile long, and I signed autographs for two-and-a-half hours today. I guarantee at least twenty of them people were crying and begging me not to go.

I'd sure like to win some money tonight. I don't wish none of them guys any bad luck, but if a couple of things happened, I could move up a few spots in the average and get out of here with thirty thousand and call it good. It hadn't cost us a whole lot this week…I would have liked to win seventy, eighty thousand, but it's not going to happen. I think I run decent and I drew worse than I roped. The thing is if you don't get off to a good start, then you start pressing and then that makes things worse. I'm trying to get back in the swing of things; I felt like I was doing everything right, but nothing ended up that way, so…

I'm not going to hang my head. I'm going to leave here with a positive attitude, and we're going to go home and have a good Christmas and start a new year.

Then, as she had so many times before, Cassie pinned his number on the back of his crisp green shirt and sent him off. However, the tenth round of his twentieth NFR did not go as Fred had hoped. He missed with his first loop, and by the time he caught with his second and tied him down, the count was into double digits. Fred Whitfield would leave Vegas with twenty-two thousand dollars…before expenses.

A small but nervous group of family and friends waited for him in the limo afterwards. All week, the after-performance limo rides had been nerve-racking affairs as Fred continued to be frustrated. If the progression continued, tonight would not be a picnic.

Instead, a boyish, buoyant Fred arrived, happier and more relaxed than anyone expected. He jumped in the car and proclaimed, "It's over."

Chapter 18

The Last Chapter

I was having dinner with Ryan Jarrett and Clint Robinson a while back and I told them both, man I'm out on all that calf tying…all that practice, all that calling and seeing who's roping, all that constant checking on everything, it don't even matter anymore. I'm going to enter and I'm going to go, and if they're roping goats, I'm going to rope one. If my goat's any good, I'm going to win something, if he ain't, I'll go on to the next one.

Cody Ohl and Blair Burk are sitting at the next table and we're kind of visiting back and forth and they said yeah, we're out on all that calf tying too. I said Blair, you never tied very many when it was time to tie. He said, "Well, you shamed me into it a few times." I still give him hell every now and then. But I told them all, there's sixty kids I never heard of over there at San Angelo and they're the ones that need to practice tying calves, not me.

The stars would really have to line up for me to win a ninth gold buckle and I've had to come to terms with the fact that isn't going to happen. The desire is still there – but this forty-five-year-old body has been ten million miles and I'm just not going to put forth that level of effort anymore. My brain is still as good as it ever was; it's just that my work ethic has subsided to a big degree, it honestly has. I put forth that level of effort for twenty-four years to be the best in the world and only recently has my approach started to change a little. Almost all of the last couple of years, I have rodeoed by myself and the worst part is always the driving. The practice, the driving, the pressure, it's all taken a toll on me and I'm just not going to put my body through the torture it takes to be dominant – it's not going to happen.

I don't know that I was born with a killer instinct; I think circumstances throughout my life created it. There were times I flat got screwed at some ropings because of the color of my skin and it built up a need in me to come out on top every time I nodded my head. I would get so fricking mad when I knew I won, but would get a bad call that was deliberate. It just built up in me to where every time I would flank and tie one, that anger was there. I knew that if I got to where I could dominate them all every time, then none of the bad calls, none of the envy, none of the jealousy, none of it was ever going to matter if I controlled what I could control.

A lot of people don't want to hear it, but it's the truth: a black man can never do enough in a white man's world, no matter what you do or how you do it. It's a fact of life, but I tell black kids all the time not to be prejudice because you've been discriminated against. You will do and be more in your lifetime if you eliminate that element from yourself. Otherwise, it will tear you down. I think that's one of the reasons I have been successful is that I had to set that part of it aside and I never talked about it because I thought it would hinder what I was doing. I honestly believed there were certain people that could have made something happen if I started running my mouth. Whether it be a bullet or brakes go out on a truck, I always been a little leery of that and have picked and chosen my battles carefully. Seriously.

Even when I got to a place where people would listen, I still didn't say much. When I won the all-around and had a chance to make some change and call some attention to it, I was real careful with what I said. I've had death threats and that nonsense and it didn't scare me, but I didn't dismiss it either. When you start teetering at the top, you've got to be careful what you say…that's the deal. Some of the stuff that transpired and some of the people I've been around showed me they had a lot more power than I gave them credit for and it was best I didn't get involved. I was accepted to a certain degree, and I didn't need to rub it in their face. I just rode the waves and when the ocean got a little rough, I stuck my oar in a little deeper and kept going. That's how one person can change the world, by never giving up.

I hadn't run a calf since the Finals and I went to a jackpot on the way to Ft. Worth in January and I don't know if what happened was done deliberately, but I know they were expecting me to throw a fit. It was two and a short round, and I was 9.5 on the first and come back with an 8.2 on the second. They took the top fifteen guys into the short round, and the number fifteen guy turned out, but they didn't turn his calf out. I said, hey, that ain't right. Ya'll are supposed to turn that calf out because it made one calf left over and I'm a calf ahead of where I'm supposed to be. The other calves had been running out of there and they're tying the hell out of them, but the gates open and mine just walked out and don't even break the neck rope. Then I roped him and run down there and he's bucking and bellering like he ain't never been roped. I just took my rope off him, coiled it up and got back on my horse.

Afterwards, at least ten people at the roping come over and said "Boy that was sure dirty how they done you." They were all telling me how bad I got screwed and I said it doesn't even matter, what's done is done. I said it's happened for twenty-three years, I didn't expect it to change in the twenty-fourth. I just took the boots off my mare, went and watered her, got on the phone and called Cassie and said I went from winning thirty-five hundred to winning five hundred. I said it ain't a big deal, I'm on my way to Ft. Worth, maybe we'll have a better one tomorrow. And that was the end of it for me.

I was getting ready to leave and the guy that had the calves came up to me and said, "Man, I'm sorry that happened." I said you're not sorry that happened, if you were sorry that happened you would have turned that first calf out and you would have made sure every one of them calves in the short round had been roped. I said that was the right thing to do. But I said all it cost me was money and I'm not that worried about it. I seen him at the slack the next day in Ft. Worth and he walked all around me and never could walk by me and look me in the eye…the sonofabitch.

I'm moving forward – they can stay stuck in the mud if they want to, but it's not affecting me like it used to. I was to the point where people could say stuff and I would fly off the handle, but now it's no big deal. The other night a guy told me, "I'm gonna tell you the things I like about you, then I'm gonna tell you the things I don't like about you." I laughed and said, are you kidding me? Then he says it again and the guy with me is wanting to whip his ass and I said it ain't even worth it – just laugh at him. He's jealous and I can see right through it.

With that said, there's an animosity in my belly that just boils…just boils and breeds…it breeds anger. I don't know the words to describe it, but it's a different kind of anger, it's the kind that always propelled me to do better in the arena. I backed in there every day, my sole mission being to whup them and make them like it. But you know what? That approach has changed. I used to be the dictator – I controlled what went on in and out of the arena and having control of everything doesn't even matter to me anymore. At one time, when I pulled up I was there to win regardless of what else happened. I mean I craved it, and I got out there and busted my ass everyday to keep that alive and now it doesn't matter. I'm just here to win a little and if it happens, I'm good with it, and if I don't, I just go on with it.

Calf roping has evolved a lot since I started. In Houston my rookie year, I tied my first one in fourteen and tied my second one in twelve and I come back in the top four with twenty-six seconds on two head. Then at San Antone this year, the top guys are around twenty-four seconds on three head. They're roping smaller calves and the barrier is much shorter, which gives everybody a chance to win. It gives a guy who doesn't rope as good as you a chance to beat you, which is the idea. It started a long time ago, but I started noticing the differences around 1997 at the NFR and that's where the precedent is set for all the other rodeos. Everybody watches the NFR on TV and everybody wants to see you tie calves fast so we're going to rope smaller calves and tie them faster. But calf roping is still calf roping – there's a million things that can go wrong. I can tie one in seven and in my mind, there's a couple of things that if I could have done them a little bit better, I could have been faster. I've made some blistering runs that still had room for improvement…but those blistering runs don't come around as often as they used to.

When the decline started, the negativity came with it and it just grew and started to poison me as things stopped going exactly the way I wanted them to. I used to be able to leave here on a weekend and win fifteen or twenty thousand; or go for a month and win thirty thousand. Then slowly the whole picture began to change until one day I'm winning fourth or fifth place instead of first place, and winning five hundred dollars instead of five thousand dollars, which drove me to being real negative. It took me three or four years until I could say winning isn't everything, I've done enough of it, I've experienced that side of it, what does it hurt to not win first every time. Turns out, I can live through it.

The negativity that I would bring from the arena to home started to shower not only on me, but on Cassie and my kids. Finally, I decided I had to focus on being happy myself and not worrying about things I can't change. This change in attitude was a long time coming and it didn't happen overnight. Cassie and I talked and she's wanted me to slow down for the last several years, but I've fought it and fought it. Until now, I haven't had a problem in my life that roping couldn't fix, not one. Then I started to make roping a problem and that is totally wrong because roping has always been my sanctuary; there's nothing about roping that should ever anger me; there's nothing about this game that should ever make me mad. I can be mad at myself or mad at a calf or upset with a horse, but there's nothing within me that should ever be pissed off about roping – nothing whatsoever.

I don't have a million dollars in the bank, I'll be the first one to tell you, but I have a great life and everything that I've got comes from me throwing my hands up. If I don't ever win another dime, roping don't owe me nothing. After all the success I had over the years, it took a long time to come to terms with that. When you've become accustomed to something being one way for more than twenty years and then all the sudden it's not that way anymore, it messes with you. You have to be a certain type of person to handle that and I am slowly becoming that person. I still want to win but when things don't go right, I'm just not going to flip my lid. I'm not angry anymore and it's a big relief.

I don't know if it was because of, or in spite of, my skin color, but I feel I have brought so many fans to the sport of rodeo. My fans could care less if I'm purple or green, it's just about good old swift competition, they like to see a guy compete. I hear from a lot of people that I made rodeo fun for them and that makes me feel good. A guy walked up to me the other day when I was signing autographs and he said "Man I want to tell you a quick story. The other day you talked to somebody's little kid and they were not really rodeo fans and didn't know much, but they've been fans of rodeo ever since they met you." Not to pat myself on the back, but I hear so many unbelievable stories from people who have been drawn to the sport because of me. Other cowboys have their fans, but nobody has fans like mine and I love them all so much.

In my mind, what I have brought to rodeo is hopefully my professionalism, the way I handle myself in and out of the arena. I thrive on competition and I've never backed down from a challenge in the arena, and never will, it's just not in my DNA. Overall, I don't think that people will remember me as the greatest calf roper ever, because there's so many greats and so many different eras. Dean Oliver had his era, Roy Cooper had his era, Joe Beaver and Cody Ohl were part of my era, so you can compare me to whoever you like. Bottom line, I'd like to be remembered as an honest guy who helped promote the sport of rodeo, and a cowboy who won when calf roping was probably the toughest it ever was. That's what I would like to be remembered for.

The only legacy I am worried about today is the one I leave with my daughters. I want to be around to watch my kids grow up and be an influence in their lives. I didn't have a fatherly influence and I missed it. I had good friends, but not a father, so I'm going to try to spend as much time as I can with them. I'm going to continue to rodeo a little bit. I'm obligated to some sponsors and I want to keep those guys happy, but mostly my life is now about my girls…all three of them.

In addition to being the world's largest live entertainment and livestock exhibition, the Houston Livestock Show and Rodeo is the richest regular season rodeo event, although it's not PRCA sanctioned and does not count toward the standings. Since 1938, the almost three weeks of festivities have included a parade, bar-b-que contests, carnivals, livestock competitions of all sorts, pig races, auctions, major concerts and the biggest names in rodeo. The fifty thousand dollar prize money paid in each event is meant to attract the best cowboys the world has to offer and it does. Participants must win their way through a series of rounds that ultimately ends with four contenders who then vie for the top prize money.

Fred Whitfield won the Houston Rodeo in 2000, but that was back when it was held in the Astrodome complex and back when it sure as hell didn't pay fifty thousand dollars. Even though it's his hometown rodeo, and even though he consistently beat the exact same competitors in other venues, the Houston Rodeo has eluded Fred for the other twenty-two years of his storied career. That never mattered to the massive crowds of fans there each year to cheer on their hometown hero in action, then stand in line for hours afterwards for an autograph. On March 16, 2013, there were 75,242 rodeo fans packed into Reliant Stadium, the home of the Houston Rodeo since 2003, to watch the Shootout round that decided who took home the fifty thousand in each event. Fred was in the final four, but he had been this close many times before.

Anthony was there as well, and it had been three years since the brothers had been together. Cassie says Fred had a good feeling about it all along, saying he thought this just might be his year. "He was confident," she says. "He was very calm and he wasn't ever angry or resentful…it just went smoothly overall." Cassie says that what was best about the Houston Rodeo this year was that Savannah and Sydney were there to see everything in person. They are too young to remember the world titles, and too old to travel with him to other rodeos, so other than the Finals, the Houston Rodeo is the biggest show they got to see him in. He and his daughters have forged a much stronger connection with Daddy having been home more the last year, which made everything that much sweeter.

I had a pretty good feeling when Houston started, just had a quiet calm, I guess. I won second in the first round of my group, I won fourth in the second round, won the average, come back in the semi-finals and had to survive one guy and I got by him. That put me in the top ten, and I was 8.6 and won first, which means I'm last to rope in the final four. I got to watch the other three go and knew I had to be 8.2 to win it.

Bob Tallman was announcing and was right in the middle of saying some great things about me and my career, calling me unbelievable and so on, when this little black calf trots out there and I run him maybe four swings and cracked it on him. I was nineteen years old again and I got off and got down there and popped this sonofabuck around and put a wrap and hooey on him. I was 7.8.

The Thomas & Mack Center holds nineteen thousand people; Reliant Stadium had over seventy-five thousand people in it that night. It was the biggest crowd I'd ever been in front of and they were all roaring for me. It was so loud in there…it was unreal. It made the hair stand up on my arms and on my neck and everywhere else. I promise you, it was unbelievable. I knew that calf would be there awhile, but with all them people screaming, there wasn't no telling what old Jewels was going to do. But she didn't let it get to her. I want to thank all the fans who over the years have been so supportive and so accepting. I couldn't go nowhere the rest of the day; people were lined up for miles to shake my hand and if I signed one autograph, I signed a thousand that afternoon and evening. They made me feel like a rock star.

And then there's the money. Hell, it's hard to win twenty thousand at one rodeo, let alone close to sixty by the time it was all over. It was an amazing feeling. I been roping at that rodeo forever and it's only been maybe six or seven years that they been paying fifty thousand to win it. I won third my rookie year, I won second a few years after that and I won the whole thing in 2000 but I had never won the fifty thousand. It's only been three or four years since Houston quit counting towards the standings and I have mixed emotions about that. Bottom line, it shouldn't count until they get a few more rodeos with that kind of money. If the wrong guy wins it and you give somebody a fifty thousand dollar lead, you're basically giving him a gold buckle. But if they had five more rodeos that paid like that, it'd be a different story. With that said, the facts are that Houston probably ain't never going to be a PRCA rodeo again because they control their own deal right now, they got the best cowboys in the world, they don't have to go by PRCA guidelines or pay them any money, so the Houston Rodeo don't need the PRCA for anything.

Certain spots have been elusive and Houston's been one of them. I've won Ft. Worth three times, I've won San Antone five times, I've won Cheyenne and Calgary several times, but for some reason, Houston has escaped my grasp other than the one year. But I just approached it a lot different way this year. I said I'm just going to go down there and rope and pretty much let the chips fall where they may. I had a quiet calm about roping there this year and everything just fell into place. I felt I could rope really good and it was set up just like I like it.

The top four were Shane Hanchey, Clint Robinson, Stran Smith and me. I got Stran's ass back because he won it a couple of years ago when I won second, so I owed him one. The only other one I wanted in there was Matt Shiozawa and he didn't make it. The thing about rodeo is when you win and there aren't a lot of big names in the round, they say well, he was supposed to win. I got to clear a lot of that up that day with those four guys being in it. To this day, I fear no man with a rope, from the biggest name to the smallest name. I rope best when I rope against the best.

For the first two days after I won, I don't think I slept hardly at all. Of all the winning I've done in my life, to win Houston at this point in my career and then come home Saturday night and try to sleep was impossible. I bet I didn't sleep two hours on Saturday night, Sunday night I didn't sleep too much, Monday I finally came off cloud nine and went to bed.

I never dreamed I would win eight World Titles. I played football until my freshman year and sometimes ponder how my life would have been different had I gone on and played football. But I never played enough to get very good at it, so I'll never know. Once I discovered I was half decent at roping, that became my priority and that never changed. I just craved it; it was the first thing I thought of every day when I woke up and the last thing I thought of every night when I went to bed and every minute in-between. Hell, I'd be sitting there in the classroom and I wasn't worried about school, I was thinking about the next calf I was going to get to rope. As soon as that two-thirty bell rang, I was out of there. Let's go rope. That's what it takes to be good at anything, whether it's education, baseball, football, it don't matter, you got to give it one hundred and ten percent. I see a lot of kids these days that don't give a hundred and ten percent and I'm totally against that. That level of dedication is behind all my success.

Roy Moffitt is still my best friend, he always has been and he always will be. Our paths have gone different ways, but we still talk two or three times a week, sometimes two or three times a day, just depends on how busy we both are. There's no telling where I'd have ended up without him. I'm thankful I was helped by good people along the way and I always give them credit, but I took advantage of everything they gave me.

To this day, I go by and visit Mrs. Moffitt. I went by the other day and took my family and visited with her for quite a while. She gave me two boxes full of clippings of me and Roy when we was kids. I look at this stuff and remember how goofy we were…just like goofy, crazy. And she's got everyone of my interviews, I mean she saved every interview I've ever done.

I'm not easy to live with, so hats off to my wife. I went through some trials and tribulations these last few years, which made me mad a lot of the time and you don't want to be around me when that happens. I can be a little uneasy. Cassie's a lot calmer than me when things are out of whack, so there's a pretty good balance. We're not filthy rich, our bills are paid and we do okay, and I'm grateful for that. I want my girls to be educated and they go to a good private school. Whether they ever ride a horse or pick up a rope that matters not to me. I just want them to be educated because with education comes money and success.

As a kid in Cypress I'd sit around and listen to guys talk about what they could have done. They were a little older than me, and they would always talk about how they could do this and how good they were at that, but they never pursued any of it. Somewhere along the way, that started something in me. I wasn't going to be one of those guys that sat around and talked about it – I was going to be a doer. This made me a highly motivated person. I came from nowhere, from nothing, and there's a certain desire in me. I've just always wanted to do better and I'm proud I turned into a pretty good person. I'm far from perfect, but I don't think I've got any major flaws. Coming from where I come from, I think I turned out pretty good. I honestly do.

A guy told me a while back, he said "Fred let me tell you something, I'm going to be straight up honest with you….I heard you defending yourself to a guy yesterday and you need to stop doing that."

I said, why's that?

He said, "Because you got eight gold buckles and they did not give you any of them, you earned them…and gold buckles don't lie."

Epilogue

Just before Father's Day this year [2013], we found out that my dad's health is declining. He don't have much time left, so we got all the kids and everybody together and had a big Father's Day celebration for him. Hell, I'm about to be forty-six years old and that was the first time in my life. It was sad, but good, I guess. It's just strange that nobody has shed a tear yet.

We had it at Anthony's house and me and my family were the first ones there. By the time everybody else got there, I saw people I hadn't seen in fifteen, twenty years. My other two sisters were there, my mom came by, a couple of Willie's mistresses were there with their kids, and we took pictures of all of us with my dad. It was weird, but we did it for him.

I called him the next day and he said he had a good time. I call him often to see how he's doing and I've spent some time with him lately. We talk about everything. We've discussed things we've never even talked about before, about things he's done in his life. He says he knows he's done more things wrong than he ever done right. He says he knows he could have been a better dad, but what's done is done and he can't undo it. That's just life. We all do things we wish we could take back; some get a chance to make it right, some don't.

I would have loved for him to have been a bigger part of what I've done over the years, but it happened like it happened. He's still my dad.

ACKNOWLEDGEMENTS

We would like to thank the following people for helping us bring Fred's story to light…

Cassie Whitfield
Savannah Whitfield
Sydney Whitfield
Miss Marie
Joanne Moffitt
Roy Moffitt
Anthony Whitfield
Doc & Sandy Currie
Casey Butaud
Stephen Perry
Shawn & Wayne Knox
David Jennings Rodeo Photography (cover)
Margaret Chapman Photography
Dave Yerxa
Ann Bleiker
Lexie Rae Graham
Shelley L. Cogdill